C4279

Pythagorean Women

Pythagorean Women

Their History and Writings

SARAH B. POMEROY

The Johns Hopkins University Press
Baltimore

© 2013 Sarah B. Pomeroy
All rights reserved. Published 2013
Printed in the United States of America on acid-free paper
2 4 6 8 9 7 5 3 1

The Johns Hopkins University Press
2715 North Charles Street
Baltimore, Maryland 21218-4363
www.press.jhu.edu

Library of Congress Cataloging-in-Publication Data

Pomeroy, Sarah B.
Pythagorean women : a social history / Sarah B. Pomeroy.
pages. cm.
Includes bibliographical references and index.
ISBN-13: 978-1-4214-0956-6 (hardcover : alk. paper) — ISBN-13: 978-1-4214-0957-3 (electronic) — ISBN-10: 1-4214-0956-9 (hardcover : alk. paper) — ISBN-10: 1-4214-0957-7 (electronic)
1. Pythagoras and Pythagorean school.   2. Women—Greece—Intellectual life.
I. Title.
B243.P63 2013
182′.2082—dc23   2012036896

A catalog record for this book is available from the British Library.

Special discounts are available for bulk purchases of this book.
For more information, please contact Special Sales at 410-516-6936 or
specialsales@press.jhu.edu.

The Johns Hopkins University Press uses environmentally friendly book materials, including recycled text paper that is composed of at least 30 percent post-consumer waste, whenever possible.

To Jørgen Mejer
and
To Nathaniel Isaac Pomeroy

CONTENTS

Acknowledgments ix
Note on Abbreviations xi
Chronology xiii
Introduction xv

1 Who Were the Pythagorean Women? 1

2 Wives, Mothers, Sisters, Daughters 19

3 Who Were the Neopythagorean Women Authors? 41

4 Introduction to the Prose Writings of Neopythagorean Women 54

5 The Letters and Treatises of Neopythagorean Women in the East 66

6 The Letters and Treatises of Neopythagorean Women in the West 99

7 The Neopythagorean Women as Philosophers 117
BY VICKI LYNN HARPER

Notes 139
Index 167

ACKNOWLEDGMENTS

Pythagorean Women covers a wide range of subjects, including literature, archaeology, and political, social, and intellectual history. I am pleased to acknowledge the assistance of those who helped me in various ways to piece together this vast mosaic. First, I wish to thank my husband, Lee Harris Pomeroy, for photographing the landscape and artifacts in Magna Graecia. I am grateful to Joseph Coleman Carter for arranging my visit to Metaponto and for commenting on the Introduction and first two chapters. Warm thanks to Francesca Silvestri for organizing my tour of the site and museum at Metaponto and for supplying the *dépliant* of the exhibit *Ornamenti Femminili in Basilicata dall'età del ferro al tardo antico: La documentazione archeologica*, Museo Archeologico Nazionale di Metaponto, Jan. 14–June 30, 1991. Thanks are also due to the American Academy in Rome for awarding me a Residency in the spring of 2010 and to Marilyn Skinner for advice offered in our long conversations at the Academy. I also wish to thank the Center for Hellenic Studies for hospitality in the winter and spring of 2011, and Marcia Mitrowski, of the Hampton Library, for obtaining interlibrary loans.

Once again I am grateful to my family history reading group for their insightful comments on two drafts of my manuscript and to Maggie Scarf for her professional insights into adultery and etiquette. I wish to thank Barbara McManus for her keen remarks on the manuscript and for supplying the photo of the scarab of Hera Lacinia. And once again I am pleased to thank Laurie Schneider Adams and John Adams, who commented on the proofs of the text and the photos. Thanks to Emily Fairey for research assistance, to Bernard Kho and Philosophy Walker for help with computer-related challenges, and to my son, Jeremy Pomeroy, for legal counsel concerning intellectual property.

I also owe a special debt of gratitude to my friend, the late and much lamented Jørgen Mejer, for supplying the idea for this book (as he also did for my previous book, *The Murder of Regilla: A Case of Domestic Violence in Antiquity*). Professor Mejer was to have written a chapter on the philosophical and historical development of Pythagoreanism. I am therefore particularly grateful to Professor Vicki Harper, who generously agreed to contribute a chapter written from a philosopher's perspective after Professor Mejer's death.

NOTE ON ABBREVIATIONS

With a few obvious exceptions, journal titles are abbreviated according to the forms in *L'année philologique* and the list published online by the *American Journal of Archaeology*. Accepted abbreviations are used for standard works. Lists of standard abbreviations may be found in reference books such as the *Oxford Classical Dictionary* and in the major Greek and Latin dictionaries. The following short titles have been used throughout the book.

Burkert, *Lore and Science*: W. Burkert, *Lore and Science in Ancient Pythagoreanism*, trans., with revisions, E. Minar Jr. (Cambridge, MA, 1972). Originally published as *Weisheit und Wissenschaft: Studien zu Pythagoras, Philolaos und Platon* (Nürnberg, 1962).

LGPN IIIA: Peter M. Fraser and Elaine Matthews, eds., *A Lexicon of Greek Personal Names,* vol. 3A, *The Peloponnese, Western Greece, and Magna Graecia* (Oxford, 1997).

P. Haun.: *Papyri Graecae Haunienses*, II, 13 (3 c. AD), ed. and trans. Adam Bülow-Jacobsen (Bonn, 1981).

Riedweg, *Pythagoras*: Christoph Riedweg, *Pythagoras: His Life, Teaching, and Influence*, trans. Steven Rendall, in collaboration with Christoph Riedweg and Andreas Schatzmann (Ithaca, 2005). Originally published as *Pythagoras: Leben, Lehre, Nachwirkung eine Einführung* (Munich, 2002).

Thesleff, *Intro.*: *An Introduction to the Pythagorean Writings of the Hellenistic Period, Acta Academiae Aboensis. Humaniora* 24.3 (Åbo, 1961).

Thesleff, *Texts*: Holger Thesleff, *The Pythagorean Texts of the Hellenistic Period, Acta Academiae Aboensis. Humaniora,* 30.1 (Åbo, 1965).

Waithe, *Women Philosophers*: Mary Ellen Waithe, ed., *A History of Women Philosophers*, vol. 1, *600 BC–500 AD* (Dordrecht, 1987).

CHRONOLOGY

Most of the dates are approximate.

Archaic
Pythaïs (mother of Pythagoras)
570–490 BC. Pythagoras*
530 BC. Pythagoras emigrated to Croton
Theano (wife of Pythagoras)
Cheilonis
Tyrsenis

Classical
Myia (daughter of Theano and Pythagoras)
Damo
450 BC. Pythagoras dead
440–400 BC. Pythagoreans dispersed
Timycha
Bitale
Aspasia
345–320 BC. Alexis, *Pythagorean Woman*, *The Tarentines*
Perictione I

Hellenistic
Fourth to third century BC
    Theano II
    Bilistiche

*Riedweg, *Pythagoras*, 43.

Third century BC
　Aesara
　Melissa
　Phintys
　Ptolemäis
Third to second century BC
　Perictione II
　Myia

Indeterminable
Arignote
Theano I (author)

Roman Empire
AD 40 to 45–117. Plutarch
AD 245–325. Iamblichus

INTRODUCTION

> They looked upon Pythagoras as divine, with the result that they turned over their wives to him in order that they would learn some of his doctrines. And so they were called "Pythagorean Women."
> —Diogenes Laertius, *Life of Pythagoras*, 41

Pythagoras was the first Greek philosopher to include women among his disciples. He was also the earliest to listen sympathetically to the pleas of married women and to impose sexual monogyny on their husbands. Some two hundred years after the death of Pythagoras, Neopythagorean women became the first women in the Greek world to write prose texts that are extant. Like Pythagoras himself, these later authors were sympathetic to the women's point of view.

Who were the Pythagorean women? Though these issues will be discussed in detail in the book (see chaps. 1 and 3), it is important to understand at the start that the Pythagorean women must be considered as two groups. First are the women who were contemporaries of Pythagoras, some of whom are named in various accounts of the life of Pythagoras by Iamblichus (ca. 245–325 AD) and by others. In the second large group are the intellectual descendants of the first: Neopythagorean women, including the authors of letters and other prose texts, some complete, some now fragmentary. The first group lived in the late Archaic and Classical periods; the second group (with one exception) is Hellenistic. The first group was composed of Dorian Greeks and at least two indigenous women.[1] The identity of the later women is less certain, but they did write in both the Doric and Ionic dialects; some are thought to have lived in Rome and Southern Italy, others in Athens and Alexandria. Literature circulated between the settlements in the east and west, for letters of Melissa and Theano were found in Egypt paraphrased in the Attic *koine* (the common language) from the Doric version in a third-century AD papyrus.[2]

The subject of this book is the social history of women who were Pythagoreans; there are, however, no previous publications on women in general in the western Greek colonies of Southern Italy.[3] Therefore, in the first two chapters I have had to paint a background picture to describe the social, cultural, and ecological context in which the Pythagoreans lived.

Chapters 3–7 treat the Neopythagoreans, some of whom wrote letters and other prose works. These texts have been edited by Holger Thesleff and published in *The Pythagorean Texts of the Hellenistic Period*.[4] The time period covered in that book is long: from the sixth century BC to at least the first century BC and possibly longer (depending on the controversial dating of Neopythagorean documents). Chapter 4 includes general observations on Neopythagorean texts by women and explores issues that arise often or are discussed at length. In the next two chapters all the writings of the Neopythagorean women appear in translation, with an introduction preceding each text and a commentary following, explaining some features specific to that document. My commentary emphasizes women's issues and social history. In chapter 7, Professor Vicki Lynn Harper discusses philosophical aspects of Pythagoreanism, especially as it pertains to women and as it appears in the Neopythagorean texts.

When I thought about writing this book, I was amazed to discover that no one had preceded me in writing a comprehensive study, even though more Pythagorean women are known by name than are women in any other Greek philosophical school. They were not "muted" like their respectable Athenian contemporaries in old Greece. These women made an impression; some of their witty and prudent remarks were quoted by later authors. Thus this book is a contribution to the historical literature concerning the Greek world beyond Athens.

Athenocentricity has warped our view of women's history, obscuring, for example, the literate women who are to be found in all periods of Greek history and at various places in the Greek world—though not often in Athens.[5] Spartan women, unlike Athenians, were neither silenced nor secluded; instead they exercised out of doors, were well nourished, were educated by the state, and exerted influence in the public sphere.[6] The connection between the women of Sparta and the women of the Spartan colony of Taranto (the home of many Pythagoreans and Neopythagoreans) is readily apparent, and cultural influences may be detected. Pythagoreans also lived in Croton and Metaponto. These cities, however, were Achaean colonies, and the women of their mother cities in old Greece have not been studied, though links between old cults of Hera and those in Magna Graecia have been traced (see chap. 2).

Although Dorian women played a larger role in public than did Athenian women, it is still true that women's history in general is more obscure than men's. For example, Theano I was the most celebrated of Pythagorean women, much quoted, influential, and adopted as a model by Neopythagoreans. Nevertheless, ancient sources differ about whether she was the wife or disciple of Pythagoras, or the daughter or wife of Brontinus. No wife other than Theano is recorded for Pythagoras, and it was generally agreed that he had children. Therefore, I will refer to Theano in this book as Pythagoras's wife (see chap. 1).

Material evidence has contributed significantly to constructing the history of Pythagorean women in Magna Graecia. The modern city of Crotone stands in the way of any extensive exploration of Pythagoras's Croton. Therefore particularly valuable are Joseph Coleman Carter's publications of the ongoing excavation he has been directing at Metaponto. *The Chora of Metaponto: The Necropoleis* is a diachronic study of the archaeology, history, and ecology of Metaponto, with particular attention to burials and grave goods.[7] His *Discovering the Greek Countryside at Metaponto* is both a detailed scholarly work and a synthesis offering one of the most complete pictures of life in a small ancient city to have been published.[8] There is no comparable study of the ecological context of the places where the Neopythagoreans lived.

Metaponto was an Achaean colony on the gulf of Taranto founded around 600 BC, just before the time of Pythagoras. Coming rather late in the history of Greek colonization, the settlers laid claim to an area with a good location on the water but already under cultivation by indigenous people. In the river valleys they found a marshy, malaria-infested site, which they proceeded to drain and convert to farmland.[9] Many Metapontines chose to live on high ground. The major drainage project took place around 500 BC, after the colonists had lived there for about one hundred years. It was no coincidence that this enormous engineering project was undertaken when Pythagoras and his disciples were politically influential. Excavations have revealed a port and a well-planned city laid out on a grid pattern.[10] Drainage ditches and sewers suggest strong, orderly government and testify to the prosperity of the city. The museum at Metaponto not only displays the findings from the site and the tombs but also reflects the breadth of Carter's vision; it contains cases devoted to artistic images of women on vases and to artifacts and utensils used by them, especially those in durable materials, including jewelry, fibulas, mirrors, ceramics, spools, loom weights, and spindle whorls. A chart of their many coiffures is displayed.[11]

Without detailed extant descriptions by a Herodotus or a Thucydides or an Aristophanes, the archaeological evidence plays an even more significant role in reconstructing the societies in which the Pythagoreans lived—though, to be sure, authors who lived much later than Pythagoras, including Livy and Strabo, conjure up the past. Grave goods supply information about the dead person and the surviving donor. For example, since Pythagoras had forbidden respectable women to wear gold, we may assume that any woman buried with gold jewelry was not a Pythagorean (or at least her survivors who buried her were not).[12] Bones have been analyzed to yield information about the gender of the corpses, their state of health, blood group, and age at death. Pollen analyses give clues to women's diet. Child burials yield dolls and miniature objects such as carts and small vases. Depictions of women in the visual arts provide information about their appearance, clothing, and habitat. Furthermore, the archaeological record at a well-excavated site like Metaponto reveals both Greek and native Italic customs and artifacts. (In contrast, the written record describing Pythagoras's interactions with women and his views about them is in Greek and limited largely, although not exclusively, to Greek women.) Architectural and engineering artifacts, including temples and canals for drainage and irrigation, suggest the material context in which these women lived, and inscriptions record contemporary public information.

The usual paraphernalia of daily and civic life in a small Greek city is important in reconstructing women's lives. We assume that women who had time to listen to Pythagoras, who owned luxurious clothing and jewelry and could make costly dedications, and who had the leisure and education to write prose that could be circulated did not personally use the pots and pans and other cooking equipment that have been excavated.[13] At most they supervised while their slaves cooked the food, though they occasionally prepared sacrificial offerings with their own hands. Since most domestic slaves were female, however, the pottery broadens the range of social classes available for our general study of women.[14] Though we cannot assume that the women buried in the graves that have been studied were Pythagoreans, some may have been. In any case, the Pythagoreans lived among or near them, subject to the same illnesses and weather, and choosing from the same food supply. At least we can be certain that Pythagoreans were members of the elite, and it is generally the graves of the prosperous that have survived to be excavated and to yield an array of grave goods.

It has been less daunting to write about the Neopythagoreans than about the Pythagoreans inasmuch as scholars, including myself, have discussed the writings of the former group. Furthermore, the Neopythagoreans lived in cosmopolitan Hellenistic cities and in Southern Italy along with other women whose lives have been studied.[15] As I mentioned, Pythagoras was the first philosopher to include women in his community. By the fourth century BC and the Hellenistic period a few women were active at Plato's Academy, as well as among the Cynics and the Epicureans. The Neopythagorean women, however, were more numerous than those associated with any other philosophical school.

Though the two groups are distinct chronologically, the Neopythagoreans preserved the traditions of the original Pythagoreans and shared the same philosophical and ethical views, and sometimes the same names. In addition, some of their writings show the influence of other philosophers, especially Plato. In this book, the two groups of women will occasionally be treated as a unified whole, but more often as distinct.

Much of the biography of Pythagoras and the history of early Pythagoreanism is unclear and controversial. Some classical scholars and social historians of antiquity tend to accept many of the early traditions, but others argue that certain evidence pertaining to the history of Pythagoras and of female Pythagoreans and Neopythagoreans was pseudonymous or untrustworthy. My intention here is not to join in the scholarly debate about these issues per se—except when they directly affect my narrative about women—but instead to use the evidence judiciously in reconstructing women's lives. In any case, considering that much of the scholarship concerning the history of Pythagoreanism has simply ignored the women who were Pythagoreans, by contributing a missing piece to the puzzle of Pythagoreanism this book may not merely expand the current picture of Pythagoras and other male Pythagoreans but alter it (see chap. 3). Meanwhile, I offer here a brief sketch that will provide guidance to the reader who is not a specialist in ancient history. This sketch will serve as a simple framework for the subject of this book: Pythagorean and Neopythagorean women. Although the intellectual experiences of these women were unique because they were Pythagoreans, what we can glean about their daily lives enhances our general knowledge of the history of Greek women.

Pythagoras was born in the middle of the sixth century BC on Samos, in the eastern Mediterranean. Like most of his disciples he traveled from the world of old Greece to settle in Magna Graecia in Southern Italy. Around 530 BC he began lecturing to the citizens of the Achaean colony of Croton and later moved to Metaponto. In addition to the contemplation of the cosmos, the nature of the soul, and subjects that were also discussed by other pre-Socratic philosophers, Pythagorean philosophy included a very elaborate ethical program, with advice to both women and men for personal conduct in everyday life.[16]

Later biographers (using the works of earlier authors) wrote about the women who actually knew Pythagoras. For example, Philochorus, who died in the 260s BC and may have known some Neopythagorean women, wrote a volume on Pythagorean women that he titled *The Collection of Pythagorean Women Heroines* (or "Founders": *Sunagoge heroidon hetoi Pythagoreion gunaikon*).[17] Philochorus may have produced his book because he noted that previous works ignored women.[18] Iamblichus named 17 women among the 235 disciples of Pythagoras whom he lists.[19] Since this catalog probably originated with Aristoxenus in the fourth century BC, when several treatises on the Pythagoreans had been written, it is likely to be accurate, but since some of the Pythagoreans named postdate Aristoxenus, Iamblichus or other biographers must have added to it.[20]

Works about the life of Pythagoras are the principal written sources for information about Pythagorean women. The most important authors are Diogenes Laertius of Cilicia (3rd c. AD), Porphyry of Tyre (232/233–ca. 305 AD), and Iamblichus of Chalcis (ca. 245–325 AD), a Neoplatonist who studied under Porphyry. Though they differ in details, there is considerable overlap among the biographies. For example, Iamblichus identifies Theano as the wife of Brontinus, while, as we have mentioned, other sources vary as to whether she was Pythagoras's wife, daughter, or disciple. Brontinus of Metaponto or Croton is sometimes identified as Theano's husband, sometimes as Deino's, and sometimes as Theano's father. There is a similar confusion about the names of Pythagoras's children. Furthermore, some sources ascribe particular quotations to Deino, others to Theano. Some of the biographers were apparently inspired by women philosophers who were their contemporaries or patrons. Thus Diogenes Laertius dedicated his work to a female Platonist.[21] In his *Life of Plotinus* (9), Porphyry mentions female students of Plotinus who were seriously committed to philosophy. Though the authors of the extant biographies wrote centuries after the original Pythagoreans lived, the biographical tradition was under way in the generation after Pythagoras's death. Pythagoras is mentioned as early as Herodotus (4.95). This early testimony thus was not totally contaminated by later influences like Platonism but rather offers some reflection of original Pythagoreanism.[22] The authors of the works that are now extant consulted these earlier biographies and incorporated them, sometimes verbatim, and often without attribution. Modern scholarship has managed to sift through much of the writing about the Pythagoreans in general and to assign authorship and dates to various traditions; these will be discussed in this book where relevant. One of the specific problems, however, encountered in studying Pythagorean and Neopythagorean women is that our ancient sources do not distinguish clearly between them, for example, conflating the Theano who was the wife and disciple of Pythagoras with the woman, or women, of the same name who wrote letters and treatises in the Hellenistic period.

In the many traditions concerning the life and doctrines of Pythagoras there is little of the misogyny that mars the teaching of other Greek philosophers and thinkers. Women do not appear as alien and inferior to men. Rather, they are the same as or equal to men, to be given the same education, to follow the same rules of conduct, and deserving of the same respect (see chap. 2). Pythagoras devoted some thought to women's habits. For example, he observed that bonds between women were strong. They would make loans of clothing and ornaments to other women who needed certain things, and they would do so without the surety of witnesses. It would not be natural for men to be so trusting. He illustrates his point with the example of the mythical Three Graiae, aged sisters who trusted one another so completely that they shared one eye among them (Iambl. *VP* 55).

The biographers agree that among the original Pythagoreans, women played an important role and participated actively in the philosophical life.[23] This phenomenon was unique in the Greek world of the sixth and fifth centuries BC. That the philosopher himself was responsible for this innovation or at least thoroughly approved it is indicated by the inclusion of his wife and daughters among the exemplary women mentioned by name.[24] According to Diogenes Laertius, Theano wrote a few things (8.43: *suggramma . . . tina*). Because he also reports that Philolaus (ca. 470 BC) was the first to publish (*ekdounai*) Pythagorean treatises, we deduce that Theano's texts were not published.[25] This deduction is consistent with an axiom of women's history: women, in general, wrote shorter and fewer works and often kept them in private or published them only under a pseudonym. Thus the tradition about Theano need not be rejected, though some influential scholars have argued that neither Pythagorean women nor Neopythagoreans could have participated in the philosophical school, nor could they have written some Pythagorean texts. For example, Richard Bentley did not believe this report about women's participation. In a discussion of the authenticity of a Neopythagorean treatise ascribed to Perictione, he wrote that the forgers of treatises simply "thought it a point of decorum to make even the female kindred of philosophers copy after the men."[26] B. L. van der Waerden continued the tradition of studying only male Pythagoreans in his *Die Pythagoreer: Religiöse Bruderschaft und Schule der Wissenschaft*.[27] In contrast, W. Burkert,[28] C. J. de Vogel,[29] and Peter Kingsley[30] remarked on the equality of women and men in Pythagoreanism.

The *Speeches of Pythagoras*, which have been dated to the late fifth or early fourth century, are an early source for the tradition about women's participation in Pythagorean society.[31] The speeches are addressed to both women and men and include discussion of appropriate behavior for women. Dicaearchus (*ap.* Porph. *Plot.* 18–19) reports that Pythagoras addressed a gathering of women and that an association of women was created for him. He goes on to discuss Theano, who was the most famous Pythagorean woman. Then he states that what Pythagoras told his intimates we cannot say with certainty, but it was generally agreed that he said that the soul was immortal, that it transmigrated into other forms of animal life, and that it was periodically reborn.[32] Although the tradition about women's participation, like other traditions concerning the life of Pythagoras, was not preserved by a contemporary author, there is no need to assume that it is a biographical fiction. The original Pythagoreans lived together in close-knit communities, abiding by a strict discipline, which extended to dietary matters, wearing apparel, and the proper times to engage in sexual intercourse. Under such circumstances, it was mandatory that both sexes understand the doctrines (see chap. 1).

Both the original Pythagorean and the Neopythagorean women must have read philosophy or sat in on classes, lectures, or informal discussions. We are told that Pythagoras addressed the women of Croton directly. With the founder creating such a precedent, there is no reason to doubt that women were included among both the Pythagoreans and the Neopythagoreans, who preserved the earlier traditions.

When I first wrote about women philosophers and writers some thirty-five years ago, at times I presented my views tentatively, knowing that some critics would refuse to be persuaded. Then it was still fashionable to theorize that works attributed to female authors were pseudonymous and that the authors had to be male. Respected scholars such as Martin West continued the tradition, traceable back to Richard Bentley. As I mentioned, Bentley had summarily dismissed the idea that women could have written the Neopythagorean treatises attributed to them, and similarly, West argued that Erinna could not have written the poetry circulated under her name. Since then, research on women's literacy has confirmed that women could well have written works that were published under their names.[33] Thus, although there are many uncertainties about where and when the Neopythagorean women (and men) wrote their letters and other prose, there is little doubt that Hellenistic women could have written such works and that Pythagorean women served as their models.

Pythagorean Women

CHAPTER ONE

Who Were the Pythagorean Women?

Iamblichus (*VP* 267) lists 235 Pythagoreans whose names are known. Following the catalog of 218 men, he names 17 women, whom he describes as "the most famous Pythagorean women." The men are classified only according to their city of origin. The women are also listed by their city of origin, and the first 8 women and the last are identified as a wife, sister, or daughter of a male Pythagorean.[1] It was natural for members of the same family, especially a married couple, to become Pythagoreans, for the philosopher ordained rules for everyday life, including dietary regulations and the proper season for sexual intercourse (Diod. Sic. 10.9.3). Moreover, the Pythagoreans were bound by secrets the wives must have shared: for example, Pythagoras's own home was called the site of mysteries.[2] The eight women whose names do not appear with that of a male relative are not necessarily completely independent or single women; it is just as likely that their male relatives are not Pythagoreans.

Most of the women are Greek and come from the Dorian strongholds of Sparta, Argos, or Achaea or their colonies. In addition, Occelo and Eccelo, sisters of the Pythagorean Lucanians Occelus and Occilus, were indigenous.[3] The indigenous neighbors of the Greeks in southern Italy were Hellenized, at least to the extent that some spoke Greek: they were particularly influenced by the Dorian traditions of the Greek colonies.[4] Sybaris, Croton, and Metaponto usually enjoyed good relations with native villages. The indigenous people in turn influenced the Greeks and in some ways created a mixed culture, but this influence cannot be detected in our study of Pythagorean women, many of whom were only first- or second-generation inhabitants of Magna Graecia.

The list of the famous women Pythagoreans, in the order in which they appear in Iamblichus, and a brief identification follow.

Timycha, wife of Myllias of Croton, is renowned for her courage in resisting Dionysius, tyrant of Syracuse (r. 396–379 BC). Dionysius had ordered that she be

THRACE
Philippi
Strymon R.
Mt. Pangaeus
Abdera
Amphipolis
Pella
Derveni
Therme
(Salonica)
Thasos
Levkadia
Stageira
MACEDONIA
Aegae
(Vergina)
CHALCIDICE
Pydna
Olynthus
Mt. Athos
Potidaea
Mt. Olympus
Dium
Torone
Mende
EPIRUS
Mt. Ossa
Lemnos
Mt. Pindus
Tricca
Larissa
Dodona
Mt. Pelium
THESSALY
Corcyra
Pagasae
Pharsalus
Pherae
AEGEAN
SEA
Ambracia
Nicopolis
C. Artemisium
Actium
ACARNANIA
Scyros
Leucas
Thermopylae
Euboea
Stratus
Mt.
Parnassus
Kalapodi
Thermum
Chalcis
L. Copais
Delphi
PHOCIS
Lefkandi
AETOLIA
Orchomenus
Chaeronea
BOEOTIA
Eretria
Ithaca
Mt. Helicon
Thebes
Delium
Patrae
Leuctra
Tanagra
Aegira
Cephallenia
ACHAEA
Plataea
Marathon
Megara
Sicyon
Mt. Pentelicum
Elis
Athens
Andros
ELIS
Corinth
Isthmia
Piraeus
Nemea
Cleonae
Salamis
Zacynthus
ARGOLIS
Mycenae
Aegina
Laurium
Mantinea
Olympia
Epidaurus
Ceos
Argos
Tiryns
Sunium
Bassae
Tenos
Tegea
Troezen
Calauria
Lycosura
Cythnos
Delos
Megalopolis
MESSENIA
Cyclades
Messene
Seriphos
Paros
Sparta
Pylos
Mt. Taygetus
Siphnos
LACONIA
Methone
Gythium
Melos
Cythera
MEDITERRANEAN SEA
Cydonia
Knossos
Crete
Phaistos
0 20 40 60 80 100 miles
0 40 80 120 160 km

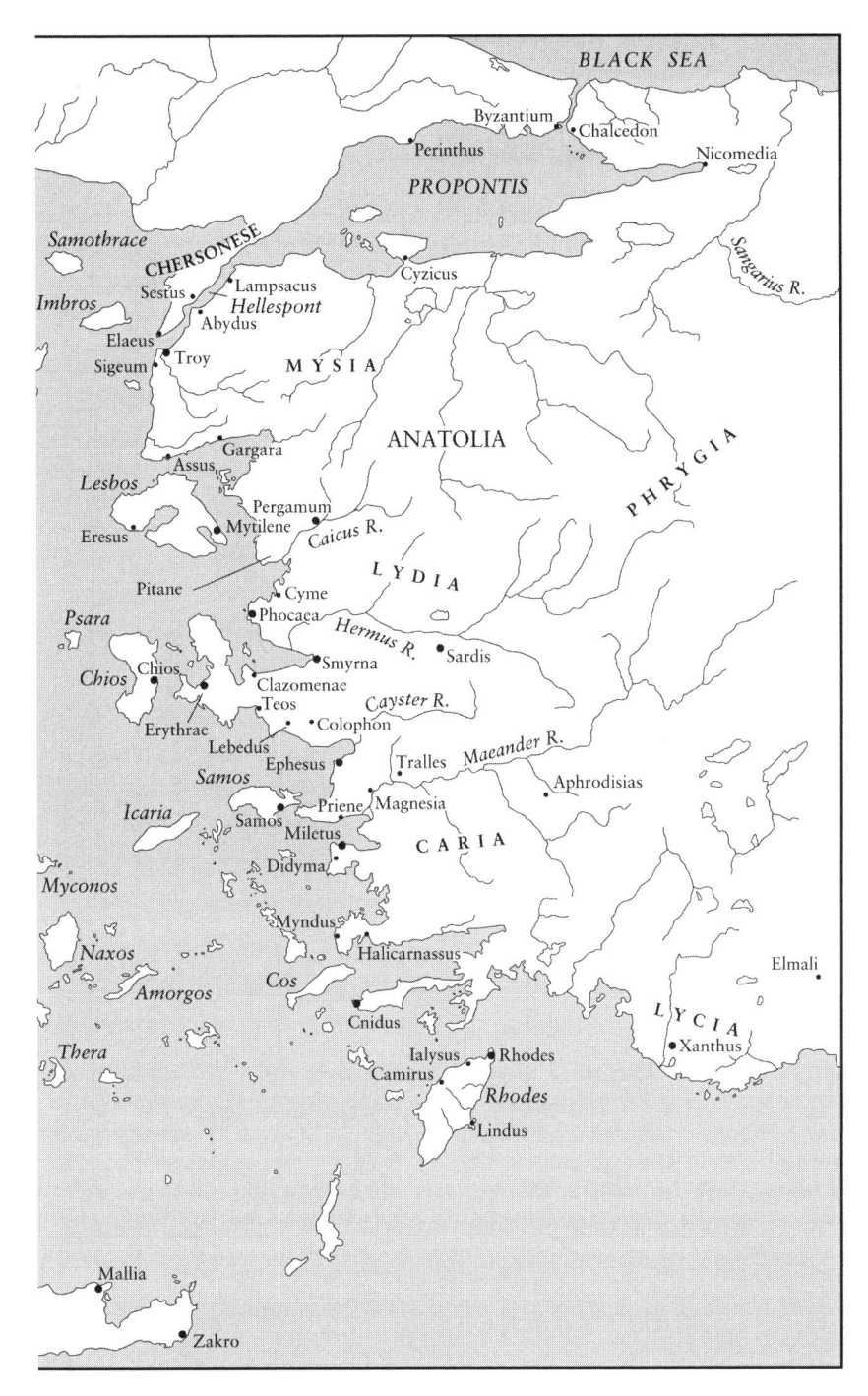

Map 1. Greece and the Aegean World. *Source*: Sarah B. Pomeroy, S. Burstein, W. Donlan, and Jennifer Roberts, *A Brief History of Ancient Greece*, 2nd ed. (New York, 2008), xxiv. Reproduced with permission of Oxford University Press.

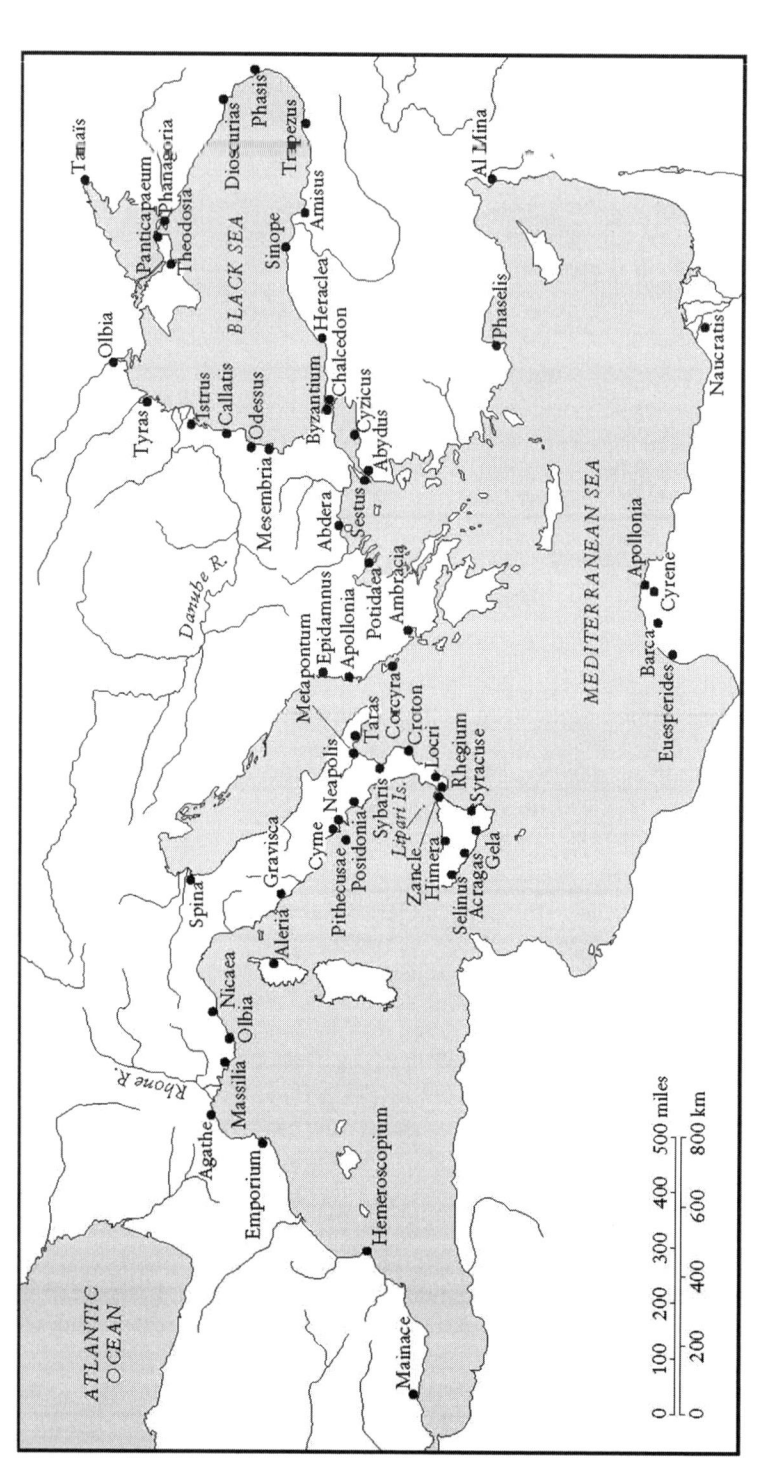

Map 2. Greek Colonization. *Source:* Sarah B. Pomeroy, S. Burstein, W. Donlan, and Jennifer Roberts, *Ancient Greece*, 3rd ed. (New York, 2012), 113, fig. 3.1. Reproduced with permission of Oxford University Press.

tortured when she was six months pregnant. Rather than reveal the secrets of the Pythagoreans, she bit off her tongue.[5] She was Lacedaemonian in descent and in her brave actions.

Philtys, daughter of Theophris of Croton, sister of Byndacus.[6]

Occelo and *Eccelo*, sisters of the Lucanians Occelus and Occilus.[7]

Cheilonis, daughter of Cheilon the Lacedaemonian. Her father was *ephor* (a powerful Spartan magistrate) in 556 BC.[8] Thus she was a contemporary of Pythagoras.

Cratesicleia the Laconian, wife of Cleanor the Lacedaemonian.[9] Cratesicleia is a typical Spartan name alluding to power and fame. This Cratesicleia may be an ancestor of a more famous Cratesicleia, who was the mother of the Spartan king Cleomenes (r. 235–?). The later Cratesicleia studied with Sphaerus, a Stoic who came to Sparta to lecture.[10] Inasmuch as Spartan women were not secluded, it is quite likely that Cratesicleia listened to Sphaerus's teachings.[11] As a result of her son's reformist policies (which she supported), Cratesicleia's and Cleomenes's children, and Cratesicleia herself, became hostages of Ptolemy III Euergetes. Eventually Ptolemy IV, Philopator, ordered that the Spartan hostages be killed. At first Cratesicleia panicked, but in the end she met her death stoically and bravely (Plut. *Cleom.* 38). If this Cratesicleia is the same as the one listed by Iamblichus, then, of course, she is a Neopythagorean with a background in Stoicism.

Theano, wife of Pythagoras, also said to be the wife of the Metapontian Brotinus (or Brontinus).[12]

Biographers of Pythagoras offer alternative genealogical solutions to the identity of Theano. It is possible that all the reports have at least some truth in them and that Theano and Brontinus married more than once. According to Diogenes Laertius (8.22) Pythagoras's wife was Theano, daughter of Brontinus of Croton. But he adds that some identify her as the wife of Brontinus and pupil of Pythagoras. According to Iamblichus, however, Deino was the wife of Brontinus.[13] Theano was the mother of Telauges and Myia, and some add Arignote. Damo was also a daughter of Pythagoras, but Iamblichus does not specifically state that Theano was her mother (Iambl. *VP* 146). No wife, however, other than Theano is recorded for Pythagoras, and it was generally (though not universally) agreed that he had children.[14] Photius (*VP* 2) reports that Pythagoras's son Mnesarchus died a young man. Telauges was another son, and Sara and Myia were his daughters. Theano was said to be not only his disciple but his daughter. Photius also states that Pythagoras lived to be 104. Scholars nowadays generally agree that Pythagoras lived circa 570–490. The various traditions can be reconciled by the conclusion that he did attain a very old age for a Greek. We may note, in passing, that his mother too was long-lived, for she must have been at least 60 when she took notes from Pythagoras, who had descended underground (see chap. 2). Perhaps the disparity in age between husband and wife led some authorities to consider Theano a daughter rather than a wife. Iamblichus reports that Aristaeus was Pythagoras's heir. As head of the school, this mysterious figure married the widowed Theano and brought up her children because he understood the doctrines.[15] Marriage of the widow of the leader of a philosophical school or of a commercial enterprise to his successor was common. In this way the legator ensured that his wife and children would be cared for economically and socially.[16]

Porphyry (*VPyth.* 19) relates that Pythagoras attracted not only men as disciples but also women, among whom was Theano. Didymus (ca. 80–10 BC) wrote that Theano was the first woman philosopher.[17] She became famous even among the neighboring barbarians, kings, and rulers. Theano also wrote some work (Diog. Laert. 8.43). Some undatable quotations and philosophical works attributed to an author named "Theano" may in fact be traceable to the original Theano (see chaps. 4 and 5). In other words, she became a famous wise woman, like the priestess at Delphi who had been Pythagoras's teacher. "Theano" was the name of the priestess of Athena in the *Iliad* (6.298, 302), the earliest and best-known Greek literature; therefore her name indicates that her parents had conceived a special destiny for her (see chap. 3). A quotation in Attic from Theano on the immortality of the soul and several apophthegms are extant (see chap. 5). For example, Diogenes Laertius (8.43) reports: "It is said of Theano that when asked how long a period of purification was necessary after a woman had intercourse with her husband, she said: the moment she leaves her own husband she is pure; but she is never pure after she leaves anyone else." She advised a woman going to her husband to take off her modesty with her clothes. This witty remark is a play on a Greek proverb also found in Herodotus.[18] Furthermore, when she was asked "what clothes," she responded "those which cause you to be a woman." This interesting response suggests that Theano believed women and men were essentially the same and that only a particular costume, which could be easily removed, constructed womanhood.[19]

Myia, wife of Milo of Croton and daughter of Theano and Pythagoras.[20] According to Timaeus (ca. 350–260 BC), before marriage Pythagoras's daughter was first among maidens in Croton, and when she became a wife, first among married women.[21] When she died the Crotoniates turned her house into a temple of Demeter and called the entrance hall a sanctuary of the Muses.[22]

Lastheneia. A Lastheneia of the city of Mantinea in Arcadia dressed as a man and studied at Plato's Academy.[23] Iamblichus states that Lastheneia came from the region of Arcadia. Thus the Pythagorean may be identical with Plato's student. We may speculate that if there were two philosophers named Lastheneia, one was the grandmother of the other. Greeks generally used the same names in alternate generations.[24] Mantinea was also the home of the philosopher Diotima, whom Socrates credits with teaching him about love in Plato's *Symposium*.

Habroteleia, daughter of Habroteles of Taranto.[25]

Echecrateia of Phlius. Probably related to Echecrates, who was one of four men from Phlius also in Iamblichus's catalog. The story in Plato's *Phaedo* is told to him. The others mentioned by Iamblichus are Diocles, Polymnastus, and Phanton. There evidently was a coterie of Platonists and Pythagoreans in Phlius. Aristoxenus mentions other Pythagoreans from Phlius, including Xenophilus, Philolaus, and Eurytus.[26] Like Lastheneia (see above), a woman named Axiothea came from Phlius in the Peloponnese to study at Plato's Academy.[27]

Tyrsenis from Sybaris.[28] Since Sybaris was destroyed in 510 BC, Tyrsenis was a contemporary of Pythagoras.

Peisirrhode from Taranto.[29]

Theadusa from Lacedaemon (*Lakaina*).[30] Another source names *Nistheadousa*.[31] These names probably refer to the same person.

Boeo from Argos.[32]

Babelyca from Argos.[33]

Cleachma, sister of the Lacedaemonian Autocharidas.[34]

The names of additional women are known through the Pythagorean biographical tradition, even though they are not listed by Iamblichus among the seventeen "most famous." Pythagoras left his memoranda (*hypomnemata*) to *Damo*, his daughter, sister of Telauges. Though Iamblichus does not include *Bitale*, Damo's daughter, in his catalog he does report that Bitale inherited the memoranda after Damo's death (*VP* 146).[35] Furthermore, during his subterranean sojourn, Pythagoras's mother, *Pythaïs*, recorded what had happened and at what time on a tablet and sent her notes down to him.[36] When he emerged he read his experiences aloud. Whether or not the story that he had visited the house of Hades is literally true is irrelevant here.[37] The Greeks, however, did believe that heroes could return from the Underworld, and certainly the mother who boasts of her son's divinity and resurrection is a historical topos not unique to the biography of Pythagoras.

This story illustrates the importance of women in Pythagorean biographical tradition. Emerging from a cave is like emerging from a womb, and therefore the presence of Pythagoras's mother is natural at her son's rebirth (see fig. 1). Pythagoras may have suffered some sort of psychotic or hallucinatory experience, as was not uncommon among Greek sages and philosophers,[38] or he may have deliberately planned a charade to increase his charisma. In any case, his mother was his trusted confidante, who protected and enhanced his reputation as a superhuman miracle worker. Pythagoras must have taken his mother with him when he emigrated from Samos to Magna Graecia, for it was customary for the Greeks in general to care for their parents, and Pythagoras, in particular, instructed his disciples to look after them. He could certainly afford to bring his mother from Samos. He came from a wealthy family, had the funds to travel in the Greek world and Egypt, is never described as teaching for pay, and was involved in the aristocratic politics of Magna Graecia. Moreover, unlike most Greek thinkers, he does not ignore women past reproductive age; rather, he refers to them in his speeches (see chap. 2).[39]

As we have seen, there are many stories about women in the biographical traditions of Pythagoras, though they have often been either ignored or dismissed as jokes.[40] Nevertheless, taken seriously, they establish a formidable link in the chain of information, not only about women, but also about Pythagoras.

We pause to reflect on literacy among pre-Socratic philosophers and among Pythagoras and the women in his circle, in particular. William V. Harris pointed out more than twenty years ago that historians of philosophy have not dealt satisfactorily with this issue, and that conclusion remains true at the time of this writing.[41] A century before Pythagoras, Anaximander and Anaximenes of Miletus published their work, followed by Xenophanes of Colophon, Heraclitus, and Solon.[42] Pherecydes wrote prose, and he was said to have been the teacher of Pythagoras. Yet Porphyry (probably using Dicaearchus as his source) reported that Pythagoras relied on his considerable rhetorical gifts and did not write anything.[43] Of course Pythagoras's *hypomnemata* (memoranda), to which Iamblichus (*VP* 146) refers, are more like notes: Porphry (*Pyth.* 57) states that Pythagoras did not leave any *suggramma* (written composition, book).[44] Thus Dicaearchus and Porphyry may have not been commenting on the memoranda but may have simply meant that Pythagoras did not write formal prose treatises or dialogs. The report just above about Pythagoras's mother sending written notes to him and about his keeping a journal while he was in a cave is evidence that he could read and write. He was also surrounded by literate women. Pythagoras's mother and wife were literate; furthermore, since he designated his daughter Bitale as the custodian of his memoranda, the chances are good that she was literate too, having learned her letters from her mother and grandmother. Consequently, during the Renaissance, the women in Pythagoras's family were cited as models of educated women.[45]

Figure 1. Red figure Apulian *lebes gamikos*, ca. 340-320 BC. Seated woman, richly adorned. Lyre on wall at upper right. Metropolitan Museum of Art, 17.46.2, attributed to the Group of New York 28, 57.10, Rogers Fund, 1917.

We observe, in passing, the female succession in the transmission of Pythagoras's memoranda, despite the existence of many male disciples and of Telauges, son of Pythagoras, who married Bitale. After the Pythagoreans were expelled by Cylon's followers in the second half of the fifth century BC, the men collected their own memoranda and written materials and made arrangements for them when they died, instructing their sons, daughters, and wives to preserve them and transmit them within the family (Iambl. *VP* 253). Women and other family members serve as the links between the traditions about the earliest Pythagoreans and such sources as Aristoxenus, whom historians nowadays find generally trustworthy.[46] Furthermore, we cannot overemphasize the strength of the oral tradition, which served as well to preserve the words and deeds of the founder among Pythagorean communities. Oral history must have been particularly accurate among the Pythagoreans, who took special care to train their memories.[47]

We also notice that biographical tradition highlights women at the very beginning—from the time of Pythagoras himself. Words of wisdom by women including Theano and Deino are quoted. Pythagoras claimed that he himself had been reincarnated three times as a man and finally as a courtesan named Alco.[48] Perhaps this last experience can be construed as the inspiration for his distaste for philandering and prostitution (see chap. 2). He also said that he taught what he had learned from Aristocleia, a priestess at Delphi (Iambl. *VP* 41).[49] In contrast to other thinkers of his time, Pythagoras did not consider women to be totally alien and inferior animals. In its explanations of how the world was organized, however, Pythagorean doctrine did relegate women to a lesser category than men. The list below—where the category on the left is superior to the category on the right—draws attention to the difference between the two. Aristotle attributed to the Pythagoreans a table of opposites, including:[50]

limit	unlimited
odd	even
right	left
male	female
straight	crooked
good	evil
light	darkness

Nevertheless, we must bear in mind that this information comes to us from Aristotle, a philosopher whose own views on women were extremely negative and who thought of women as creatures with minds that did not function.

The known origins of famous women Pythagoreans include 3 from Croton, 2 from Lucania, 2 from Sparta, 2 from Laconia, 2 from Taranto, 2 from Argos, and 1 each from Metaponto, Arcadia, Phlius, and Sybaris. Seven women of the total seventeen are seen to have come from Sparta and cities associated with Sparta, namely, Laconia and Taranto. In comparison, out of a total of 218 men, there are 43 from nearby Taranto and 3 from Laconia.[51] Pythagoreanism would seem to have a special attraction for Spartan women. The largest contingent of women were Spartans (Cheilonis, Theadusa, Cleachma, Timycha, and Cratesicleia) or from the Spartan colony of Taranto (Habroteleia and Peisirrhode). The idea that prescribed commandments and structure might govern the minutiae of life in an entire community was familiar to Spartans.[52] The lifestyle advocated by Pythagoras was favorable to women and in some ways similar to the wholesome regime of Spartan women. For example, childbearing at a mature age was recommended. Pythagoras's prohibition against cosmetics in an age when white lead was commonly used as face powder was salutary. The Pythagorean regimen was consistent with Spartan ideals of austerity, decorum, and education. Moreover, Sparta enjoyed cultural ties with Samos, Pythagoras's native land.[53] Thoughtful women who enjoyed the luxury of choosing how to live were likely to choose to become Pythagoreans. Thus it is no coincidence that Spartans, some of the most autonomous women in the Greek world, were listed as disciples.[54]

As we have shown, some of the women were contemporaries of Pythagoras and some later. Although the veracity of Iamblichus is sometimes questionable, scholars generally believe that much of Iamblichus's catalog goes back to Aristoxenus and thus is reliable evidence for the early Pythagoreans.[55] Iamblichus (*VP* 267) gives the names of 218 known male Pythagoreans and mentions that doubtless there were many others whose names are not known. To this remark we may add that a large proportion of the Pythagorean men must have been married, since Pythagoras speaks to them about conjugal relations. That Iamblichus states that he is listing the famous women suggests that there were others. Pythagoras, however, discouraged women from becoming known. In his address to the women at Croton, he urged them to speak little their whole lives and to see to it that others would not malign them (Iambl. *VP* 55). Though the majority of the names of the wives of known Pythagoreans are not included in Iamblichus's catalog of the 17 most famous Pythagorean women, surely a large number of them must have been followers of Pythagoras. As was usual in the ancient world, simply as a result of their gender, women were less likely to be noticed by historians. They spent less time in public than men did, and consequently their activities failed to be recorded, and even those who did make it into the pages of history are frequently ignored by later scholars (see Intro. and chap. 3). Moreover, fewer women than men were literate, so they did not write about themselves or about topics of interest to future philosophers and historians. Nevertheless Iamblichus reports that Pythagoras addressed the wives of his followers at Croton.

Not only did Pythagoras care about the women, but he knew that his program for men could not be successful without women's participation. Being a Pythagorean was not a part-time commitment for a man to practice for a few hours when he left his home and joined other men each day. Rather, Pythagoreans followed detailed, nonintuitive rules that encroached on private life, including regulations for diet, clothing, bedding, sexual intercourse, and childrearing; it would have been virtually impossible for a married man to adhere to Pythagoreanism if his wife did not. In view of the patriarchal structure of Greek society, even wives who did not share their husbands' enthusiasm for Pythagoreanism would have had to follow the rules for daily life. Furthermore, an enticement was the harmonious music that infused Pythagorean life, for it must have been both a pleasure to hear for its own sake and a means of creating a shared happiness. Pythagoras "used to employ the following choral arrangement: he seated someone holding a lyre in the middle. Those who could sing sat around him in a circle. Thus while the first one played the lyre, they sang paeans together, through which they thought they would feel joyful, and become harmonious and rhythmical."[56]

There is archaeological evidence for lyres constructed from tortoise shells in the area where the original Pythagoreans lived,[57] and lyres are also a common theme in Neopythagorean literature. Philosophers considered the Dorian mode the best, for it was manly and dignified.[58] In any case, as we will show in the next chapter, Pythagoreanism offered an attractive way of life for women, a life in many ways superior to that of the ordinary, noncommitted Greek.

Pythagorean doctrine was sympathetic to women; the proof that bears repeating is that Pythagoras required the same sexual monogamy of husbands that was mandatory for wives.[59] Because Pythagoreanism pervaded everyday life women had to know the regulations governing diet, dress, sexual behavior, religious obligations, and other essential aspects of life. Lunch consisted of bread with honey or honeycomb, no wine, with the caveat that one should not break bread—lest friendships be broken apart.[60] Their breads were made of barley and of wheat, which grew locally.[61] As on the mainland, those who could afford wheat came to prefer it. They also ate *opson*, consisting of raw and cooked vegetables, fruits, especially figs and olives, and meat from sacrificial animals.[62] They cultivated grapes and made wine from varietals they had brought from the Greek mainland and from those they found in Italy. Their sugars included honey and dried fruit. Analyses of bones and teeth from Metaponto indicate that women consumed more sugars than men, and men consumed more protein than women.[63] The olive was raised for consumption and even more so for the production of olive oil. The local diet was similar to that of Southern Italy nowadays and included a variety of legumes. Pythagoras, however, banned foods that cause flatulence, including beans, which were a staple of the ancient diet.[64] Nor should his followers step on beans.[65] Although they lived on the coast, unlike other Greeks, they did not eat much fish or seafood. The inner circle was to abstain from eating fish that were sacred to the gods (red mullet, black-tail, sea barbell, sea anemone) and from eating white cocks.[66]

Pythagoreans also abstained from eating living food. The sources on their vegetarianism disagree, but it seems that the most committed Pythagoreans were vegetarians, while others followed various less restrictive diets.[67] Like those nowadays who follow kosher, halal, or Jain rules, their eating practices identified Pythagoreans as a minority group, different from their relatively omnivorous neighbors. Their diet is another indication that Pythagoreans were wealthy; they could choose their food according to their rules rather than according to what happened to be in season and was abundant and cheapest in the market, and they could indulge in wasteful practices, such as serving luxurious banquets that they looked at but were not allowed to eat (Diod. Sic. 10.5.2). The average height of women in Pantanello was 60.2 inches, of men 63.7 inches.[68] Because the Pythagoreans were wealthy and probably better fed than the general population, they may have been slightly taller.

During the day Pythagoreans did not drink wine, but at dinner they did consume wine.[69] Spartan women drank, but Athenian women did not, except as portrayed in the topsy-turvy world of Athenian Comedy. Following Doric tradition, Pythagorean women probably drank wine. They wore clean white linen and used linen bedding, which is nowadays touted as providing a superior sleeping environment.[70] Pythagoras may have learned about linen during his visit to Egypt. Though linen was not yet common in Magna Graecia, it had been used in the Greek world since Homeric times.[71] Pythagoreans did not use fleeces, since as vegetarians they did not regularly slaughter animals for meat. In contrast to fleece, linen is easily cleaned and not likely to harbor lice.[72] Freeborn women were forbidden from wearing gold.[73]

The regimen was all-embracing, from dawn to bedtime. The Pythagoreans exercised; their daily routine included a private walk. This attention to physical exercise for both women and men shows Spartan influence, although the Pythagorean version was milder. Xenophon (*Oec.* 10.11, 11.15, 18), too, who admired the Spartan educational system, also advised that men and women take walks, and Aristotle (*Pol.* 1335b12–14) suggests that pregnant women should too. Although Iamblichus (*VP* 165–66) does not specify women, there is no reason to suppose that women did not also participate in the following activities that he describes: "They particularly valued the memory and devoted themselves to its care and exercise. . . . A Pythagorean would not rise from bed before recalling what had happened the previous day trying to bring to mind the events of the whole day, eagerly attempting the disciplined recollection of everything, just how each thing had occurred. And if there was plenty of time on waking up. . . . trying to recover the events of the day before that in the same way."

In addition to learning the unique rules governing the domestic life of Pythagoreans, the Pythagorean women had to know the basic system of housekeeping that was common to households in Magna Graecia. Like other Greek housewives they managed the domestic economy, in particular, feeding and clothing the members of the *oikos* (household, estate), including the family, slaves, and dependent freedmen.[74] Staples were raised on the family farm, and an excess might be sold or traded. Most clothing was also produced at home. The wife was in charge of her daughters until they married and of her sons until at least age seven. She also trained, supervised, and even nursed the domestic slaves and kept track of the household goods, lest any be lost or stolen. It was her responsibility to make sure that there was always an adequate amount of food kept safely in storage in case bad weather or a poor harvest suddenly interrupted the food supply.

The Lives of the Pythagoreans

That the Pythagoreans were wealthy is suggested immediately by their having had time to listen to the speeches of Pythagoras.[75] Pythagoras's first speeches at Croton are addressed to an elite who seem to have been as luxurious and dissipated as their neighbors in their rival city Sybaris. The speeches allude to ostentatious expensive items in their lives, including concubines, numerous slaves, and gold jewelry. Wealth enabled these people to make choices about how to live their lives and to enjoy the freedom to become disciples of the philosopher.

Pythagoreans were wealthy landowners. There is no mention of any Pythagorean in the group working for wages.[76] They were recruited from Greek colonies along the Ionian coast of Puglia, Basilicata, and Calabria, including Taranto, Metaponto, Croton, Sybaris, and Locri. The wealth of the people in these areas derived from animal husbandry and from growing grain (*triticum aestivum*) and six-rowed barley.[77] Emmer (*triticum dicoccum, farro*) was probably grown only for local consumption.[78] Through major land reclamation efforts involving draining marshes and digging canals, Pythagoreans increased the arable land. They also grew grapes, fava beans, and olives.[79] Their domesticated animals included goats, sheep, pigs, cattle, poultry, asses, mules, hinnies, aurochs, oxen, and horses.[80] Sheeps' and goats' milk was used for cheese. Horses and oxen were used for transportation and oxen especially for plowing. Duck, deer, and other edible wild animals were plentiful. Sheep were also raised for wool, but most of the other animals were used for work or local consumption. Though the Pythagoreans themselves did not wear woolen garments, their slaves probably did. Excavations of the city centers and the countryside have revealed homes, sanctuaries, cemeteries, and public buildings. Though there is no archaeological evidence specifically linked to the Pythagoreans, it is reasonable to suppose that—subject to the specific restrictions of their regimen—they lived like their wealthy neighbors in these areas, for they were recruited from these populations. The coins of these cities advertise their prosperity. Women in these regions wore abundant jewelry as well. Necklaces, large earrings, and other ornaments and clothing embroidered in metallic thread are clearly depicted in Apulian vase painting (see fig. 1).

The record shows change over time. Archaeologists have discovered that houses in the area gradually grew larger and more comfortable.[81] Farmhouses were domiciles and places of work. Some houses had two stories; the ground floor was devoted to farming, storage, weaving, and sheltering animals, and the family lived in the upper level.

Reforming the Lives of the Pythagoreans

The charismatic Pythagoras, however, found that, despite their relative ease and prosperity, some elite members of the population were ripe for change. He introduced sumptuary measures that affected both women and men. With rhetorical flourishes, Justin (20.4) relates Pythagoras's opposition to luxury:[82]

> The Crotonians ceased to exercise their valor, or to care for distinction in the field. They hated the arms which they had unsuccessfully taken up, and would have abandoned their former way of life for one of luxury, had not Pythagoras arisen among them. This philosopher was born at Samos, the son of Demaratus, a rich merchant, and after being greatly advanced in wisdom, went first to Egypt, and afterwards to Babylon, to learn the motions of the stars and study the origin of the universe, and acquired very great knowledge. Returning from there, he went to Crete and Lacedaemon, to instruct himself in the laws of Minos and Lycurgus, which at that time were in high repute. Furnished with all these attainments, he came to Croton, and, by his influence, recalled the people, when they were giving themselves up to luxury, to the observance of frugality. He used daily to recommend virtue, and to enumerate the ill effects of luxury, and the misfortunes of states that had been ruined by its pestilential influence; and he thus produced in the people such a love of temperance, that it was at length thought incredible that any of them should be extravagant.
>
> He frequently gave instruction to the women apart from the men, and to the children apart from their parents. He impressed on the female sex the observance of chastity, and submission to their husbands; on the rising gen-

eration, modesty and devotion to learning. Through his whole course of instruction he exhorted all to love temperance, as the mother of every virtue. He produced such an effect upon them by the constancy of his lectures, that the women laid aside their clothing embroidered with gold, and other ornaments and distinctions, as instruments of luxury, and, bringing them into the temple of Juno [Hera], consecrated them to the goddess, declaring that modesty, and not fine apparel, was the true adornment of their sex.[83]

How profligate the character of the youth had become can clearly be gauged from the stubborn depravity that he overcame among the women.[84] Three hundred of the young men, however, being united by an oath of fraternity, and living apart from the other citizens, drew the attention of the city upon them, as if they met for some secret conspiracy; and the people, when they were all collected in one building, proceeded to burn them in it. In the tumult about sixty lost their lives; the rest went into exile.

In his sumptuary measures and in advocating austerity, Pythagoras was in agreement with other lawgivers in Magna Graecia, including Zaleucus of Locri, with the laws of Syracuse, and in particular with the laws attributed to Lycurgus of Sparta.[85] It is also interesting to compare Solon's laws concerning women in Athens early in the sixth century with Pythagoras's recommendations more than half a century later. It is necessary to remember, however, that Solon's legislation affected the entire Athenian population and was commissioned and enforced by the authority of the state, whereas Pythagoras's rules were private, devised for his elite group to follow voluntarily. Solon had been granted dictatorial powers; Pythagoras met with the elite Crotoniates and used persuasion to convince them that his recommendations had merit.

Furthermore, Solon's laws were quite detailed and fell disproportionately on women. They included the following provisions, largely limited to the proper conduct at weddings and funerals rather than to the minutiae of daily life that Pythagoras dealt with:

— The *prothesis* ("laying out of the body") must be held indoors;
— the *ekphora* ("transporting the corpse to its place of burial") must be held before sunrise on the succeeding day, with men walking in front of the cart, and women behind; only women over the age of 60 or related to the deceased within the degree of second cousin are permitted to participate, with the latter also permitted to return to the house after the burial;
— women must not wear more than three *himatia* ("cloaks"), nor must the dead be interred in more than three;

— laceration of the flesh, singing of prepared dirges, or bewailing anyone except the person whose funeral is being held is forbidden;
— and trousseaux were limited to three dresses and some other paraphernalia of little value.[86]

Since women were neither lawgivers nor voting citizens, they had no say in framing the sumptuary prescriptions in Athens or in Magna Graecia. Clearly, sumptuary measures everywhere affected the wealthy more than the poor. We do not know if Athenian women were pleased by the laws of Solon, but we suspect that they were not, inasmuch as they curtailed women's influence and restricted their opportunities to meet with other female members of the family. By restricting the means by which the wealthy displayed their prosperity and power, Solon's sumptuary measures created at least the appearance of equality among Athenian citizens. Similarly, by promoting austerity among his followers and adopting the Spartan ideal of frugality he may have learned about at Sparta and Taranto and even in his native Samos (which had ties to Sparta),[87] Pythagoras also created a kind of community of goods.[88] He rejected the *truphe* (luxury) associated with Sybaris. Furthermore, the inhabitants of the Spartan colony of Taranto, asserting that they were following their ancestral laws, were also influential in spreading Spartan ideals in Magna Graecia.[89]

Adherence to sumptuary measures distinguished the followers of Pythagoras from other wealthy inhabitants of Magna Graecia: the women were particularly noticeable, for the men renounced their concubines, but their external appearance continued pretty much as usual. The women, however, had to make radical changes in their appearance and dress. As Thorstein Veblen observed, women serve as a means of displaying the family's wealth. They are vehicles of conspicuous consumption.[90] By their lack of adornment and simple attire, Pythagorean women would stand out from the crowd, neither flaunting their wealth nor dressed like the poor. Even if most of them remained anonymous, their unique garb would have identified them as a distinctive group, members of a cult.

Although the Pythagoreans were wealthy and members of the elite, they were subject to the same environmental forces as everyone in Magna Graecia, though we may speculate that their peculiar diet and fastidious lifestyle may have given them some advantage over their neighbors. Nevertheless, they could not escape from malaria, which was endemic in southern Italy. Evidence from the Pantanello necropolis at Metaponto shows that, beginning in childhood and lasting throughout their lives, the population also suffered from nonvenereal syphilis (*treponema pallidum*), causing pain and disfigurement.[91] The life expectancy of females was thirty-nine years, and of males, forty-one.[92]

Also endemic were traumas caused by human interaction. When the Pythagoreans migrated to Magna Graecia, they did not leave political and military conflict behind them. Rivalries and animosities among political factions and between cities flourished. This is not the place to give a detailed history of the continual hostilities in and among the cities in Magna Graecia. We have mentioned the conflagration and violence against the young men in Croton as related by Justin. One additional example will suffice. Croton and Sybaris were the homes of many Pythagoreans. In 510 BC Croton annihilated Sybaris so thoroughly that even now it is difficult for archaeologists to find traces of this once-flourishing and wealthy polis. The Pythagoreans were elite, wealthy, and numerous, and they constituted a formidable political faction recruited from various cities. Sometimes they held power, at other times they were expelled from cities and assassinated. Thus the lives of Pythagorean women were not always tranquil and harmonious.

CHAPTER TWO

Wives, Mothers, Sisters, Daughters

More than any other early thinker, Pythagoras paid attention to improving family relationships. In contrast to Solon, whose family legislation largely reflected traditional practices,[1] Pythagoras proposed new ways of creating harmony within the nuclear family. His program for daily life included advice to husbands about the proper treatment of their wives; to wives about the relationship with their husbands; to children about the appropriate behavior toward parents; and to parents about the proper nutrition and upbringing of children.

Wives

Pythagoras was the first Greek thinker to propose a single standard for the sexual behavior of husband and wife: he advocated strict monogamy for both. Men should not conduct extramarital affairs. A husband may have intimate knowledge of his own wife exclusively, and a wife should not commit adultery even when her husband has abused her or in reaction to his adultery. Marriage is a religious bond, and the wife is a suppliant at the hearth in her husband's house.[2] As part of the traditional Greek wedding, the bride was introduced to the gods of the bridegroom's hearth, supplicating them to accept her as a member of the household.[3] Pythagoras extended the period in which the wife was to be treated as a suppliant from the initiation of a marriage to its duration. Since throughout Greece a suppliant was to be treated with hospitality and respect, we may deduce from the simile that Pythagoras forbade violence and wife abuse. As a way of avoiding conflict, he also advised that a woman should not contend with her husband but consider it her triumph when he wins (Iambl. *VP* 54).

Moreover, Pythagoras declared that a husband should be an exemplar of *sophrosyne* (Iambl. *VP* 48). *Sophrosyne* was a personal virtue with a wide range of connotations, including discipline, self-control, and orderliness.[4] Though here the husband is to set the example, *sophrosyne* was the most characteristic virtue attributed to women. As a traditional female virtue, it bore the connotations of inhibition, chastity, and self-restraint.

The people of Croton who were attracted to Pythagoras's doctrines concerning rebirth and transmigration of the soul also listened to Pythagoras's more mundane advice.[5] The women asked Deino to persuade Pythagoras to urge self-restraint on their husbands, particularly in the sphere of sexual relations.[6] The only request that the women of Croton made of Pythagoras was that he tell their husbands to give up their concubines. That they limited their demands to this single item underlines its importance. This request is the earliest explicit report in Greek literature that women did not accept the double standard of sexual conduct. Pythagoras told the men what their wives had requested. Consequently, the men gave up their licentious behavior. They dismissed their concubines and had no erotic involvement with any women to whom they were not lawfully married, only with their wives (Iambl. *VP* 132, 152). The words Iamblichus uses are *pallakai* (concubines) and *anegguioi gynaikai* (unmarried women). In the fourth century BC an Athenian orator distinguishes *hetairai* and *pallakai* from legitimate wives: mistresses were for pleasure; concubines for daily service to the body; but wives for producing legitimate children and to be the faithful guardian of the inside (*tas men gar hetairas hêdonês henek' echomen; tas de pallakas tês kath' hêmeran therapeias tou sômatos, tas de gunaikas tou paidopoieisthai gnêsiôs kai tôn endon phulaka pistên echein*: Ps. Demos. 59, 122.) *Hetairai* were at the top of the social scale of prostitution. Many of them, in addition to physical beauty, had intellectual training and possessed artistic talents, attributes that made them entertaining companions to men. Concubines were more likely to live with a man in a more or less permanent union.[7] Current discussions about adultery suggest that to a wife, the long-term relationship her husband has with another woman is the most injurious.[8]

An anecdote about a Pythagorean who moderated a quarrel between two men, one of whom was accused of seducing the wife of the other, indicates that one woman, at least—though not necessarily a Pythagorean—dared to conduct an extramarital affair (Iambl. *VP* 125). In his address to the women of Croton, Pythagoras noted that Odysseus showed his loyalty to Penelope by refusing Calypso's offer of immortality, which would have meant abandoning Penelope (Iambl. *VP* 57). This example was riveting: instead of citing the faithful Penelope (who was the obvious example), Pythagoras mentioned Odysseus, who had many sexual partners but ultimately resisted a most attractive temptation from Calypso. Pythagoras cited the epic hero as a challenge to the women of Croton to show equal fidelity. Calypso's home, Ogygia, was said by some to be located off the coast of the Lacinian Cape, where Pythagoras addressed the women. This alleged proximity may have prompted Pythagoras's reference.

Conjugal Relations

Pythagoras approved of orderly marital sexual relations. Anecdotes record that Pythagorean women approved as well. Deino made the famous remark (which some claim was Theano's): "The wife should sacrifice on the very day she woke up in her husband's bed" (Iambl. *VP* 132). This dictum meant the wife who had just had intercourse with her husband remained pure, whereas a woman who woke up in the bed of a man to whom she was not married was polluted. Pythagoras's view contrasted with the traditional Greek idea that all sexual intercourse, even conjugal, was polluting (Iambl. *VP* 55). A husband was not merely to abstain from extramarital sex but rather had an obligation to be with his wife.[9] Pythagoras added the authority of Hades to this principle. When he returned from the underworld Pythagoras reported that men who did not wish to be with their own wives were punished.[10] Though we may well doubt that any underworld existed and that Pythagoras actually visited it (see chap. 1), the report attributed to him is consistent with beliefs about marriage that he expressed at other times. He thought that the successive life stages of women reflected the divine: Core (bride), Nymphe (a childbearing woman), and Meter, or Maia (the woman who produces children by means of her children, i.e. grandmother).[11] Thus the normal processes characteristic of these stages could not incur pollution. Pythagoras may have reached these original conclusions after making a serious study of sacrifices and ceremonial purity while visiting Egypt (Isoc. *Bus.* 28). In passing we note that Pythagoras divided man's life into four phases: childhood, youth, manhood, and old age.[12] Girls, in contrast, married so young that they were not thought to have a period of adolescence.

Anecdotes about Pythagorean women show some recognition of the idea that seductiveness and sex play within marriage are positive goods. For example, Diogenes Laertius (8.43) reports that Theano told a woman who was joining her husband to put away her shame with her clothing. Furthermore, Theano once exposed her hand as she was arranging her cloak. "What a beautiful arm," said someone. "But not public property," she replied.[13] Thus we deduce that the sight of a wife's arm can be sexually provocative, and the wife ought to reserve it for the husband.[14] Like his wife, Pythagoras was very attractive; he was tall, with the face of a free man, charming in speech and manner (Porph. *VPyth.* 18). Pythagoras's

Figure 2. Helen, born from egg of Leda and Zeus, disguised as a swan. Museo Archeologico Nazionale di Metaponto. Photo by Lee H. Pomeroy.

overarching view was that sexuality should be controlled. Sexual relations should take place only in the winter, and even then moderately. When asked whether a man should indulge in sexual pleasure, Pythagoras responded, "when you want to be weaker than yourself."[15]

The women of Croton were reputed to be beautiful. Probably in the early fourth century Zeuxis, from nearby Heraclea in Lucania, assembled the women of Croton to select five models for his painting of Helen.[16] Helen was Dorian, and many of the known Pythagorean women also came from Sparta, Laconia, and the Spartan colony of Tarentum. Helen was beautiful; the women of Croton were therefore appropriate models for Helen's portrait (fig. 2).

Mothers

Pythagoras and his followers advocated limiting sexual relationships to those that would produce legitimate children.[17] Furthermore, Pythagoras stated that a husband records his contract with his wife in their children (Iambl. *VP* 47). Pythagorean men were to abstain from intercourse with anyone except their own lawful wife not only because the wives demanded it but also because a husband's intercourse with a courtesan, or a slave, or with another man's wife was merely to satisfy lust and not to produce children. Thus Pythagorean regulations differed from pronatal policies in some other known Greek societies, which never seemed to have enough men, owing to death in war and natural factors, and which elevated to limited citizenship children born of a citizen father and of a noncitizen mother to whom the father was not legally married.[18] Pythagoreans were an elite corpus, and the philosopher was not overtly intent upon urging them to increase their numbers. Pythagoreans were to reproduce thoughtfully, leading healthy and temperate lives both before and during gestation, eating moderately, and not becoming inebriated (Iambl. *VP* 211–13).

A person must have children so that they will worship the gods, but certain restrictions were imposed (Iambl. *VP* 83, 86). A man should not endeavor to have children by a wealthy woman (Iambl. *VP* 84). Immature women should not bear children (Iambl. *VP* 209). Boys should not be introduced to sexual intercourse before they reach twenty (Iambl. *VP* 210). Men should come to procreative intercourse sober, not having eaten too much (Iambl. *VP* 211).[19] Perhaps Pythagoras did not need to mention the wife's sobriety because, though Spartan women regularly drank wine, they were not reputed to overindulge. Following this tradition, Pythagorean women probably drank modestly as well. Other Greek women in the classical period were not tipplers, except in Comedy.[20] The Pythagorean rules for conjugal intercourse are similar to those at Sparta, where women were not married until their bodies were fully mature; in contrast, in Athens girls were given in marriage at puberty. The Spartan bridegroom was also required to come to his bride perfectly sober.[21]

Heterosexuality is assumed, for obviously any other relationships are not procreative. The limitation of sexual relations to procreation would mean that postmenopausal women were to abstain, though this life stage is not treated in the sources except in the mention of Pythagoras's mother and of Meter, or Maia. The average age of menarche in classical Greece was fourteen.[22] The age of menopause was typically forty to fifty.[23] Thus the majority of women did not live to reach menopause, but surely some did.[24] Nevertheless, Greek men usually did not consider them sexually attractive: youth was more titillating. Furthermore, once the years of childbearing had passed, and loss of teeth and wrinkles had transformed a woman's appearance, she was considered "old," even if she had not actually reached menopause. As we have mentioned above, the life expectancy of the rural population in Metaponto was thirty-nine for women.[25] The average Greek woman married soon after puberty, but if the Pythagoreans followed

Spartan customs, their women married at about eighteen, when they were fully mature. The interval between childbirths was about four years.[26] The average woman gave birth to 4.3 children, of whom 1.6 died young and 2.7 survived to adulthood. The fertility of Pythagorean women was likely to have been lower than that of the average Greek woman as a result of Pythagoras's recommendation that sexual intercourse take place only in the winter, as well as the generally ascetic practices of the group. Thus they would have endured the rigors of childbirth less frequently and had better survival rates than the average Greek woman.

Interestingly enough, women outnumber men by almost two to one in burials at Metaponto.[27] This ratio is the reverse of the ratios in necropoleis in old Greece. The reason may be that at Metaponto women were held in higher esteem than in poleis like Athens, where female infanticide was practiced.[28] There is no evidence for female infanticide at Sparta, and it may well be that Dorians in general did not practice it.[29] Consequently the Dorian colonies in Magna Graecia were also free of this. Furthermore, at Metaponto the population was stable, and children and husband and even parents may have seen to the burial of a woman, especially one who died in her childbearing years.[30] Such concerns were consistent with Pythagoras's principles that husbands should treat wives with respect and that children should honor parents (see below).

Pythagoras believed that conjugal relationships should be temperate not only for the good of the married couple but also for the benefit of the baby who might be conceived. Conjugal relationships should be inspired by the wish to create children, not by lust. Temperate, sober intercourse would produce children who were also temperate and orderly. Bestial, thoughtless intercourse would produce intemperate, disorderly offspring.

A modern married woman might find congenial much of Pythagoras's advice advocating treating a wife as a suppliant, abstaining from violence in conjugal relationships, and most importantly, male sexual monogamy; evidently the women who became followers of Pythagoras did too. In antiquity, as now, male extramarital sexual relationships were common. In the *Oeconomicus* Xenophon portrays a relatively enlightened husband in the fifth century BC who believes himself exemplary and is proud of his treatment of his wife. This paragon nevertheless contemplates sexual intercourse with slaves in the house. A veiled threat to the wife may be detected in his declaration: "for compared with a slave, the appearance of a wife who is unadorned and suitably dressed becomes a sexual stimulant, especially when she is willing to please as well, whereas a slave is compelled to submit."[31]

Pythagorean doctrines about the family and individual ethics were sympathetic to women. The maxim that a wife be treated like a suppliant ensured gentle treatment in a world where wife abuse and domestic violence were not illegal. In antiquity wives might suffer not only the mental abuse inflicted by a philandering husband but also physical abuse, ranging from beating to murder. Before advocates for women succeeded in some countries in making such abuse a crime punishable by the state, it was a private matter and rarely entered the historical record—though there is scattered testimony from Greece and Rome.[32] In the seventh century BC Semonides of Amorgos (originally from Pythagoras's native home, Samos) wrote of a foxy, crafty wife: "She yaps it out even if there's no one to listen. Her husband can't stop her with threats, not even if he flies into a rage and knocks her teeth out with a rock."[33] Corporal punishment for freeborn children was normal in antiquity, and wives were, in some respects, legally the same as children. The Roman husband, however, was expressly forbidden to kill his wife for any offence without consulting the woman's kinsmen, but this law was flouted in at least one noteworthy instance.[34] Valerius Maximus (a Roman historian of the first century AD who wrote of moral exemplars) noted that in early Rome a husband cudgeled his wife to death for drinking wine. Nevertheless, he was not criticized, for it was generally agreed that drinking was a prelude to the loss of a woman's virtue.[35] In the second century AD Herodes Atticus ordered his freedman to beat his wife, Regilla, for trivial reasons. She died in premature childbirth from a blow to her abdomen.[36] Writing about his mother's tolerance of her husband's behavior, Augustine observed that the faces of many women were scarred as a result of being beaten by their husbands.[37] Plutarch suggested that married women need protectors to whom they were not married.[38] In view of the lifespan in antiquity, it was most likely that the father of a married woman would die and that she would turn to her brother for aid against her husband.

Pythagoras elevated the private sphere by comparing the governance of the *oikia* (household) and the *polis* (city-state: Iambl. *VP* 183). Furthermore, he stated that the relationship a man enjoyed with his wife, children, siblings (*adelphoi*), and relatives (*oikeioi*) should be characterized by friendship (*philia*: Iambl. *VP* 229). There must be as little harm as possible in friendship; this peaceful situation will develop if both people know how to control their anger, especially the younger person. Older people should admonish younger ones with kindness and respect. Friendship is secured by trust and undermined by lies (Iambl. *VP* 101–2, 232). Friendship with non-Pythagoreans was avoided (Iambl. *VP* 233). In other words, women, men, children, and other relatives were linked in the family and the larger Pythagorean community by the bonds of friendship, but separated from nonbelievers. Because most Pythagoreans, like Pythagoras himself, were first- or second-generation immigrants, they would not have had access to a wide range of extended family. Therefore they were open to making new ties, whether with other Pythagoreans or with their spouse. Furthermore, demographic realities will have curtailed the opportunity for three-generational families to develop and for parents to become grandparents. Nevertheless, some people did survive to old age. In fact, Pythagoras himself died at around eighty years as a result of violence;[39] otherwise he might have lived even longer.

Sisters

Iamblichus (*VP* 267) identifies four of the seventeen famous female Pythagoreans as sisters. Occelo and Eccelo are listed as disciples, along with their brothers Occelus and Occilus, who are also listed among the Pythagorean men. Philtys, daughter of Theophris of Croton, is cited as a sister of Byndacus, though neither her father nor her brother is included in the catalog of male Pythagoreans. Cleachma is identified as a sister of the Lacedaemonian Autocharidas, who is also listed separately among the men. These women may have converted their brothers to Pythagoreanism or they may have been drawn to this philosophy through a brother's enthusiasm. Similarly, in the second half of the fourth century BC, following her brother Metrocles, Hipparchia became a disciple of the Cynic Crates (Diog. Laert. 6.94, 96–98).

Daughters

Pythagorean doctrine mandated many of the same principles for the education of girls and boys.[40] Girls and boys must be brought up with hard work, exercise, endurance, and a diet appropriate for a laborious, self-controlled, and patient way of life. Iamblichus (*VP* 50) reports that after addressing the men and women of Croton separately he spoke to the children (*paides*) at the temple of Pythian Apollo. Parents were delighted to see their children in his presence rather than attending to their own business, and the children were eager to become his students. Isocrates also reports that Pythagoras was popular among the young (*Bus.* 29). Iamblichus uses the common word *paides*, which means "children of both sexes" or "boys."[41] The words Isocrates uses for children (*hoi neoteroi, hoi paides*) are masculine, but the Greeks always used the masculine, whether they were writing about both males and females or males only. Therefore, it is possible to question whether girls were invited to the lecture at the Temple of Apollo or whether only boys could attend.[42]

It seems likely that since Pythagoras lectured to the women, he must not have excluded the girls (who would eventually become women). He did not ignore girls but compared them to the divine *Core*. Furthermore, Pythagoras was influenced by the Spartan educational system, and at Sparta the state regulated an educational system for girls as well as for boys, with some similar features in the curricula of both and some features designed for each gender, respectively.[43] Though the Pythagorean educational system was not as rigorous as the Spartan, it too included elements of totalitarianism. It would have been ludicrous to exclude girls from learning the doctrines and to see them, for example, step on beans or hear them clamoring for gold jewelry, fleece bedclothes, and other items forbidden to the Pythagoreans. If they were not indoctrinated along with the boys, they would have become inadequate brides for them indeed.

Furthermore, Damo, daughter of Pythagoras, was reputed to be first among the girls, and when she grew up, first among the women.[44] In view of her lineage and immersion in Pythagoreanism, it was natural that Damo was the best. Interestingly enough, we do not hear that any particular boy, not even Pythagoras's son Telauges, was singled out as the best. Being first among the girls suggests a competitive educational framework in which a girl might be the best dancer in a chorus, or the sweetest singer, or the fastest and most graceful runner, or simply the most beautiful. Alcman's *Partheneia* allude to such rivalry among girls at Sparta.[45] It is thus reasonable to assume that Pythagoras included girls in his audience from the very beginning, when he addressed the elite at Croton.

Pythagoras's directives for the relationship between parents and children were unusual for the Greeks of the time in that he singled out mothers for special attention, just as he had chosen his own mother to be his record keeper during his miraculous subterranean sojourn. He said that mothers as well as fathers deserve honor, for among the gods there are both mothers and fathers (Iambl. *VP* 39). It was said of the Pythagoreans that "after what is due to the gods and the divine [they thought it necessary] to pay the greatest attention to parents and laws.... They approved upholding the customs and laws of their fathers, even if they should be somewhat inferior to those of others."[46] He said children owed gratitude to their parents for having given them life and for being their first benefactors (Iambl. *VP* 38, 40). Children should learn not to contradict their elders so that they themselves will be obeyed later (Iambl. *VP* 50). Children are also dear to the gods, for Apollo and Eros are portrayed as children (Iambl. *VP* 51–52).

Pythagoras was known as a versatile speaker: when he was invited to speak to the children, he composed childlike speeches for them; for the women speeches suited to women; for the archons speeches suited to archons; and for the ephebes speeches in a youthful style.[47] He began by telling the children not to initiate a quarrel or respond to one (Iambl. *VP* 51). He also preached that *sophrosyne* should be the goal of boys as well as girls and of married women, the elderly, and especially the young (Iambl. *VP* 41). Controlling desires of all kinds—whether for food or sex or other pleasing indulgences—was essential.[48] As a warning to the youth he cites the lack of self-control that allowed the lesser Ajax to rape Cassandra, priestess of Athena, and the thousand-year punishment that fell on the maidens of his polis, Opuntian Locri, in expiation for their ancestral hero's lack of sexual continence. The maidens of their colony Locri Epizephyrii (Locri) may have shared this burden.[49] Some girls from Locri may have been in Pythagoras's audience to be reminded of this frightening myth, for ten of the men in Iamblichus's catalog of known Pythagoreans came from Locri (Iambl. *VP* 267). According to the myth, Locrian maidens landed at Troy at night and had to reach the temple of Athena unobserved while the Trojans tried to kill them.[50] If they reached the temple, they were forced remain virgins for their lifetime and to serve as temple slaves. The tribute may have become a kind of initiation rite for Locrian girls that was enacted annually in historical times by only two girls.[51]

Pythagoras also dealt with the potential conflict a woman might have as both a daughter and a wife. He is reported to have urged the women to think about their marital relationships, noting that even fathers permitted a woman to love her husband more than her father (Iambl. *VP* 54). He noticed that parents of both sexes compete for the love of their children (Iambl. *VP* 39). The bonds between generations are precious. The worst crime is to cause dissension between parents and children (Iambl. *VP* 49).

As we have noted above, the *oliganthropia* (shortage of men) that has been detected at cemeteries in Metaponto may be attributed to the high regard Pythagoras and his Dorian peers had for women, at least in comparison with the attitudes in Athens and old Greece. According to various biographical traditions, Pythagoras himself had only one son, Telauges, but raised three daughters, Myia, Damo, and Arignote. We hear of only one grandchild, Bitale. The skewed sex ratio in favor of women at first seems unusual for the Greek world.[52] That more mirrors have been discovered in burials at Metaponto than anywhere else in the Greek world is a result of both the numerous female burials and the wealth of the survivors and perhaps the dead women. The explanation for the sex ratio may be found in Spartan customs. Sparta practiced male infanticide but does not seem to have culled female infants.[53] Spartan men were constantly being lost at war, while Spartan women enjoyed a healthier life style than their contemporaries in, say, Athens. Perhaps we can generalize from Sparta to the Dorian population of Magna Graecia.

Immortal Wives, Mothers, and Daughters

Pythagoras spoke to the women of Croton in the temple of Hera Lacinia.[54] This temple was not only important to all Crotoniates and all inhabitants of the region, but it also became particularly important to Pythagoras's female followers. Pythagoras commented that women are most suited for piety, and he addressed the women of Croton on religious rites, connecting traditional religion with Pythagorean ethics (Iambl. *VP* 54).

Pythagoras's selection of the temple of Hera Lacinia as the site of his mesmerizing first address to the women of Croton was significant. At Croton the worship of Hera was concentrated at two major locations: the "Vigna Nuova," and the Lacinian Cape.[55] Pythagoras might have directed them to assemble at the "Vigna Nuova" or somewhere else within the city where they could have gathered for an hour and rushed back home. Instead he chose as his podium a much larger site to accommodate the crowd, a famous sacred place where the women would gather as an elite group, beyond the confines of home, marriage, and the city. The temple was six miles from the city; we assume that some of the women walked, but many drove or were driven there in carriages. Visitors to the temple of Hera Lacinia left their homes at sea level, an area that was often swampy and malarial. After trudging up the promontory or riding in wagons through fields of wild flowers, they reached the Sacred Way and the temple precinct, a glorious sight (fig. 3).

The temple perches high on a bluff. The name Lacinia comes from the location on the Cape of the same name (now also called Capo Colonna), which Thetis presented to Hera as a gift.[56] This name, in turn, may ultimately derive from the Italian hero Lacinius. The women who had migrated from the Greek mainland and islands in the east probably remembered catching sight of the Cape joyfully from a ship, as their first view of civilization after their long voyage to Magna Graecia. It would take the women of Croton a good part of a day to reach the site and to listen to the lecture. On the journey back home they would have plenty of time to think about and to discuss what Pythagoras had said. The women of Croton must have traveled with wagons laden with baskets of offerings and food for themselves, delighted to have an excuse for a picnic and a day in the country.

Since temples were homes for the gods, not for crowds of worshippers, the

Figure 3. The Via Sacra, approaching the temple of Hera Lacinia. Photo by Lee H. Pomeroy.

women gathered in the temple precinct, and in Building B, which they reached before approaching the temple (fig. 4). Building B was built for worshippers and people who had come to celebrate festivals. It had fourteen square rooms, which must have contained *klinai* (dining couches). Ceramics for cooking and eating were excavated there.

Livy (24.3.1–8) gives a lengthy and inspired description of the place:

> Six miles from this famous city there was a still more famous temple to Juno Lacinia, an object of veneration to all the surrounding communities. There was a grove here enclosed by a dense wood and lofty fir-trees: in the middle was delightful pasture.[57] All kinds of cattle, sacred to the goddess, used to feed without any herdsman, and at nightfall the different herds separated each to their own stalls without any beasts of prey lying in wait for them or any human hands to steal them. These cattle were a source of great profit, and a column of solid gold was made from the money gained and dedicated to the goddess. Thus the temple became celebrated for its wealth as well as for its sanctity, and as generally happens in these famous spots, some miracles also were attributed to it. It was commonly reported that an altar stood in the porch of the temple, the ashes on which were never stirred by any wind.[58]

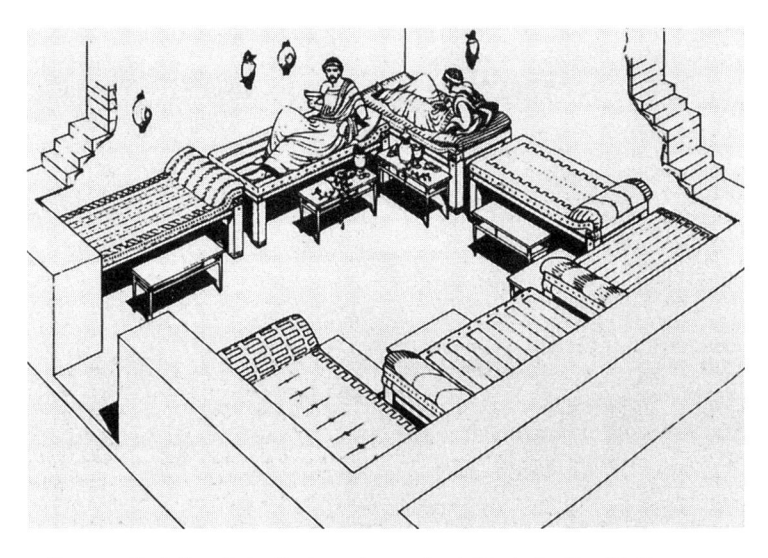

Figure 4. Building B, in the temple precinct. Photo by Lee H. Pomeroy.

Though Livy is a late source for the ambience of the Temple in the days of Pythagoras, religion is conservative; traditions at sanctuaries are likely to be maintained or at least remembered. To the reader who has not visited the site, Livy's description might appear to be that of a *"locus amoenus"* (a pleasing place), that is, a literary description of an idyllic pastoral scene with elements of an idealized golden age. Greek and Roman literature is replete with such descriptions. To the visitor nowadays, however, the site is truly a lovely place. Palm trees flourish in the subtropical climate, and the hill teems with small wildlife, including bees and lizards It is still numinous—like, for example, the Amphiaraeon in Attica, where it is possible to understand why worshippers believed they were in the presence of the divine.

The temple was surrounded by groves where statues of Olympic victors, including the famous Milo, were erected (Philostr. *VA* 4.28). Milo was not only an athlete but also a famous warrior. Statues of the priestesses who served the goddess were also dedicated on the site, as was usual at Greek sanctuaries (Diod. Sic. 12.9.5–6, Pliny *HN* 34.31). Festivals were celebrated here, some with athletic games. All the Italian people attended the festival of Hera, and the temple also became the assembly place of the Greeks of Magna Graecia (Athen. 12.541a–b). At least one epigram of the third-century BC poet Nossis, which is connected with a dedication at the Lacinium, was probably inscribed on a stone tablet placed near the object it describes.[59]

Figure 5. Single remaining column of the temple of Hera Lacinia. Photo by Lee H. Pomeroy.

The temple was built in the sixth century BC, then enlarged, reusing the earlier foundation, in the early fifth century: this period includes the time of the Pythagoreans' sojourn in Croton.[60] Six Doric columns on the short ends and fourteen on the long sides rose 8.35 meters on a high stylobate. Here Hannibal slaughtered two thousand Italian mercenaries and dedicated a bilingual inscription (in Punic and Greek) on a brass tablet, advertising his victories. Polybius mentions it as a source for his history of the Punic Wars.[61] Livy, Pliny (*HN* 2.240), and Valerius Maximus (1, 8, ext. 18) were impressed by the structure of the altar, which protected the flame from the surrounding winds.

The temple was clad with Parian and Pentelic marble. Q. Fulvius Flaccus stripped the marble tiles in 173 BC (Livy 42.3). In 1600 AD the temple was still almost intact, but it was demolished by a bishop called Lucifero. Two columns were left. One was overthrown by earthquake in 1638.

Dedications to Goddesses

Having been persuaded by the first address of Pythagoras, the women of Croton abandoned luxury and dedicated their superfluous possessions at the temple (Iambl. *VP* 54, 56). Pythagoras had specified that they prepare their dedications themselves and carry them themselves and not employ slaves.[62] He told them not to offer bloody sacrifices, which made their task easier. Nevertheless, slaves would have been helpful, but they would also have served as an aspect of conspicuous consumption, and Pythagoras was urging his followers to abandon luxury and not to think about their appearance. Moreover, he may not have wished to share his precious esoteric insights with slaves. Their dedications must have been light enough for the women to carry at least from the wagons. Women could certainly carry incense, round cakes, pastry of barley meal, honeycombs, jewelry, and clothing. These offerings were vegetarian and did not require the services of a butcher or any other assistant.

Over the years the temple came to possess great riches. The dedications were not made anonymously. We must imagine that the Pythagorean women were identified among the donors and thus brought glory to themselves and their group. The Museo Archeologico Statale at Croton displays a rich array of dedications to Hera Lacinia, including gold and silver jewelry and bronze figurines of common archaic female monsters, for example, a sphinx, a siren, and a gorgon of the mid–sixth century BC. There is also an unusual bronze model of a ship, perhaps dedicated by a voyager who alighted below the temple of Hera.[63] Less valuable dedications included mirrors, ceramics, and terra-cotta heads of *korai*.

A gold diadem that probably crowned the cult image has been discovered (fig. 6).[64] The crown was decorated with leaves and berries, reminiscent of the crown of Hera at Sparta, which was decorated with chrysanthemum and galingale (sedge: Ath. 15.678a, 681a). The crown and other valuable dedications date from the middle of the sixth century BC,[65] so they may well be connected with dedications made by the wealthy citizens of Croton at the urging of Pythagoras. It is conceivable that some of the women's property was sold, or their gold jewelry melted down, as a contribution to the crown. The crown was manufactured in two phases. First it was fashioned as a diadem with horizontal geometric braided ornamentation; after the middle of the sixth century BC, the floral decoration was added.[66]

The women dedicated their luxurious clothing to Hera, adding to the abundant riches at the huge temple. Doubtless many chose to dedicate their wool clothing, since Pythagoreans were forbidden to wear wool.[67] Thereafter they prob-

Figure 6. Golden diadem dedicated to Hera, decorated with myrtle, berries, and maple or vine leaves. Croton, Museo Archeologico Statale. *Museo Archeologico Nazionale Crotone. Itinerari dei Musei, Gallerie, Scavi e Monumenti d'Italia*, no. 58 (Rome, 2002), 34. Photo by Lee H. Pomeroy.

ably wore linen and dedicated it to Hera as well, a tradition that continued at least to the third century BC, when the poet Nossis made a dedication of linen (see below).[68] Pythagoreans favored wearing white clothing in general, especially for religious ceremonies.[69] Thus the clothing of the Pythagoreans imparted an immediately visible identity, separating them from their neighbors. Since it can be cold in southern Italy, the women probably wore many layers of cloth—like the Japanese women who wear twelve silk kimonos. Plutarch (*Isis and Osiris* 4) points out that linen is suited to all kinds of weather. Thus, though they were not wearing precious jewelry, their uniform displayed the wealth of their families through textiles.

The women of Croton offered many tens of thousands of *himatia* (garments).[70] Some, or all of them at different times, may have been draped over the cult image. These items are not to be compared to our donations of used, no-longer-stylish clothing to the Salvation Army and thrift shops. The *himatia* were extremely valuable and wearable, generation after generation. Vases from Magna Graecia portray women dressed in elaborate, sumptuous, showy clothing (see chap. 1, fig. 1). In a typical scenario, the wool was produced by sheep on the estates of the wealthy. The herds were maintained by slave shepherds or free workers; in either case the labor was costly. The textiles were produced by slave women and, voluntarily, by the free women in the household, who took the raw wool, cleaned, spun, dyed, and wove it. Textile manufacture was the sole productive activity by women that the Greeks recognized as making an economic contribution, and it certainly was a substantial and visible one.[71] In Xenophon's treatise Ischomachus, the successful estate owner displays the stores of textiles belonging to his *oikos* (*Oec.* 9.3.6). Such textiles constitute some of the liquid wealth of a household, kept in reserve and regarded as capital, to be exchanged for food or cash in hard times. Because Greek clothing was not sized, but would fit subsequent generations, textiles were a constituent part of dowries and inheritance; Demosthenes (27.10) includes clothing as part of his inheritance and mentions that clothing and bedding served as security for a loan. Some textiles are valuable enough to be locked in the innermost chamber of the house (*thalamos*).[72] In the *Oeconomicus* (8.41) Xenophon mentions doubling a slave's value by teaching her to spin. Also in the fourth century BC Aeschines (1.97) enumerates the skilled slaves inherited by Timarchus. Among them he makes specific and detailed mention of a woman skilled in working flax who produced sheer textiles for the market. The *scholion* comments that these goods were very valuable.

Iamblichus reports that Pythagoras urged his wealthy female followers to dedicate their luxurious clothing and ornaments to Hera Lacinia. There are many examples of the dedication of women's clothing to female divinities. Textiles are recorded in temple inventories, for example, that of Artemis Brauronia.[73] Textiles constituted part of the wealth of temples. Cult centers often were storehouses of treasures donated by the pious, functioning almost like museums: their ancient, costly, unusual, or artistic possessions attracted visitors to the sites. The clothing dedicated by the female Pythagoreans must have been valuable, and it would have been recorded item by item in inventories on inscriptions. A wealthy woman could dress in linen, or in the superb Apulian wool, or in silk from Cos or even China. Not only was the wool valuable, and the dyes and embroidery threads costly, but the weaving of the cloth and the fashioning of the garment represented many hundreds of hours of labor.[74] Thus a dedication of clothing was not solely an act of piety but was itself not only an act of renunciation but also, paradoxically, an opportunity for ostentation.

By dedicating their luxurious clothing, the Pythagorean women were making a substantial contribution to the treasury of Hera Lacinia. The dedication is further evidence of their affluence. Among the many parallels for the dedication of women's clothing to goddesses we may cite the inventory of clothing dedicated to Artemis Brauronia,[75] as well as the dedication to Demeter of the clothes of his murdered wife, Regilla, by the wealthy Herodes Atticus.[76]

Numerous sanctuaries have been excavated in the areas inhabited by the Pythagoreans, including the great temple of Hera Lacinia and other temples of female and male divinities, Hera, Artemis, and Athena, among them. The cults of female divinities required the service of female attendants because the bodies of the images representing the goddesses needed to be bathed and dressed periodically. Thus holding priesthoods offered women an opportunity to serve the community in public. Often the expenses incurred by the holders of Greek priesthoods were not insignificant, though they might also receive compensation for their services.[77] Therefore the numerous temples serve as additional evidence of the prosperity of the region and of the elite.

The women of Croton particularly favored Hera, for she was a goddess of marriage. Hera was the model spouse.[78] Indeed, that Hera's husband Zeus was a philanderer with many illegitimate children made her an appropriate model for mortal wives, who often faced the same problem, and in particular for the women of Croton, whose husbands had only recently agreed to give up their concubines.

Hera wielded a large array of powers and attributes in Magna Graecia, far more than anyone familiar with the worship of Hera only at Athens would imagine. In Magna Graecia Hera's spheres of influence overlapped with those of other powerful female divinities.[79] As the armed Hera, especially as a younger virgin warrior, she trespassed on territory usually allocated to Athena.[80] Hera, "cow-eyed" in Homer, always retained a special relationship with cattle. The use of this totem, however, does not exclude her caring for other animals, as did Artemis.[81] Hera enjoyed a special relationship with nature, especially with animals and vegetation.[82] Like Artemis, Hera Lacinia was connected with childbearing and the nurture of infants. The cult of Hera Lacinia also bore some similarities to the cult of Aphrodite.[83] In this it resembled the cult of Hera in Sparta, where mothers of brides sacrificed to Aphrodite-Hera.[84] That among the Pythagoreans Aphrodite would have links with marriage is suggested by their positive attitude toward marital sex.

The pomegranate, alluding to chthonic powers and fertility, was special to Hera as it was to Persephone.[85] Fertility was a particular concern to all members of an ancient community. Thus, Hera was a goddess of women and men of all classes. For example, she was worshipped by horsemen as Hippia (horse-goddess) and given dedications such as a bronze bridle.[86] A man with a horse usually rode in the cavalry and was almost certainly a member of the upper class. Obviously the cult of Hera Lacinia was also congenial to men: therefore it was a cult of the polis.[87] At the other extreme of society, Hera Lacinia as Eleuthe-

Figure 7. Scarab showing head of Hera Lacinia. Getty Villa, Malibu.

ria (Grantor of Freedom) gave asylum to slaves, and manumitted slaves offered dedications to her.[88]

Hera was so important that some cities built more than one temple to her. In Metaponto she was given two major temples, one in the urban center and another on a hill outside the city. A fragment of the cult statue from the temple beyond the city walls wearing a peplos has been excavated.[89] The statue of Hera, reconstructed, would have stood 170 centimeters high. A marble head that originally had little horns allows the identification of another figure found in the city sanctuary near Temple A2 as Hera's priestess Io. Other fragments indicate that she was wearing a peplos and *himation*. Similarly, at Croton the worship of Hera was concentrated at two major sites: the Vigna Nuova, and the Lacinian Cape.[90] The external temple was probably where the Greek colonists mingled with their indigenous neighbors, the urban temple where primarily Greeks worshipped. Thousands of dedications to Hera, ranging from inexpensive terra cottas made in molds to the lavishly adorned gold crown of Hera Lacinia, have been excavated in Croton and Metaponto and the surrounding territory (see above).

Greeks, of course, did not risk incurring the wrath of any divinity by ignoring her or him. The area of Magna Graecia that was home to the Pythagoreans was studded with temples to the pantheon of gods, female and male. Goddesses connected with fertility and rebirth were particularly important. Not only Hera, but Demeter and Persephone (Core) were honored with sanctuaries and thousands of offerings. For example, more than three thousand cups decorated or undecorated, small jars, amphorae, and terra-cottas made in molds as multiples and dedicated to Demeter Thesmophorios at Parapezzo (Locri Epizephryii) have been excavated. The dedications also included statuettes (all female) from the first half of the fifth century BC. These offerings are overwhelmingly small and inexpensive, indicating that the dedicators came from all social classes. Pythagoras held that women were pious, and his observation suggests that most of the donors to these popular female divinities were women. Though these dedications are not specifically tied to Pythagorean women or to any particular group of women, Pythagoras's statement about women's piety in general surely pertains to his own female followers. Also discovered in Locri, though now displayed in the Museo Nazionale della Magna Graecia in Reggio di Calabria, were fine archaic *pinakes* depicting aspects of the life of Persephone.[91] Some plaques show that, as with the cult of Hera Lacinia, the worship of Persephone at Locri was linked to the cult of Aphrodite, clearly an advantage for goddesses of marriage. At Locri the cult of Persephone emphasized the rape, marriage, and annual return of Persephone to the world above.[92] Although Persephone did not bear children herself (perhaps because she was always shown as young in comparison to her mother, Demeter), her saga as the archetypal bride and her attributes, including the pomegranate, pine cone, and a sheaf of grain, were connected to human marriage and the fertility of the family, crops, and society.

Eleven of the male Pythagoreans in Iamblichus's catalogue (*VP* 267) were Locrians. The foundation myth of Locri was similar to that of Tarentum, but the family structure was unusual in the Greek world. When the men of Locri were away fighting in the twenty-year-long Second Messenian War (ca. 650 BC), their wives had children by their male slaves. The mothers and their illegitimate children left Greece and became the founders of Locri Epizephyrii, now known as Locri.[93] At Locri nobility was traced matrilineally, back to the founding mothers.

Thus we find that the poet Nossis, who lived in Locri in the third century BC, identifies herself as descended from her mother and grandmother in an epigram written to accompany an offering to Hera Lacinia:

> Most reverend Hera, you who often descending from heaven
>   Behold your Lacinian shrine fragrant with incense,
> Receive the linen wrap that with her noble child Nossis
>   Theophilis daughter of Cleocha wove for you.[94]

As already mentioned, Pythagoras believed that women were akin to the divine as Core (bride), Nymphe (a childbearing woman), and Meter, or Maia. Reversing this perspective, we may say that the goddesses were anthropomorphic. Their worshippers shaped them in their own image and according to their own roles and needs. Persephone, Demeter, and Hera were anthropomorphic goddesses whose experiences were often replicated in the life cycles of their female worshippers. The countless dedications, sanctuaries, and costly temples to these divinities indicate their importance to the life of the community. These female divinities were primarily associated with fertility, with the growth of crops and of livestock, and with the perpetuation of families through marriage. Persephone was the archetypal Greek bride, captured by her bridegroom at puberty. Her virginity was secure, for she was usually chaperoned by her mother and girlfriends. Though her marriage was a surprise to Persephone and her mother Demeter, following the pattern of normal Greek marriages it resulted from a prior arrangement between her father and her bridegroom. Furthermore, like many Greek brides, including Bitale, who married her uncle Telauges, Pythagoras's son, Persephone married a close relative, in this case her uncle Hades. When Persephone was abducted, she cried out to her father Zeus for help, but since he had already approved of the marriage and the rapist was his own brother, he did not rescue his daughter.

To their sorrow, many Greek brides were separated from their natal families forever. For the immortals, however, there was a happier ending. Persephone became a queen, albeit in her husband's gloomy Underworld domain, and Demeter, wielding supramortal powers, was able to secure an annual visit from her daughter. Pythagoreans were more likely to have married within the group. As deduced above from Pythagoras's directives concerning the relationship between parents and children, from his bequeathing his memoranda to his daughter, and from his discussion of the conflicting loyalties a married woman may have toward her father, on the one hand, and her husband, on the other, Pythagorean mothers, fathers, and daughters seem to have been able to maintain their ties.

Map 3: The Hellenistic World. *Source*: Sarah B. Pomeroy, S. Burstein, W. Donlan, and Jennifer Roberts, *Ancient Greece*, 3rd ed. (New York, 2012), 480, fig. 12.5 (adapted). Reproduced with permission of Oxford University Press.

CHAPTER THREE

Who Were the Neopythagorean Women Authors?

The largest number of women philosophers in the Hellenistic period were Neopythagoreans; some of them were authors of letters and treatises.[1] These writings constitute the only extant body of Greek prose literature by women in the pre-Christian era.

The names of the authors and the recipients of their letters follow, arranged according to Holger Thesleff's designation of their place of origin and date (see further below):[2]

— Theano I
— Perictione I
— Arignote
— Theano II (to Euboule, Nicostrate, Callisto, Rhodope, Euclides, Eurydice, Timareta, and Timaionides)
— Ptolemaïs
— Aesara
— Melissa
— Phintys
— Perictione II
— Myia (to Phyllis)

Iamblichus does not distinguish between an original and later bearer of the same name. Theano and Myia are authors whose names also appear in Iamblichus, where they are members of Pythagoras's immediate family. None of the recipients is named by Iamblichus or otherwise known. Rhodope is addressed as "philosopher," but she is not necessarily a Pythagorean, for other contemporary philosophical groups admitted women (see below, and chap. 5, Theano to Rhodope). Euclides the physician is also not listed by Iamblichus. In the prosopography of ancient Greeks a man is usually identified by his given name and patronymic and often in addition by his place of origin or citizenship. A woman may be identified by her patronymic and her father's polis, but frequently she is known only by her given name. Thus it is not surprising that the Neopythagorean women writers are identified only by a given name.

Ptolemaïs deserves further discussion here because, until the publication of Flora Levin's *Greek Reflections on the Nature of Music* in 2009, she had received little attention.[3] Ptolemaïs came from Cyrene to Alexandria sometime after 300 BC. Porphyry, who quotes extracts from her work, does not call her a Pythagorean, but neither does he call attention to an even more startling fact, that is, that she is a woman (see chap. 5). Indeed, she is the only ancient woman known to have written about musical theory. Although in a dispute between the Neopythagoreans and Peripatetics she supported the doctrines of the latter, because of her subject matter scholars have considered her a Neopythagorean. As Flora Levin points out, Ptolemy also criticized the Pythagoreans, but nevertheless he remained a Pythagorean himself.[4] Ptolemaïs certainly could not have been a Peripatetic: Aristotle was notorious in his disdain for women's intellectual capacity, and there are no women Peripatetics known from antiquity. Therefore Thesleff has rightly included her in both his books on Neopythagorean texts.[5] Levin suggests that Ptolemaïs was the granddaughter of Ptolemaïs of Egypt (the daughter of Ptolemy I Soter), the fifth wife of Demetrius Poliorcetes, and the mother of Demetrius the Fair, who lived in Cyrene in the mid-third century BC.[6] In any case her name, accompanied by a place name, indicates that she was of the upper class and possibly of royal blood. Thus she was of a higher class than the other Neopythagorean authors and eschewed writing about mundane matters.

The texts by women comprise letters and treatises preserved completely or in fragments embedded in quotations by later authors. The dating is controversial. Estimates range widely. Conjectures about their dates range from the fourth century BC to the second century AD. In the past scholars like E. Zeller thought the works were written in the first century AD or later.[7] A survey of scholarly opinion on the dating beginning with the publication of Thesleff's *Introduction* and *Texts*, arranged chronologically, follows. Thesleff proposed some of the earliest dates for the corpus. W. Burkert disagreed with Thesleff about the dating.[8] In a number of publications over the years Burkert suggested dates ranging from the second century BC to the late third century AD. Influenced by Burkert's advocacy of a later date, a decade after he had published *Introduction* Thesleff stated that, although the third century might be too early, an early Imperial date was too late.[9] Burkert, however, also dates the earliest Neopythagorean texts to the third century BC.[10] P. M. Fraser suggests the first century BC, if not earlier, for the emergence of Neopythagoreanism in Alexandria.[11] Though Fraser does not argue for his hypothesis, it is consistent with the meticulously detailed picture he paints of the social and intellectual life of Ptolemaic Alexandria. Alfons Städele gives dates as late as the second century AD.[12] Charles Kahn dates the earliest texts to the third or second century BC.[13] Mary Ellen Waithe assigns some of the letters to the original Pythagoreans rather than to the Neopythagoreans of the Hellenistic period.[14] Consequently, although she follows Thesleff for the most part, a few of her dates are earlier.

Some recent scholarly publications on Neopythagoreans still reject Thesleff's dating.[15] Despite all their virtues, these works are incomplete inasmuch as they ignore the traditions about the original female Pythagoreans and fail to examine the Neopythagorean texts by women as well as the work by female scholars on these texts.[16] The writings of Neopythagorean women constitute approximately 23 pages of a total of 245 pages of Greek in Thesleff, *Texts*.[17] In view of the woeful survival of literature from antiquity, these works by women are a significant body of original sources. By not studying these texts, some scholars have ignored nearly 10 percent of the Neopythagorean work and jeopardized the validity of their conclusions. Thus, for example, in his authoritative survey Huffman refers to the Neopythagorean texts as "pseudepigrapha," and he examines them almost exclusively in terms of their relationship to Plato and Aristotle. Nevertheless, he does not mention Perictione I, Plato's mother, who is the author of a long letter and who is an obvious link between Pythagoreanism and Platonism. Huffman's generalization may be an appropriate description of the writings by Neopythagorean men: the content of the majority of the texts by women, however, has little to do with Plato and Aristotle, but rather deals with topics of women's daily life, including philandering husbands, cosmetics, jewelry, luxurious clothing, wet-nursing, and childrearing.[18] Though some historians of ancient philosophy agree with Thesleff that some of these texts were composed in Alexandria and others in Italy, others do not seem aware of the lives of women in these places in the time periods they advocate when they reject Thesleff's framework.[19] Holger Thesleff, who edited all the texts, is the only scholar who demonstrably read all the texts by both women and men; therefore his views on the dating, which are based on painstaking linguistic analysis of each author, paying equal attention to female and male writers, should take precedence. Moreover, knowledge of the social contexts in which the authors composed their texts supports Thesleff's dating and general arguments for the origin of the texts.

Since Thesleff published his two books on Neopythagorean texts some new evidence confirming his dating of the texts by women authors has emerged. The principal new evidence consists of the publication of a papyrus fragment of a previously known text; a rare gem portraying a woman writing (see below); extensive excavations in southern Italy, where communities of Pythagoreans lived; recent excavations and papyri that give information about Hellenistic Alexandria; and subsequent discoveries in women's history (see below), that lend support to the earlier dating proposed by Thesleff, which I adopted in 1977 and follow here.

The Hellenistic period from the death of Alexander the Great in 323 to the death of Cleopatra VII in 30 BC was the heyday of the Greek bluestocking. Archaeological evidence, including inscriptions, terra-cotta figurines, sculptured reliefs on tombstones, and a rare gem, portray women reading, writing, and engaged in other activities classified as the musical arts.[20] Since the fourth century BC women were again writing poetry, and some women wrote extremely pedantic prose texts. There is evidence for women in the philosophical schools, including Plato's Academy, Cynicism, and Epicureanism. The Neopythagorean texts show that a woman might read esoteric works on musical theory, and one woman lent a copy of Plato's *Parmenides* to another.[21] Phintys observes that many think women should not philosophize, but the texts themselves, including her own, serve as evidence for the existence of female philosophers (see below, chap. 6). The texts by women also refer to the luxurious and dissolute lives of the Greek upper classes, known especially in cosmopoleis like Hellenistic Alexandria and Athens. Hellenistic queens set a highly visible example of erudition to other Greek women. Thus Arsinoë II and Berenice III were patrons of allusive, pedantic literature, and Phila (mother of Antigonus Gonatas, king of Macedonia, third century BC) is portrayed in a fresco at Boscoreale engaged in a discussion with a philosopher (see below). Phintys's rejection of governance by women would seem to be a reaction to the public power exercised by Hellenistic queens and would almost certainly mean she lived before the death of Cleopatra VII (see chap. 6). If Perictione I was Plato's mother, her letter can be no later than the first half of the fourth century BC. Furthermore, as we have mentioned, Flora Levin has recently argued that Ptolemaïs of Cyrene, author of a treatise on Pythagorean and Peripatetic musical theory, should be dated to the middle of the third century BC. A reference to Plato's *Parmenides* in the letter of Theano II to Rhodope makes it clear that the author lived after the mid-fourth century BC.[22] In sum, both new discoveries, as well as internal evidence, continue to validate Thesleff's detailed framework for the dates and origins of the Neopythagorean women.

There is also controversy about the place of origin of the various texts. Despite challenges from other scholars, the view of Holger Thesleff that some of these writings originated in Alexandria or possibly Athens, and others in southern

Italy or Rome, is still persuasive. There is evidence for the emergence of Neopythagoreanism in these areas. Even the texts that were probably composed in Italy, however, include Greek names and were not only written in Greek but reflect a Greek social context. Upper-class Roman women could write Greek, but they did not publish personal advice to other women. Indeed, they would not have tolerated husbands like those described in some of the Neopythagorean letters. Roman women had more options than Greeks. Furthermore, there is no mention in the texts of matters that distinguish Roman women from Greek, such as the status and role of the *matrona* or Roman laws on prostitution.[23] The status and role of the Greek housewife and of the Roman *matrona* differed considerably, but both Roman and Greek wives (with the exception of wives of Pythagoreans) were obliged to accept the double standard, even though they might lament it. Despite the vast difference in Greek and Roman laws on prostitution, the lives of ordinary prostitutes in the Greek and Roman worlds were similar and do not show very much change over time. Prostitutes in both were unfortunate women who existed to provide a sexual outlet for bachelors and married men alike (see chap. 4, below).

In addition to the text attributed to Perictione I, comic playwrights attest to the existence of female Neopythagoreans in Athens in the fourth century BC. Learned Pythagorean women were lampooned in at least three Middle Comedies. Cratinus (second half of 4th c. BC?) wrote a play titled the *Pythagorean Woman*.[24] He also wrote in his *Tarentines* that it was the custom of these pedants, if they came upon a stranger, to examine him on doctrines and to confuse and confound him with antitheses, conclusions, errors, and magnitudes. For example, Aesara's treatise on human nature is replete with the kinds of definitions and abstractions that the comic poets found laughable when stated by women (see chap. 6). That the women are depicted as walking about freely and talking to strange men indicates that the play was written after the Peloponnesian War, when respectable Athenian women were no longer strictly secluded.[25] Alexis, who was born in Thurii around 375 BC and whose plays were performed in Athens in the 350s at the earliest, also lampooned women in his *Pythagorean Woman* and probably (like Cratinus) in his *Tarentines*, which is set in Tarentum.[26] The *Tarentines* was performed around 345–320 BC.[27] This play confirms that some Pythagoreans were still living in southern Italy.

The bluestockings in comedy are an indication of women's education, which spread in the Greek world in the fourth century and the Hellenistic period.[28] Schools existed in the Hellenistic world. Some of these were endowed and provided a free education for children of both sexes. The curriculum for girls and

Figure 8. Terra-cotta figurine showing a girl reading. The cloak suggests schooling outside the home. Alexandria. Greco-Roman Museum. Photo by Sarah B. Pomeroy.

boys was the same. Otherwise, education was private. The wealthy, like Hellenistic royalty, would obtain private tutors—often slaves—who instructed children at home. A Hellenistic gemstone depicts a woman writing on a diptych.[29] There are many images of girls reading. Terra-cotta figurines portray girls and young women looking at diptychs in their laps (figs. 8 and 9). Terra-cottas were not manufactured for a wealthy elite. They were mass-produced in molds and priced accordingly. The historian must assume that the activities portrayed on terracottas record the realities of the everyday life of people comfortable enough to afford more than the bare necessities. The letter of Theano II to Rhodope (see chap. 5) shows that women owned books of philosophy and lent them to one another. Many of the texts by Pythagorean and Neopythagorean women are extant because they are quoted by Stobaeus (5th c. AD anthologist): he prefaces his quotations without reservation, often with a statement such as "from Perictione the Pythagorean" or "Theano writes."

Terracottas also depict girls and young women dancing and playing musical instruments. Music and dancing were two facets of *mousike* (the musical arts). Musical accomplishments could enhance the reputation of a respectable woman. On the grave stele of Nico, an Alexandrian, the dead woman is seated in a mournful pose. A small girl offers her a lyre (see chap. 5 and fig. 10). Thus the

Figure 9. Terra-cotta figurine of girl reading a papyrus roll. Hamburg, Hamburger Museum für Kunst und Gewerbe, inv. no. 1898.53.

Pythagorean women who refer to music and the strings of a lyre in their texts are simply part of a larger group of elite women who were competent in music. It is in this context that Ptolemaïs composed her treatise on musical theory, of which approximately fifty lines are extant.[30]

After the Pythagoreans had been dispersed and some driven out of southern Italy by their political enemies in the last third of the fifth century BC,[31] some of them, at least, may have been forced to abandon their comfortable lifestyle for a time. For example, Pythagoras's daughter Damo had become very poor after her father died.[32] In Middle Comedy Pythagoreans appear as scruffy, unbathed, and poorly fed and dressed.[33] On the other hand, their austere diet, simple clothing, and lack of jewelry and cosmetics may have made them seem poor to outsiders, when in reality women who had time to philosophize were clearly not obliged to do their own housework or childcare or to undertake income-producing work for sustenance. The Neopythagorean women's letters—mostly dating at least a century after Middle Comedy—reflect their economic ease: they range over such topics as hiring a wet nurse; the treatment of slaves; overfed children raised in luxury; advice against wearing gold or emeralds or appearing in public with a large retinue of slaves; and husbands who lavish money on other women. Biographical information on Plato attests to the wealth and distinction of the family of his mother, Perictione, who may be the author of one of the extant texts. As was true for the original Pythagoreans, there is no mention of any author working for wages or struggling with financial problems.

The center of Greek philosophy had moved from Athens to Alexandria by the first century BC, and some Neopythagoreans may have gone to Egypt along with refugees from other philosophical groups.[34] Pythagoreanism apparently survived in southern Italy through the Hellenistic period; in any case, there is no doubt that it was formally revived in Rome by Cicero's friend Nigidius Figulus. In both Egypt and Italy the Neopythagorean women found notable literate women to emulate, including, as was noted above, the Ptolemaic queens, who were patrons of writers and scholars, and Cornelia, mother of the Gracchi, whose letters were published.[35] They lived in or near large cosmopolitan cities with people from all over the ancient world and with many other Greek-speaking inhabitants. Their letters reflect the new social position of Greek women in the Hellenistic period.[36] They have the autonomy to initiate a divorce and the freedom to write letters to men who are not their kinsmen. They can also make purchases and contracts for a substantial sum of money, for example, buying a slave wet nurse, or hiring or renting one for a year (if she is to nurse a girl) or for two years (if she is to nurse a boy). They may also be tempted to participate in orgiastic cults, which were popular in the Hellenistic period, such as the cult of Cybele, which was attractive to the Greek population in Alexandria and elsewhere and was officially brought to Rome at the end of the third century BC.

The domestic responsibilities of Neopythagorean women did not differ considerably from those of their counterparts in Southern Italy in the days of Pythagoras (see chap. 1). Most women, no doubt, were concerned with children, husband, food, clothing, and domestic slaves. In a big city like Alexandria, however, food and fabrics might be purchased with cash, rather than produced at home or on the family farm.[37]

Neopythagorean works originating in the east tended to be written in the Ionic dialect, while those from the west used Doric.[38] We note that the original Pythagorean women were Dorians, but the Neopythagoreans included both Dorians and Ionians. Literature, however, circulated between the two Hellenistic settlements, and one papyrus fragment indicates that the dialect was changed in the copy. Moreover, Alexandria was an international city with inhabitants and visitors drawn from all over. For example, in *Idyll* 15 (89–93) Theocritus depicts two women speaking Dorian at a festival in Alexandria sponsored by Arsinoë

II. Therefore, the dialect of the extant texts is not a perfectly secure guide to the place of origin, but lacking much other evidence, it is a useful one.

The texts by women discuss private and philosophical matters and do not refer to specific geographical locations or political events that might help locate them in space and time. The subjects they discuss are of perennial interest, especially to women. Though, as we have noted, some reflect the general changes in women's lives in the Hellenistic period, the corpus does not show change from century to century. Nor are there discernible differences between thoughts and attitudes of female authors in the east and those in the west. Adherence to Pythagorean doctrine imposes a uniformity on their work. Thesleff dates the texts and their origin primarily on the basis of a detailed analysis of language. He distributes the women authors geographically and assigns dates as follows:

EAST
Fourth to third century BC
    Theano (I): some works
    Perictione I: "On the Harmonious Woman"
Indeterminable or later
    Arignote
    Theano (II): most works
    Ptolemaïs[39]

WEST
Third century BC
    Aesara
    Melissa?
    Phintys
Third to second century BC
    Perictione II: "On Wisdom"
    Myia

Authenticity

Some scholars have doubted that the authors of the Neopythagorean letters and treatises were actually women, suggesting that men who adopted the names of earlier female disciples and relatives of Pythagoras as pseudonyms wrote them.[40] In other words, they claim that Neopythagorean women writers never existed. The arguments against female authorship consist basically of two parts: (1) the names of the women authors are pseudonyms, and (2) the treatises were written by men using the pseudonyms.⁴¹

Some of the authors have unexceptional names, such as Melissa and Phintys. These names occur elsewhere in the Greek world, and though Aristotle's daughter was named Melissa, such names have no particular significance in a philosophical context. There would have been no point in forging works under a name like this unless such a name had been found among Pythagoras's female disciples. Other authors are named for Theano (wife or disciple of Pythagoras), Myia and Arignote (his daughters), and Perictione (Plato's mother). Several of the male authors of the Neopythagorean so-called pseudepigrapha—for example, Archytas, Cleinias, Megillus, Milon, and Lysis—also bear names that appear in earlier Pythagorean and Platonic traditions.

It is likely that the names are authentic, for, as a declaration of identity, Neopythagoreans would give their daughters names that had occurred earlier in the Pythagorean tradition. The names of children often reflected their parents' religious persuasions or intellectual interests.⁴² Naming children for their ancestors shows family solidarity; by naming their offspring after earlier Pythagoreans, the Neopythagoreans strengthened their bonds with their spiritual forebears.

Moreover, disciples sometimes marry the daughters of their teachers. Thus Aristotle's will directed that his daughter marry his nephew Nicanor or Theophrastus, his successor as head of the Lyceum, and later, among the Neoplatonists, Theagenes, benefactor of Marinus, married the learned Neoplatonist Asclepigenia, daughter of Archiadas.⁴³ Female disciples may marry the teacher himself, for some sources report that Theano was first Pythagoras's student and then his wife, and in the same way Hipparchia became a follower of Crates the Cynic and then married him.⁴⁴ Couples such as these expressed their spiritual affiliation and their blood filiation simultaneously in choosing names for their children. Thus it is easy to see why the writings of the latter group could have been attributed to the former.

In the Hellenistic period there are many examples of female philosophers. Women participated in some of the other Hellenistic philosophical groups, including Platonism, Epicureanism, and Cynicism.⁴⁵ Moreover, for the period just after the one being discussed here, there is ample evidence for women's involvement in philosophical and religious groups, particularly in the eastern part of the Roman Empire.⁴⁶ Some of the early anonymous Christian literature has been attributed to female authors.⁴⁷ In the case of Neopythagoreans, however, we are dealing not with anonymous literature but with a substantial amount of writing with female bylines.

Often, but not always, female philosophers were related to male philosophers. In the case of Hipparchia, her brother Metrocles was the catalyst. Crates the Cynic visited Metrocles, who had been a Peripatetic, and inspired him to become his disciple. Hipparchia was captivated as well.[48] Magnilla, a philosopher who was both a daughter and a wife of philosophers, is named in an inscription from Apollonia in Mysia.[49] Phila of Macedonia, though not a full-fledged philosopher herself, apparently was attracted to philosophy through the influence of her son Antigonus Gonatas. Antigonus was himself a philosopher and entertained other philosophers at his court. A painting from Boscoreale after a Greek original of the middle of the third century BC depicts Phila and Antigonus listening to a philosopher who may be the Cynic Menedemus of Eretria. Phila is in the foreground, gazing up at the philosopher, showing much more interest than Antigonus.[50] Thus the Neopythagorean authors, especially those bearing philosophically significant names—like other creative women working in philosophy, scholarship, and art—often chose to adopt their male relatives' interests. In the case of Plato, however, not only Socrates but also his mother, Perictione, may have been his inspirations.

Considering that other Hellenistic women, including Hestiaea and Agallis, were capable of writing scholarly works on more arcane subjects than those discussed in most of the Neopythagorean letters and treatises (such as who had invented ball-playing and whether the Trojan War had been fought around the city named Ilium in the Hellenistic period), there is no reason to believe that the education of women would not have rendered them competent to compose these letters and treatises.[51] Furthermore, even though some scholars have designated the women's letters as "Pseudepigrapha," Ptolemaïs's authorship of an erudite treatise on Greek musical theory has not been challenged.[52] Although she is the only woman we know of who wrote about musical theory, Porphyry, who quotes from her work, does not comment on the fact that she is female. Arguing *ex silentio*, we may hypothesize that his lack of interest in her possible uniqueness indicates that there were others. A learned woman like Ptolemaïs did not seem as unusual to Porphyry as she does to us, for he knew of women philosophers in the circle of Plotinus, and his contemporary Iamblichus gave the names of many Pythagorean and Neopythagorean women (see Intro. and chap. 1, above). The first Greek woman who wrote about astronomy was Diophila, who worked, at the earliest, in the late fourth or early third century BC.[53] The study of astronomy and musical theory was based on a knowledge of mathematics, and mathematics was an essential part of Pythagorean philosophy. This tradition goes back to women who lived in the days of Pythagoras himself. In her work "On Piety"

Theano I discusses Pythagorean number theory.[54] Plutarch also urges that women learn mathematics because of the ethical influence of such study (*Advice to the Bride and Groom*, 48).

In any case, if other contemporary women did not write letters and prose treatises, and if the very notion that women could write such works was considered outlandish, there would have been no point in circulating such literature under women's names. Furthermore, as was true of the original Pythagoreans, it was necessary that the wife of a Neopythagorean understand the rules about diet, dress, childrearing, sexual relationships, and other aspects of the daily Pythagorean regimen. In addition, the biographical tradition about Pythagoras left no doubt that women, in particular Pythagoras's own mother, wife, and daughter, were very much part of his inner circle, and the Neopythagoreans would scarcely have ignored the wisdom of their founder in this respect.

It has been argued that because women are often the subject of the letters and treatises, these works were published under women's names to win them credibility among their readers.[55] For example, two Greek sex manuals were purportedly written by women, but their female authorship was doubted even in antiquity.[56] Similar arguments have been proposed to support the claim that the female poet Erinna did not write "The Distaff." Because the extant fragments of the poem deal with girlhood and mention dolls, a mother, and young wives, it has been asserted that the man who wrote the poem cleverly adopted a female pseudonym to lend the flavor of authenticity.[57] I have argued elsewhere that Erinna is, in fact, the author.[58] Nevertheless, assuming that such an argument has validity, it is necessary to examine whether this argument might apply to the Neopythagorean writings attributed to women. A large portion of the work by women does deal with the proper conduct of women, but not all of it does. For example, Perictione I wrote about wisdom, and Theano II wrote about the theory of numbers and the immortality of the soul as well as about conjugal relations. Furthermore, many male writers also spoke of women without finding it necessary to adopt a female pseudonym. Works on women's obligations in religion and marriage, their general conduct, and the need to avoid luxury were attributed to Pythagoras himself. We cannot stress enough, however, that the Neopythagorean texts consistently employ a woman's perspective; they comprise the earliest prose literature to examine these subjects from a female viewpoint and to assert strongly that the double standard in conjugal relations is painful for married women.

Adhering closely to Pythagorean doctrine, the works by women and about women discuss the proper behavior of women, recommending chastity, control of one's appetites, and tolerance of a husband's vices. Many of the ideas in these writings were traditional in Greek thought. Precedents can be found even in the most misogynistic of earlier authors, including Hesiod and Semonides, though presented from a masculine point of view. Yet these attitudes need not persuade us that the Neopythagorean texts were written by men. It would be unreasonable to expect the Neopythagorean women to write like modern feminists, but they certainly do present these traditional concepts from a woman's perspective. Orthodox writings by women were much more likely than radical works to gain publication and circulation and thus be preserved.

That the writers often urge their readers to accept the status quo, which favors men, does not mean that they were men, deviously controlling women. Life as a single woman was not an attractive choice. From the archaic through the Ptolemaic period there was no room in Greek society for a respectable spinster or divorcée. They were prey to men: in the same sentence Pythagoras himself had directed the men of Croton to avoid both concubines and unmarried women (see chap. 2). If a woman were to divorce a philandering husband and remarry, her subsequent husband might be even worse. Since according to Greek and Roman law children belonged to their father, a divorcée would be separated from her own children and would have no descendants to care for her in her old age. It was not unlikely that she would become a stepmother, recruited to raise the children of her next husband. The texts of the Neopythagorean women authors reflect the realities of the strongly patriarchal Greek society to which there simply were no alternatives.

CHAPTER FOUR

Introduction to the Prose Writings of Neopythagorean Women

The Neopythagorean letters and treatises discussed in this book are the earliest extant examples of literary Greek prose by women. Some poetry by women, including Sappho, is earlier. Poetry precedes prose among male writers as well. In the corpus of Greek literature, women's voices are extremely rare. The Neopythagoreans are among the first women in the Greek world to write letters that were circulated and published, but they are not the only ones who wrote letters. For example, in the second half of the fourth century BC, Olympias wrote to Alexander warning him of a plot against him (Diod. Sic.17.32.1).

Some of the Neopythagorean authors are thought to have lived in Alexandria in the Ptolemaic period (see chap. 3). Therefore it seems particularly relevant to look at the nonliterary letters of women in Egypt during the same time period. These letters, written on papyrus, have been translated and published in Roger S. Bagnall and Raffaella Cribiore, *Women's Letters from Ancient Egypt, 300 BC–AD 800*.[1] Some of the Ptolemaic letters are petitions and requests addressed to government officials and estate managers, while others are private letters from women to members of their family and include discussions of birth, death, religion, household management, and legal matters. The letters in the latter category are well written, employing complex sentence structure and displaying an understanding of the epistolary medium and good knowledge of the Greek language.[2] Yet the women who sent them did not live in the sophisticated cosmopolis of Alexandria; rather, the writers were women who lived in smaller cities and Greek settlements in Egypt. Thus, like the Neopythagorean women, the writers of the personal letters on papyrus were sufficiently educated and wealthy enough to indulge their wish to communicate in writing with others. The letters by other women on papyrus serve as additional evidence that women were indeed the authors of the Neopythagorean texts attributed to them. The fulsome greetings and endings of many of the papyrus letters indicate that the women had plenty of time to write them and did not need to stint on the use of papyri. Several sheets of papyrus could be glued together for longer letters. The lengthy literary letters of the Neopythagorean women would have been written on papyrus rolls comprising numerous sheets glued together. Thus it has been postulated that the papyrus containing a *koine* paraphrase of Melissa's letter to Clearete and the opening of Theano II's letter to Euboule was originally part of a papyrus roll containing additional Neopythagorean letters.[3]

The majority of the Neopythagorean texts are letters; a few are treatises. The texts are didactic. The treatises expound philosophical ideas, and many of the letters offer words of advice from women to women; the only exception is a letter to a male physician. The recipients of the letters generally face domestic problems, ranging from coping with unfaithful husbands to the rearing of children and the treatment of slaves. That advice is offered implies that the recipients had not been managing their lives successfully. The texts also treat the perennial subject of women's virtues, especially *sophrosyne* (chastity, self-control, moderation). Sometimes the letters seem personal, though they are nevertheless prescriptive, literary letters and lack the effusive greetings and closings of the nonphilosophical letters collected by Bagnall and Cribiore. Often the Neopythagorean letters resemble treatises. Because the problems and topics they discuss were common, the Neopythagorean letters can be understood as addressed to a specific reader while offering advice general enough to be read by any woman in need of it. (A parallel would be Plutarch's *Letter of Consolation to His Wife*, which contains intimate details about her breastfeeding history but nevertheless were read by readers in addition to the letter's addressee.) For this reason, as we have mentioned, some letters of Melissa and Theano II circulated between the Neopythagorean communities in the east and west.[4] We note that Thesleff assigned Melissa to the west, and both letter writers named Theano to the east (see chap. 3). This circulation of texts is further evidence that although some Neopythagoreans lived in the east and some in the west, their views on perennial social and personal problems were similar, and the letters constitute a consistent corpus.

We need not picture the authors of these texts as necessarily sitting at a desk, nibbling their quill pens, and staining their fingers with ink. Even if they knew how to write, upper-class women (like men) would often dictate to male scribes. The scribes who wrote the letters in Bagnall and Cribiore's *Women's Letters from Ancient Egypt* were professionals, who may have been slave or free: they were normally hired by individuals to write a single letter. In contrast, since the Neopythagorean women were wealthy, their scribes were probably personal slaves; therefore it is certainly unlikely that they dared to alter the woman's words to suit male sensibilities.⁵ In slave-owning societies, civil status trumped gender. Thus we may still hear the women's voices. Because the women authors could employ scribes, they themselves did not need to know how to read and write. By the Hellenistic period, however, literacy among upper-class women was not uncommon (see Intro. and chap. 3, above). Nevertheless, wealthy literate people often employed slave secretaries to write as they dictated and slave readers to read aloud to them. Thus, despite the intimate discussions of sex, infidelity, and scandal in some of the letters, a mistress would not have hesitated to employ a slave to write or read them aloud. Slaves were ubiquitous in antiquity, and life proceeded as if they were part of the furniture. Despite their presence, they were not intruding on the writer's privacy.

Women Philosophers

Pythagoreanism provided the largest number of examples of female philosophers. In *A History of Women Philosophers*,⁶ Gilles Ménage names twenty-six female Pythagoreans, while women affiliated with all the other schools (including Platonists, Cynics, Epicureans, Stoics, and others) total only twenty-four. Furthermore, there are no philosophical treatises by women other than the Neopythagoreans extant from this period. Women were intimately involved in Pythagoreanism from its founding in the sixth century BC, far longer than they were connected with any other Greek philosophical school. Pythagoreanism survived among women also because some of its tenets were later absorbed into Platonism, which admitted female disciples. Tradition connected Platonism to Pythagoreanism through a female link: Plato's mother, Perictione. Both Pythagoreanism and Platonism emphasized mathematics as having not merely a material value but also a spiritual power, and music was an audible expression of mathematical relationships.

Plutarch is also a good source for the pragmatic but intellectual currents of Hellenistic philosophy as they affected women. In the area of conjugal relations Plutarch was not an original thinker, but rather an industrious and eclectic one.⁷ The Neopythagorean treatises and letters on marriage were one of his sources for his *Advice to the Bride and Groom*. Similarities abound. Plutarch gives detailed instructions for the proper behavior of the wife, counseling her to live for her husband, to tolerate his vices, to think no private thoughts, to avoid adultery, and to consider the marriage bed sacrosanct. The husband in turn was urged, though not obliged, to be sexually monogamous. In his *Advice to the Bride and Groom*, Plutarch advised the bride Eurydice to behave like a philosopher. Thus Plutarch notes that "a woman who understands mathematics will be ashamed to dance," and he refers in his Introduction to "the tunefulness of marriage and home" and to "discourse, harmony, and philosophy."[8] Pythagoreanism was a particularly appropriate model for Plutarch's view of marriage, for its tenets applied to the daily lives of married couples, though wives rather than husbands were obliged to make the majority of the accommodations necessary for a harmonious marriage.

We may compare Pythagoras's adamant stand against adultery to the more lenient approach of Plutarch in *Advice to the Bride and Groom* (44): "What does drive women mad is their husbands' . . . association with other women. It is therefore wrong to cause such pain and disturbance to wives for the sake of a little pleasure. Better to treat a wife as we treat bees, which are believed to become angry and pugnacious towards those who have just had sexual relations with a woman, and so keep yourself pure and clean of intercourse with others when you go to your wife's bed."

Plutarch recommends that women stay in their homes like turtles and talk only to their husbands or through them (*Advice*, 32). Nevertheless upper-class women in Hellenistic Greece were not secluded and were subject to extramarital temptations. For example, before her marriage Eurydice had studied with Plutarch, who was not her kinsman. The letters by Neopythagorean women also show that the women were neither secluded nor forbidden to meet with men who were not their relatives; a virtuous Neopythagorean woman could be conversant with a male philosopher and a male physician, and she could contemplate the notion and consequences of being in bed with a man who was not her husband. Beginning with Perictione I's admonitions to women against committing adultery, the warnings suggest that the authors would not inveigh against such infidelity if it were nonexistent. Any kind of adultery by wives would threaten to destabilize the small community of Neopythagoreans even more than extravagant philandering by husbands. Clearly, women in the Hellenistic period enjoyed more autonomy than their classical counterparts. Both the Neopythagorean letters and Plutarch state that a wife may initiate a divorce without mentioning any need for male assistance.[9] This social context helps to confirm the date of the letters as Hellenistic.[10] Probably because women's concerns are generally remote from the worlds of war and politics, and Neopythagoreans were further insulated in their cult, the letters lack references to events that could date them more specifically. In any case, as literary letters their content is timeless.

Plutarch and the Neopythagoreans are also in agreement about their disdain for cosmetics, jewelry, and luxurious and ornate clothing: thus, if the bride Eurydice would not only read but also memorize the treatise Plutarch's wife wrote on adornment, she would eschew the use of cosmetics ("*Advice*," 48). Plutarch and the Neopythagoreans both find much to admire in the Spartan way of life. In particular, they both approve of many aspects of the Spartan system of education.

In the letters it becomes clear that women exercise authority over their own appearance and over their children and household slaves. They cannot, however, control their husbands, for there was no Pythagoras around in the Hellenistic period to enforce his ban on extramarital sexual relationships. It is clear, however, that the problem of unfaithful husbands was as acute and painful to wives as it had been in the days of the original Pythagoreans (see chap. 2). Nevertheless, observant Neopythagoreans, men as well as women, lived according to Pythagoras's ethical advice. The male author of the Hellenistic treatise titled "Charondas" advocated limiting sexual relationships to those that would produce legitimate children.[11] "Charondas" states that each man should love his wife according to custom and law, that the man should ejaculate his seed only into his legitimate wife, and that the couple should produce children.[12] "Ocellus" in *On the Nature of the Universe* (written ca. 150 BC) also asserts that sexual intercourse should be limited to a married couple with the goal of reproduction.[13] Any sex outside marriage is brutish and animalistic.[14]

Accordingly, the letters of Neopythagorean women discussing adultery are both private and public; they deal with an individual woman's struggle with her husband's infidelity and with a general social problem that afflicted marriages. The letters are especially persuasive because their authors are women, addressing other women who are their social equals. Most of the letters are a form of communication between two women, and it is possible to glean a glimpse of both author and recipient in addition to their names. The letters are a medium of self-presentation. Sometimes the description is overt, for example, when Myia describes herself as an older more experienced woman than her correspondent Phyllis, who is a new mother. The writers' stance is sympathetic, and there is no doubt that they are interested in the reader's well-being, though in discussions of marital difficulties, they never discuss their own personal experience. Theano I, in particular, serves as a model for other women (see chap. 1). The authors present themselves as sophisticated, knowledgeable, and well-spoken. We also occasionally detect more flexibility in the writers' views of propriety than in Pythagoras's stern admonitions against wearing cosmetics and expensive clothing. Thus Melissa in her letter to Cleareta describes the virtuous woman as having made her face beautiful inexpensively and wearing clothing that is not overly costly.[15] The frequent reminders to avoid excessive expenditures and conspicuous consumption, such as not wearing jewels or purple, or bathing too much, create a palimpsest of the life of luxury available to elite women in the Hellenistic world. We deduce that although the Neopythagorean women were quite willing to perpetuate Pythagoras's strictures on female dress and be immediately identifiable in their appearance as Pythagoreans, they also wanted to be physically attractive. Although the male gaze assessing women is almost ubiquitous in Greek literature, in these letters we encounter the female gaze.

Neopythagorean letters by women to women display the same bonds of friendship that may be observed between Pythagorean men. Pythagoreans were famous for their concern for each other, and numerous anecdotes are told about their altruism.[16] The letters by and to women are characteristic of Pythagoreanism in showing the concern of older women for younger, less experienced women, or for women married to adulterers, advising them as a mother would a daughter.

We may note briefly that the Neopythagorean letters should be categorized as letters of exhortation. Techniques for writing such letters were taught formally in the rhetorical schools and could be observed in published letters and in the harangues of rhetoricians and philosophers in public places. Since women in the Hellenistic period were not secluded, they would have witnessed these performances. The rules of style were also available in manuals such as the *Typoi Epistolikoi*. This work was attributed to the Peripatetic Demetrius of Phalerum, who was born in the middle of the fourth century BC and ended his colorful career by serving as librarian in Alexandria under Ptolemy I, but it has been dated between 200 BC and AD 300, probably as a result of modifications over the centuries.[17] The Neopythagorean letters conform to Demetrius's advice. They show a judicious blend of the graceful and plain styles and are conversational while eschewing the informal diction of dialogue. They are expositions "of a simple subject in simple terms."[18] The letters are an appropriate length; the longer texts, such as those by Perictione I and Perictione II, are treatises. We may speculate that although the letters were originally addressed to individual women, like the Neopythagorean treatises and like Plutarch's letter of consolation to his wife, they were copied and circulated among other like-minded readers and perhaps even more widely, and that is how they came to be preserved.

"The Other Woman"

The letters from women to women mirror concerns recorded in the biographies of Pythagoras (see chap. 2). They are consistent with Pythagoras's teachings and consistent with each other, though they do not reflect or reiterate all his ideas about women.[19] In the body of letters as a whole there are no internal contradictions in the advice about conjugal relations. Pythagoras focused more on male behavior; the letters, in contrast, emphasize the effect of husbands' behavior on their wives. By far the most attention is paid to anguished wives whose husbands consort with other women, especially with courtesans. This betrayal is recognized as the most painful experience for a wife and has the potential to cause the most profound disturbance to a wife's inner harmony. No fewer than three letters, including two very long ones, discuss the unfaithful husband at length, and the topic is raised, in passing, in others. In two letters Theano II offers sympathy and advice to Eurydice and Nicostrate, whose husbands are ensnared by courtesans (*hetairai*).[20] Perictione I as well advises the wife whose husband consorts with other women.[21] In these texts more words are devoted to how a wife should treat a philandering husband than how to live with a faithful spouse.

We draw attention to the fact that the "other woman" is the subject that recurs most frequently in these letters. In contrast, the effect of a husband's infidelity on his wife is not a topic of any major interest in any corpus of prose composed by male didactic or philosophical authors in the classical or Hellenistic period. That these Neopythagorean letters, written by women to women, pay special attention to the response of wives to unfaithful husbands supports the thesis that they were, in fact, written by women rather than by men using pseudonyms. Neopythagorean women recognize the devastating effect that the husband who engages in sexual relationships with other women has on his wife, providing a rare insight into how these wives felt.

Furthermore, the philandering husbands described in these letters are breaking not only the rules of sexual conduct for Pythagoreans but also the rules for Greek gentlemen. Though the double standard of behavior was acknowledged as normal and permissible, the husbands in these letters have gone too far: they are breeching the social limits regarding decorum and self-control. These men are so besotted that they have forgotten to be discreet. They ignore their wives' feelings and are totally enslaved to passion. What they are doing is the modern-day equivalent of a married man buying an expensive apartment for his mistress in the same neighborhood where his wife resides and boldly taking the mistress out to restaurants and on trips where they may be seen and become the subject of gossip.

Greek society at large was tolerant of a husband's infidelity as long as the husband did not flaunt the other woman and as long as the extramarital relationship did not cause an intolerable drain on the family's finances. The idea of irresponsible expenditure and waste of a family's livelihood from a husband's associations with courtesans appears as well in Theano's letter to Nicostrate.[22]

The double standard is obvious in the law codes and texts composed by men. For example, the wealthy orator Lysias visited a courtesan named Metaneira regularly and brought her to Athens to be initiated into the Eleusinian Mysteries ([Dem.] 59. 21–22). But he was married to his niece and his elderly mother lived with them. Therefore he kept his relationship with Metaneira strictly separate from his marriage and lodged her in Athens with a bachelor friend. Such behavior was considered acceptable for a married man. As we have mentioned, even Plutarch (*Advice*, 44) is tolerant of a husband's infidelity, though he admonishes a bridegroom not to go directly from a courtesan to his wife because recognizing where he had been [i.e., the smells of her perfume and of the stale sex] would provoke the wife and cause her to sting like an enraged bee. He also excuses the husband who commits an offense with a mistress or servant. He tells the wife not to be angry with him but to reflect that it is his respect for her that makes her husband share his intemperance with another woman (*Advice*, 16).

The letters of respectable Neopythagorean women paint the courtesans as demons and temptresses who entice husbands for the sake of money and who are a wife's rivals for attention and love. Yet the lives of these unmarried women might seem glamorous and attractive. The authors of the letters suggest that husbands patronized courtesans because they considered them more exciting and interesting than their wives. Unlike the Pythagorean women, they could wear brightly colored clothes, paint their faces lavishly with cosmetics, and wear gold jewelry.[23]

Although it is understandable that wives demonized and glamorized them, in reality courtesans were at least as much victims of the patriarchal society as were the betrayed wives. Their only power, if they were free, was to accept or reject a man as a client. Popular courtesans might choose among clients, but the period when their youthful beauty would attract well-paying men vying for their favors was brief. Without dowries or male kin to protect them, their welfare was precarious and their lives were sordid. Considering the frequency with which they had intercourse and the unreliability of contraceptives, they were often pregnant, either enduring abortions or bearing children whose futures were as uncertain as those of their mothers. Their mothers had no financial security and were especially vulnerable when they had lost their youthful charm and had no families to provide support.[24] For example, when Pythagoras told the men of Croton to summarily abandon their concubines, all those women suddenly needed to find other partners or a new source of income (see chap. 2).

It is often said that Greek society condoned extramarital sexual relationships for men, but since the testimonia are overwhelmingly by men, that generalization applies only to male attitudes. Differences between the views on adultery expressed, on the one hand, by Neopythagorean women and, on the other hand, by Plutarch indicate that the letters are by women for women. Women endure a husband's infidelity, but they do not accept it as Plutarch does. In contrast, Plutarch advises both husband and wife to abstain from extramarital intercourse, but in case the husband does indulge, he recommends discretion.

The letters recognize that the husband who engages in an extramarital sexual relationship inflicts mortal pain on his wife's psyche. They acknowledge the anguish of the betrayed wife and seek to offer sympathy and instruction in dealing with the problem. Much of the advice and the excuses supplied for the husband's behavior are strikingly familiar and modern—e.g., the relationship with the other woman is unimportant in comparison to marriage; the husband will soon tire of his mistress; he was emotionally needy; his lust was overwhelming; he fell in love.[25]

There were several categories of women with whom a husband could have extramarital intercourse. Some were free of cost throughout Greek history: these were slaves in his own house or those whose owner granted him permission. It may well be that the woman described in Theano's Letter to Callisto who whips her slave is enraged because the husband has chosen that slave as his favorite (whether the slave was willing or not).

The dictum of Pseudo-Demosthenes (59.122) in the fourth century BC sums up gender relations from a male perspective: "We have mistresses (*hetairai*) for the sake of pleasure, concubines (*pallakai*) for daily service to the body, and wives (*gynaikai*) for the bearing of legitimate offspring and to be the faithful guardians of the house." (We pause to point out that no Greek woman—mistress or concubine or wife—could have made the equivalent statement about men.) The *hetairai* in this context must include all women who were paid for their sexual favors, from high-priced courtesans to prostitutes. A concubine was a woman whom a man supported and with whom he had a long-term liaison. Pythagoras had urged the men of Croton to give up their concubines (*pallakai*).[26] In contrast, the Neopythagorean letters are most concerned about *hetairai*. Theano II, writing to a betrayed wife, uses the word *hetaira*.[27] This choice of words probably indicates an actual difference in the identities of "the other woman." Croton in the days of Pythagoras was wealthy and prosperous, but it was hardly the mecca for famous *hetairai*. The profession of the *hetaira* evolved along with the development of coinage and commerce in the Greek world. Thus Solon, whose legislation strengthened Athens as a commercial center, established state-owned brothels.[28] The young male client handing a purse to a *hetaira* is a common theme in Athenian vase painting.[29] Aspasia, Phryne, and Neaera, *hetairai* who practiced their trade in the fifth and fourth centuries BC in Athens and Corinth, are some of the best-known women in Greek antiquity. Hellenistic Alexandria, with its prosperity and glamour, was the home of even more powerful and wealthy *hetairai*. For example, in the third century BC, Bilistiche was a mistress of Ptolemy II, Oenanthe was a mistress of Ptolemy III, and Agathoclea was the mistress of Ptolemy IV; these women enjoyed great riches and even managed to wield political power.[30] Bilistiche owned racehorses that were victorious at Olympia, and Agathoclea was a ship owner.[31] Their highly visible success was doubtless a factor that attracted other courtesans to Alexandria, a city where there were plenty of men with money looking for adventure and a good time. The Ptolemaic kings were married, and their flagrant adultery served as a model and excuse for errant husbands; to counter this licentious behavior, some marriage contracts included a monogyny clause.[32] After the second Punic War, Rome as well became a cosmopolitan wealthy city where courtesans plied their trade.[33] Courtesans needed to be clever to survive and to be skilled at attracting men. With their wide range of sexual experiences they were able to be more entertaining in bed than the respectable wife who had learned about sex only from her husband and from her female relatives and friends.

In her letter to Nicostrate, Theano II distinguishes the reasons a husband frequents a hetaira from those that make him return to his wife: if he associates with the courtesan with a view toward pleasure, he associates with his wife with a view toward the beneficial. He goes to the courtesan in order to be frivolous, but abides with his wife in order to share a common life. He loves his wife on the basis of good judgment, but the courtesan on the basis of passion. Theano II goes on to distinguish the good wife from the courtesan by her orderly conduct toward her husband, her attention to her home, and her sensitive handling of children and associates.

Wives may also be involved in adulterous relationships. Often, but not always, the wife is provoked by her husband's infidelity. In her letter to Nicostrate, Theano II cautions a betrayed wife not to seek revenge by copying her husband's behavior. In her essay "On the Harmonious Woman" Perictione I advises a betrayed wife to tolerate a husband who cohabits (*suggenetai*) with other women because men are forgiven for this error in judgment, but women never are. As we have mentioned above, women were no longer secluded as they had been in Athens before the Peloponnesian War; rather, they were vulnerable to temptations.

Perictione I also urges women not to dress provocatively and to avoid becoming involved with other men.[34] Phintys cautions married women not to become intimate with strange men.[35] She urges women to make sure that their children resemble their father.[36]

In their advice, the Neopythagoreans reflect the mores of the days of Pythagoras, when an anecdote was told about a Pythagorean man who moderated a quarrel between two men, one of whom was accused of seducing the wife of the other (Iambl. *VP* 125). A statement attributed to Deino or Theano I alludes to a wife who had sex with another man and slept in his bed (see chap. 2). Thus, even in classical Magna Graecia, it was not inconceivable for a wife to have an affair, but such liaisons must have been extremely rare, as they were also in the days of the Neopythagoreans.

What is the betrayed wife to do? The letters agree that she should not be brutalized by jealousy and anger but should preserve her inner harmony. She should endeavor to continue to live a harmonious life and not lower herself to the level of her husband and his mistress. Theano II warns Rhodope not to reproach her husband for licentiousness or to take revenge. She interprets Nicostrate's husband's infatuation with a courtesan as madness and cautions the troubled wife to endure his infidelity, for it will not last long. Similarly, Perictione I declares that a wife must put up with a husband who sleeps with other women.[37] Revenge on the part of the wife is demeaning to her; divorce will surely bring either another husband (who may have the same faults) or spinsterhood.

The general tenor of the rest of the women's advice urges the wife to accommodate her husband's moods, to be sexually faithful, and to love her husband and children. The authors of the letters view this not as subservience, but rather as self-development, for it allows the wife to retain her own internal harmony, an important component of Pythagorean philosophy. The Neopythagoreans who lived after Perictione I reiterated her advice:

> A woman must live for her husband and according to law and in actuality, thinking no private thoughts of her own, but taking care of her marriage and guarding it. For everything depends on this. A woman must bear all that her husband bears, whether he be unlucky or does wrong out of ignorance, whether he be sick or drunk or sleep with other women. For this latter wrongdoing is peculiar to men, but never to women. Rather it brings vengeance upon her. Therefore, a woman must preserve the law and not emulate men. And she must endure her husband's temper, stinginess, complaining, jealousy, abuse, and anything else peculiar to his nature. And she will deal with all of his char-

acteristics in such a way as is congenial to him by being discreet. For a woman who is affectionate to her husband and treats him in an agreeable way is a harmonious woman.[38]

Parents

The Neopythagorean advice about relationships between the generations is similar to that attributed to Pythagoras himself. It is basically traditional Greek thought about caring for parents. That this advice is found frequently in letters to married women suggests that, despite marriage, they would continue to see their parents, though of course the treatment of parents includes parents by marriage. Perictione I, in "On the Harmonious Woman," declares that a woman must revere her parents and observes that they act in the interests of their grandchildren. Sarah Hrdy, in *Mothers and Others: The Evolutionary Origins of Mutual Understanding*, has recently pointed out the beneficial evolutionary effect of grandparents, especially of grandmothers.[39] This insight was rare among the Greeks, who usually considered an older woman a liability.[40] The Neopythagoreans evidently married within the community, and women were not secluded in their husband's home but enjoyed access to their natal families.

CHAPTER FIVE

The Letters and Treatises of Neopythagorean Women in the East

The Greek version of the texts in chapters 5 and 6 is cited as published in Thesleff, *Texts*, followed by page and line numbers. References to Hercher are to the monumental R. Hercher, *Epistolographi Graeci*.[1] The letters of Melissa, Myia, and Theano II have also been published in Alfons Städele, *Die Briefe des Pythagoras und der Pythagoreer*.[2] Städele showed that the manuscripts present the letters in varying sequences. Thesleff arranged the texts alphabetically by the authors' names. The texts are presented here chronologically by author, following Thesleff's dating.[3] Since there is proof that the texts traveled beyond their place of origin, a chronological arrangement will reveal any influences of early authors on later ones. The translations cited in Waithe, *Women Philosophers*, are by Vicki Lynn Harper. Any small changes in the Harper translation are indicated by italics.[4] I have taken the liberty of substituting other English words for "sin" (*hamartano, hamartia*) because the word is anachronistic and misleading. Stobaeus is cited from C. Wachsmuth and O. Hense, *Ioannis Stobaei: Anthologium*.[5] The references introducing particular passages in the Commentaries refer to Thesleff's *Texts* and to the English translation. Further philosophical commentary on many of the letters in chapters 5 and 6 appears in chapter 7, below.

Theano I. "On Piety"

Thesleff, *Texts*, 195, trans. Sarah B. Pomeroy

INTRODUCTION

Theano I was the wife of Pythagoras (see chap. 1), while Theano II was a Neopythagorean, or several Neopythagoreans named Theano, whose works have been collected under the rubric Theano II. Apparently the hypothesis that more than one woman author bore the name Theano is due to the large number of extant texts by her; no one has detected any differences in style or content among them. Thesleff comments that the dates of the statements attributed to Theano I are indeterminate, and he dates some of these writings or apophthegms to the fourth to the third century BC.[6] Apophthegms from Theano I were quoted by 300 BC.[7] These bon mots could have been authentic quotations, as Diogenes Laertius reports that Theano wrote a few things.[8] Theano lived in the time of some highly literate Greek women, including the lyric poets and wise women; one priestess was said to have instructed Pythagoras and Cleobuline, daughter of the philosopher Cleobulus, who composed riddles in verse.[9] The Pythagorean women are not unique insofar as having their words quoted by later generations. Although Athenian women were a muted group, Spartan women of the classical period were encouraged to speak out and were quoted and their pithy sayings collected.[10] The Spartans were renowned for their excellent memories: for example, they did not have a written law code because they all knew the laws by heart. Theano's writings cover a wide range of subjects, including human morality, proper etiquette, daily conduct, and the numerical structure of the universe.[11] The following fragment shows that in its emphasis on mathematics, Pythagoreanism is akin to Platonism.

TRANSLATION

"I have learned that many Greeks think Pythagoras said everything is created from number. This statement itself raises a question. How can what does not exist think and reproduce? But he did not say everything is derived from number, but everything is generated according to number, that the primary order is in number. By being part of it [the primary order], a first and second and the rest that follow are the order for things that are counted."

COMMENTARY

Pythagoras had observed that women were especially pious: hence, perhaps, the title of Theano's treatise. The extant fragment, however, deals with another key feature of Pythagorean doctrine. It was popularly believed that Pythagoras considered number the origin of everything that exists. W. Emmanuel Abraham, referring to Aristotle's *Metaphysics,* explains: "Things are ontic constructs, not number aggregates; as ontic creatures, they exist through relations of numbers and through conformity to those relations."[12] Aristotle, however, who did not believe women were capable of philosophizing, apparently had not read Theano's text or he ignored it, for he reported:

The so-called Pythagoreans, who were the first to take up mathematics, not only advanced this study, but also having been brought up in it they thought its principles were the principles of all things. Since of these principles numbers are by nature the first, and in numbers they seemed to see many resemblances to the things that exist and come into being—more than in fire and earth and water (such and such a modification of numbers being justice, another being soul and reason, another being opportunity—and similarly almost all other things being numerically expressible); since, again, they saw that the modifications and the ratios of the musical scales were expressible in numbers;—since, then, all other things seemed in their whole nature to be modelled on numbers, and numbers seemed to be the first things in the whole of nature, they supposed the elements of numbers to be the elements of all things, and the whole heaven to be a musical scale and a number.[13]

Thesleff, *Texts*, 195.13–14. "How can what does not exist"
Burkert remarks on the noteworthy idea that number does not exist and argues that equating "being and corporal being" suggests a Hellenistic date and disagreement with Aristotle.[14] If Burkert's hypothesis is correct, this passage should be attributed not to Theano I, wife of Pythagoras, but to some later Theano.

Theano I. Apophthegms, trans. Sarah B. Pomeroy

Apophthegm: "If the soul is not immortal, then life is truly a feast for evildoers who die after behaving iniquitously."[15]

COMMENTARY

This apophthegm seems to be directed against philosophers who doubted the existence of the afterlife, including Democritus (5th c. BC) and his atomist theory. Pythagoreans believed in the immortality of the soul and the transmigration of the soul after death to a destiny appropriate to the life that had been lived. Thus a person who had lived a disorderly and amoral life might be reborn as a promiscuous beast. Here Theano considers the order of the world not as numerical concepts but rather in moral anthropocentric terms.

Apophthegm: "There are things which it is fine to discuss; about these things it is shameful to remain silent. There are also things which it is shameful to discuss; about these things it is preferable to remain silent."[16]

COMMENTARY

Theano could also offer practical everyday advice.

Apophthegm: It is better to ride a horse without reins than to be an unreflective woman.[17]

COMMENTARY

"horse": In her letter below, Phintys of Sparta considers the possibility of a woman riding a horse.
"unreflective": Theano also spoke of the necessity for a woman to be thoughtful. That the soul has no sex and that women may be as rational as men is a theme that is repeated in the writings of female Neopythagoreans.

Apophthegm: Being asked what is love (eros), Theano said it is a condition of "an unoccupied soul."[18]

COMMENTARY

In other words, passion and desire will not afflict those who are busy thinking virtuous thoughts. That *eros* could cause irrationality and personal loss of control was a traditional Greek idea. Sappho had written: "Eros, loosener of limbs, whirls me,"[19] and "I'm in love! I'm not in love! / I'm crazy! I'm not crazy!"[20] This concept, however, did not prevent Theano from approving of sexual attraction within the marriage relationship (see chap. 1).

Perictione I. "On the Harmonious Woman"

Thesleff, *Texts*, 142–45, Stob. 4: 688–93, 631–32, trans. Flora R. Levin[21]

INTRODUCTION

Thesleff identifies the dialect as Ionic with a few Doricisms. He also finds that an author named Perictione uses a "fairly consistent Doric" in "On Wisdom" (*Peri Sophias*),[22] and he therefore concludes that there were two traditions for authors named Perictione. "On the Harmonious Woman" was written in the east in the fourth to third century BC, and "On Wisdom" in the third to second century BC in the west.[23] The earlier text was addressed to women, the later treatise was written for both women and men. These authors are referred to in this book as Perictione I and Perictione II. Thesleff dates Perictione I to the fourth to third century and believes the author was probably Plato's mother.[24] Upper-class Athenian women married at puberty and could be mothers by the age of fifteen. Since Plato was born around 429 BC, if his mother lived as long as he did, she could well have written philosophical texts even as late as the second quarter of the fourth century; this hypothesis is consistent with Thesleff's earlier date. Perictione would thus be the first Athenian woman to have written not only an extant philosophical text but also any extant literature at all. She may have been influenced by philosophers in the Pythagorean diaspora in Athens or by Plato himself, who visited Sicily and Tarentum, where he was friendly with the Pythagorean ruler Archytas.[25] Judging simply from their respective ages, it is likely that Perictione I wrote her essay before Plato wrote his dialogs. Some upper-class women in the classical period were literate. For example, in Xenophon, *Oeconomicus* (9.10), the wife of the wealthy Ischomachus keeps the household accounts.[26] For female philosophers as predecessors we need look no further than Aspasia, Diotima, Lastheneia, and Axiothea in Plato's circle and works. In quoting from Perictione at such great length, Stobaeus may be paying tribute to Plato's mother. On the other hand, the name Perictione was an obvious one for a Neopythagorean to give to a daughter, since Plato had had links with Pythagoreanism and, like Pythagoras, had had female pupils (see chap. 1 and Theano II to Rhodope, below). Even if the identity of Perictione I is uncertain, it is at least clear that she is not the same woman as the later Perictione, who wrote "On Wisdom" (see chap. 6).[27]

The historical Perictione was born into a very wealthy family and then married well, so her concerns about lavish adornment and expensive jewelry would reflect her personal experience as well as that of her elite audience. While criticizing extravagant and seductive makeup and attire, she does believe harmonious women may bathe and wear adornments and attractive clothing in moderation. She apparently was not one of the scruffy Pythagorean women portrayed in Athenian comedy (see chap. 4).

In this text Perictione I ranges over ethics, religion, dress, adultery, politics, household, and philosophy: these topics will recur in many of the texts written later by Neopythagorean women. She adapts Pythagorean theory to the actual lives of married women, for her treatise is not theoretical, but practical, with goals that could have been achieved by women in the fourth century and the Hellenistic period. Despite serious provocations, the harmonious woman will exercise self-control, will obey her parents, and will be at peace within herself. In such a condition she will be an integral part of the natural order of the universe and will be living the Pythagorean life. *Harmodzo* means "I fit together," as a carpenter might join pieces; thus it came to mean "to accommodate." *Harmonia* refers to a joint between two parts of a whole and also connotes "temperament," "music," and "order."[28] In a harmonious person, reason and the passions are in total balance and attunement—like the stretched strings of a lyre. Such a person is neither "high-strung" nor "slack" or "loose." In keeping with the musical metaphor, *sophrosyne* has been translated as "temperance," but it also connotes chastity and self-restraint. Traditionally, *sophrosyne* was a virtue of women and as such connoted inhibition, self-restraint, and chastity, but the Pythagoreans and Socratics extended the meaning to include both genders. For Pythagoras *sophrosyne* was not confined to private life but also permeated all aspects of human existence (Iambl. *VP* 6.32, 27.132, 31.195). The Pythagoreans may have influenced Plato's views on *sophrosyne* in the public sphere,[29] and Xenophon's views on *sophrosyne* in both the public and private spheres,[30] and the views of these two Socratics, in turn, may have contributed to Neopythagorean theories. Several of the Neopythagorean letters refer directly to *sophrosyne* as a virtue in both women and men, especially in the context of marriage and education (see, e.g., Theano II to Eurydice, below).

The first three beneficiaries of a woman's virtue (husband, children, and home) are traditional in Greek thought. The one good type of woman listed in Semonides' *Diatribe against Women* (7th c. BC) causes her husband's "property to grow and increase, and she grows old with a husband whom she loves and who loves her, the mother of a handsome and reputable family."[31] That a woman can win acclaim by governing is a more unusual idea, perhaps inspired by contemporary Macedonian queens or by earlier female monarchs, for example, Artemisia I, or (less likely because of the chronology postulated just above) by the female guardians in Plato, *Republic* 5. It should be observed, in contrast, that Phintys, a member of the western group of Neopythagoreans, declared that women should not take part in government (see chap. 6).

The two fragments of this treatise are presented in the order in which they are printed in Thesleff, *Texts*. They are not recorded in a continuous order in Stobaeus (5th c. AD anthologist), where, in fact, Fragment II precedes Fragment I. Stobaeus quotes Fragment II in his chapter on duties toward parents (*hoti chre tous goneis tes kathekouses times*), and Fragment I in his chapter on household or estate management (*Oikonomikos*). Since Fragment I ends with a Pythagorean climax, there is a strong possibility that it constituted the last part of the treatise and that Fragment II came somewhat earlier in the treatise.

TRANSLATION

"We must deem the harmonious woman to be one who is well endowed with wisdom and self-restraint. For her soul must be very wise when it comes to virtue so that she will be just and courageous [lit., "manly," *andreie*] while being sensible and beautified with self-sufficiency, despising empty opinion. For from these qualities fair deeds accrue to a woman for herself as well as for her husband, children, and home; and perchance even to the city, if in fact such a woman were to govern cities or people, as we see in the case of a legitimate monarchy. Surely, by controlling her desire and passion, a woman becomes devout and harmonious, resulting in her not becoming a prey to impious love affairs. Rather, she will be full of love for her husband and children and her entire household. For all those women who have a desire for extramarital relations [lit., "alien beds"] themselves become enemies of all the freedmen and domestics in the house. Such a woman contrives both falsehood and deceits for her husband and tells lies against everyone to him as well so that she alone seems to excel in goodwill and in mastery over the household, though she revels in idleness. For from all these activities comes the ruination that jointly afflicts the woman as well as her husband. And so let these precepts be pronounced before the women of today.

"With regard to the sustenance and natural requirements of the body, it must be provided with a proper measure of clothing, bathing, anointing, hair-setting, and all those items of gold and precious stones that are used for adornment. For women who eat and drink all sorts of extravagant dishes and dress themselves sumptuously, wearing things that women are given to wearing, are decked out for seduction into all manner of vice, not only the bed but also the commission of other wrongful deeds. And so, a woman must merely satisfy her hunger and thirst, and if she is of the poorer class, her chill, if she has a cloak made of goatskin. To be consumers of goods from far-off lands or of items that cost a great amount of money or are highly esteemed is manifestly no small vice. And to wear dresses that are excessively styled and elaborately dyed with purple or some other color is a foolish indulgence in extravagance. For the body desires merely not to be cold or, for the sake of appearances, naked; but it needs nothing else. Men's opinion runs after inanities and oddities. Therefore a woman will neither cover herself with gold or the stone of India or of any other place, nor will she braid her hair with artful device; nor will she anoint herself with Arabian perfume; nor will she put white makeup on her face or rouge her cheeks or darken her brows and lashes or artfully dye her graying hair; nor will she bathe a lot. For by pursuing these things a woman seeks to make a spectacle of female incontinence. The beauty that comes from wisdom and not from these things brings pleasure to women who are well born.

"Let a woman not think that noble birth and wealth and coming from a great city and having the esteem and love of illustrious and royal men are necessities. For if a woman is well off, she has nothing to complain about; if not, it doesn't do to yearn. A clever woman is not prevented from living without these benefits. Even if allotments be great and marvelous, let not the soul strive for them, but let it walk far away from them. For they do more harm than good when someone drags a woman into trouble. Treachery, malice, and spite are associated with them, so that a woman so endowed could never be serene.

"A woman must reverence the gods if she hopes for happiness, obeying the ancestral laws and institutions. And I name after [the gods], her parents, whom she must honor and revere. For parents are in all respects equivalent to the gods and they act in the interest of their grandchildren. A woman must live for her husband and according to law and in actuality, thinking no private thoughts of her own, but taking care of her marriage and guarding it. For everything depends on this. A woman must bear all that her husband bears, whether he be unlucky or does wrong out of ignorance, whether he be sick or drunk or sleep with other women. For this latter wrongdoing is peculiar to men, but never to women. Rather it brings vengeance upon her. Therefore, a woman must preserve the law and not emulate men. And she must endure her husband's temper, stinginess, complaining, jealousy, abuse, and anything else peculiar to his nature. And she will deal with all of his characteristics in such a way as is congenial to him by being discreet. For a woman who is affectionate to her husband and treats him in an agreeable way is a harmonious woman and one who loves her whole household and makes everyone in it well disposed. But when a woman has no love in her, she has no desire to look upon her home or children or slaves or their security whatsoever, but yearns for them to go to perdition just as an enemy would; and she prays for her husband to die as she would a foe, hating everybody who pleases him, just so she can sleep with other men.

"Thus, I think a woman is harmonious if she is full of sagacity and temperance. For she will not only help her husband but also her relatives, slaves, and her whole household, in which reside all her possessions and her dear kin and friends. She will conduct their home with simplicity, speaking and hearing fair words and holding views on their common mode of living that are compatible, while acting in concert with those relatives and friends whom her husband extols. And if her husband thinks something is sweet, she will think so too; or if he thinks something bitter, she will agree with him. Otherwise, she will be out of tune with her whole universe."

COMMENTARY

Thesleff, *Texts*, 142.20. "courageous" [lit. "manly," *andreie*]
In the works of radical Socratic philosophers, including Xenophon and Plato,

women may share masculine traits and virtues. See below on Theano II to Euboule (Thesleff, *Texts*, 196.17), chap. 6; below on Phintys; Plato, *Resp.*, esp. bk. 5; and Jeremy McInerney, "Plutarch's Manly Women," in *Andreia: Studies in Manliness and Courage in Classical Antiquity*, ed. Ralph M. Rosen and Ineke Sluiter (Leiden, 2003), 320–44, esp. 323–24.

Thesleff, *Texts*, 142.24–143.1. "a woman were to govern cities or people, as we see in the case of a legitimate monarchy."

In Plato's *Republic* women and men of the guardian class are given the same education, and there is no gender difference in the *psyche* (soul). Therefore, theoretically the state may be governed by a Philosopher King or Queen. Perictione I would also have been aware of historical queens, including Artemisia I and II, who ruled their kingdoms on the periphery of the Greek world.

Thesleff, *Texts*, 143.5. "enemies of all the freedmen and domestics in the house."

The loyalties of slaves and freedmen would be compromised since they would know of the adultery and be forced by their mistress to lie to their master.

Thesleff, *Texts*, 143.10. "a proper measure of . . . bathing," 143.26; "bathe a lot."

Before the great baths built by Roman emperors for the general population, Greek men bathed at the gymnasium. Immersion baths for women were a luxury, requiring the services of slaves to fetch and empty the water and fuel to warm it, and demanding that the bather own a bathtub and enjoy sufficient leisure time to bathe and to relax afterwards. Thus, according to Athenaeus (12.519e), the Sybarites had tubs that allowed them to stretch out. In contrast, Pythagoreans discouraged conspicuous consumption as well as the sensual, sexual, and seductive feelings that bathing could arouse.

There were precedents for luxurious bathing for the Neopythagorean women in both the west and the east. Immersion baths and hipbaths were excavated in Magna Graecia from the late fourth century BC and on the Greek mainland from the fifth century BC.[32] Luxurious baths have also been found in private dwellings in Ptolemaic Egypt.[33] In Alexandria, the wealth and imagination of Ptolemaic women allowed them to invent extravagant ablutions like the fabulous asses' milk baths of Cleopatra VII.

Pythagoreans cared about cleanliness. Phintys stresses the importance of washing with water and wearing clean clothes (see chap. 6, below).

Myia advises Phyllis to prevent the nurse from bathing the infant too often because of the enervating effect. See chap. 6, below, Thesleff, *Texts*, 123.31–32. These references to excessive bathing are additional evidence of the high economic status of Neopythagorean women.

Thesleff, *Texts*, 143.18–19. "dyed with purple" [lit. "dipped in dye from the shellfish"]

Purple dye was made from a vein in certain shellfish. The process was invented by the Phoenicians: hence the dye was known as Tyrian purple. Like gold, gemstones, and perfume, mentioned later in this paragraph, purple was extremely expensive and thus a symbol of power, luxury, and even decadence. In the Greco-Roman world purple was worn by people of high status, especially royalty, and by freeborn Roman children (see Pliny *HN* 9.60–63).

Thesleff, *Texts*, 144.9–10. "A woman must live for her husband and according to law and in actuality, thinking no private thoughts of her own, but taking care of her marriage [lit. "bed"] and guarding it."

Plutarch (*Con. Praec.* 14) advises: a wife should have no feelings of her own, but share her husband's seriousness and sport, his anxiety and his laughter. We note, however, that Perictione's emphasis is on sexual fidelity, whereas Plutarch is interested in emotional harmony in marriage. In the fifth century BC Sophocles, *Oedipus* fr. 909 (Nauck, 2d ed = 545A in *Tragicorum Graecorum Fragments*, ed. Kannicht), had written: "It is pleasing too, if her husband has had some bad experience, for a wife to put on a sad face with him and to join in sharing his pains and pleasures. [lacuna] You and I—when you suffer, I will be content to suffer with you." Both passages are clearly consistent with the status quo in the patriarchal Greek world, which endured, despite some significant changes in women's status and education, in the Hellenistic period. Parallel passages like this one about a wife having no private thoughts cannot be used to argue that Perictione I and Plutarch were contemporaries.

Thesleff, *Texts*, 144.12–14. "For this latter wrongdoing is peculiar to men, but never to women. . . . and not emulate men."

Perictione I is the first woman writer in western literature to acknowledge the double standard, the view that sexual relations preceding or outside of marriage are permissible for men, but not for women. Women are taught to perpetuate the double standard: life is over for the woman who has committed adultery. The wife must make the choice to endure a husband's unharmonious behavior in order to preserve harmony in their marriage. *Nomos* can refer to custom or to legislation: in patriarchal societies—where men make the rules—both custom and law conspire to approve chastity only for respectable women and to allow men to be sexually polygynous. Prostitution served as an institution that preserved the chastity of respectable women while allowing men sexual freedom.[34] Pythagoras, however, advocated a strict standard of monogamy for both married women and men and required men to stop consorting with women to whom they were not married (see chap. 2). By curbing her own sexual desires and jealousy when her husband is a slave to lustful appetite, the wife displays more virtue than he does and shows herself to be a more faithful Pythagorean.

Thesleff, *Texts*, 143.22–23. "stone of India . . . Arabian perfume"

Herodotus (3.107) wrote that Arabia was the only country where frankincense, myrrh, cassia, cinnamon, and ladanum (rock-rose resin) grew. Even after Alexander's campaigns in the East, the idea that aromatics were found only in Arabia survived.[35]

Thesleff, *Texts*, 145.5–6. "Otherwise, she will be out of tune with her whole universe" (*anarmonios*).

Perictione closes with a typical Pythagorean *sphragis*, a reference to [the lack of] harmony.

Perictione I. "On the Harmonious Woman," fr. 2.

Thesleff, *Texts*, 145–46, Stob. 4.25.50, pp. 631–32

INTRODUCTION

Care for parents was traditional in Greek society and even codified at Athens by the laws of Solon.[36] At Sparta the same views prevailed, as is clear from the anecdote about younger men giving their seats to older people, but not to bachelors, because a bachelor would not produce children who would rise in turn for their elders (Plut. *Sayings of Spartans* 227.14, *Lyc.* 15.2). There were no established state or privately run charities to care for the elderly; indeed, a major incentive to produce children was that they would care for their parents when they grew old.

Pythagoras had advised his disciples to respect and obey their parents (see chap. 2). The migrations of the Pythagoreans themselves, however, probably separated many from their extended kinship networks. Hence it was necessary to reaffirm the principle that adults should obey and care for their parents. For sons to care for parents was traditional. That a daughter was obliged to care for her parents too may be attributed to the social upheavals of the Peloponnesian War and subsequent migrations, during which there were fewer constraints on women than had been in force earlier, as well as to the high economic and social status of some women, which enabled them to care for their own parents.[37] In fact, if this Perictione was Plato's mother, she may have been inspired to write this section of the treatise owing to her own experience with her children. Perictione had three sons, including Plato, and one daughter by Ariston, and another son when she remarried after Ariston's death. After the execution of Socrates, Plato left Athens. He traveled to Sicily and Magna Graecia three times and was held hostage by pirates. In these tumultuous times, we speculate that at least the elderly Perictione could turn to her daughter Potone, who had married and become the mother of Speusippus.

TRANSLATION

"We should neither speak ill of our parents nor do them harm, but obey those who generated us in both trivial and important matters, and in every state of the soul and body, in inner and external matters, both in peace and in war, in health and in sickness, and in wealth and poverty, in fame and obscurity, whether they are private individuals or public officials. It is necessary to keep in step and never desert them, but to obey them even to the point of madness. Such conduct is considered wise and honorable by pious people.

"If someone should have contempt for her parents, plotting any sort of evil in private, her wrongdoing is recorded by the gods whether she is living or dead. People will hate her, and with the impious in their place under the earth forever she will be harmed by evils in behalf of justices and of the gods below who are appointed to supervise these matters.

"Divine and beautiful is the sight of one's parents, so too is the reverence and the care of them, as great as the sight of the sun and all the stars which heaven wears and twirls, and whatever else anyone may consider something greater to view. It seems to me not even the gods are angry when they see this occur. It is necessary to revere them when they are living and when they have departed and never to mutter against them even when they behave senselessly because of illness or deception, but rather exhort and teach and in no way hate them. There is no greater error and injustice among human beings than not to revere one's parents."

Theano II to Euboule

Thesleff, *Texts*, 195–97, Hercher, 603, nr. 4, Theodoret, *De Vita Pythagoras* (1598), 163–65, trans. Vicki Lynn Harper, in Waithe, *Women Philosophers*, 42–43

INTRODUCTION

This letter was written in the Attic *koine*. The advice is consistent with the teachings of Pythagoras concerning childrearing (Iambl. *VP* 51, 201–4; Myia to Phyllis, chap. 6, below; and see chap. 2). It is also consistent with the views of other philosophical schools and with traditional Greek ideas about the malleability of children. What is missing here is the corporal punishment that parents often used to discipline children.[38] Furthermore, the Pythagoreans are distinctive in their concern about spoiling their children with too much comfort and luxury. The conspicuous consumption and abundance of material goods the Greeks encountered in such places as Hellenistic Alexandria was at variance with Pythagorean ideals. Most Greeks in other places and in other time periods did not enjoy such a surfeit that they needed to worry about giving children too much food or too many baths or keeping them too warm. According to Theano II, children should be trained to be Pythagoreans, to be comfortable with austerity, and to exercise self-control and temperance. This letter also reflects the influence of the Spartan educational system on Pythagorean childrearing. Like Pythagoras himself, the historical Spartans, and the guardian class in Plato's *Republic* (which reflects Spartan practice), the Neopythagorean women authors do not differentiate between boys and girls in such a way as to give the girls an inferior education. The Spartan *agoge* was revived in the Hellenistic period. If Theano II was a member of the group of Neopythagoreans living in Alexandria (see chap. 3), she may have even met Cratesicleia who was the mother of the Spartan king Cleomenes (r. 235 BC). Cratesicleia's and Cleomenes' children were hostages of Ptolemy III Euergetes and killed by Ptolemy IV (Plut. *Cleom.* 38, and see chap. 1).

In Athens mothers looked after daughters until they left their parents' house to be married; but mothers raised sons only until the age of seven, when they entered the father's milieu and were turned over to male tutors, pedagogues, and relatives. As in Sparta, the Pythagorean mother's contribution to the education of her children of both sexes and her continuing responsibility for the adults that they become is emphasized. We would expect the role of the mother to be discussed in a letter from one woman to another, but it is interesting to note that the role of the father is not mentioned at all.

TRANSLATION

"I hear that you are raising your children in luxury. The mark of a good mother is not attention to the pleasure of her children, but education with a view to temperance. Look out lest you accomplish not the work of a loving mother, but that of a doting one. When pleasure and children are brought up together, it makes the children undisciplined. What is sweeter to the young than familiar pleasure? One must take care, my friend, lest the upbringing of one's children become their downfall. Luxury perverts nature when children become lovers of pleasure in spirit and sensualists in body, mentally afraid of toil and physically soft. A mother must also exercise her charges in the things they dread—even if this causes them some pain and distress—so that they shall not become the slaves of their feelings, greedy for pleasure and shrinking from pain; but rather, shall honor virtue above everything and be able both to abstain from pleasure and to withstand pain.

"Don't let them be sated with nourishment, nor gratified in their every pleasure. Such lack of restraint in childhood makes them unbridled; it lets them say anything and try everything; especially if you take alarm every time they cry out, and always take pride in their laughter—smiling indulgently even if they strike their nurse or taunt you—and if you insist on keeping them unnaturally cool in summer and warm in winter, giving them every luxury. Poor children have no experience of such things; yet they grow up readily enough. They grow no less, and become stronger by far. But you nurse your children like the scions of Sardanapalus, enfeebling their manly natures with pleasures. What would one make of a child who, if he does not eat sooner, clamors; who, whenever he eats, craves the delights of delicacies; who wilts in the heat and is felled by the cold; who, if someone finds fault with him, fights back; who, if someone does not cater to his every pleasure, is aggrieved; who, if he does not chew on something, is discontent; who gets into mischief just for the fun of it, and stutters about without living in an articulate way?

"Take care, my friend—conscious of the fact that children who live licentiously become slaves when they grow to manhood—to deprive them of such pleasures. Make their nourishment austere rather than sumptuous; let them endure both hunger and thirst, both cold and heat, and even shame before their peers or their overseers. This is how they turn out to be brave in spirit no matter whether they are exalted or tormented. Hardships, my dear, serve as a hardening-up process for children, a process by which virtue is perfected. Those who have been dipped sufficiently in them bear the tempering bath of virtue as a natural thing. So look out, dear, lest, just as vines which have been improperly tended are deficient in fruit, your children produce the evil fruit of licentiousness and utter worthlessness, all because of luxury. Farewell."

COMMENTARY

Thesleff, *Texts*, 196.7–11. "A mother must also exercise her charges in the things they dread—even if this causes them some pain and distress . . . and to withstand pain."

These lines evoke the Spartan *agoge*, which was revived in the late third century BC. Boys were hardened to endure heat and cold, were whipped, and competed in contests displaying endurance of pain: Xen. *Sp. Const.* 2.2–9, see further Nigel M. Kennell, *The Gymnasium of Virtue: Education and Culture in Ancient Sparta* (Chapel Hill, NC, 1995).

Thesleff, *Texts*, 196.14. "even if they strike their nurse"
Wealthy Greek children were served by slaves from the moment of birth. Like their parents, children might regularly hit slaves and otherwise treat them as subhuman. See Theano II to Callisto; below chap. 6; and see further Keith Bradley, "Images of Childhood. The Evidence of Plutarch," in *Plutarch's "Advice to the Bride and Groom" and "A Consolation to His Wife,"* ed. Sarah B. Pomeroy (New York, 1999), 183–198, esp.188.

Thesleff, *Texts*, 196.17. "their manly natures"
This phrase does not necessarily indicate that Theano II has been writing about the rearing of boy children exclusively. Greek masculine pronouns and nouns may apply to women (see chap. 2, above). The Spartan educational system was quite detailed and specific concerning the rearing of Spartan girls: see further Sarah B. Pomeroy, *Spartan Women* (New York, 2002), chap. 1. As in Xen. *Oec.* 10.1, a woman may have a masculine intelligence (see further Sarah B. Pomeroy, *Xenophon Oeconomicus: A Social and Historical Commentary* [Oxford, 1994], 303). Perictione I, "On the Harmonious Woman" (this chapter, above), notes that a woman may be courageous [lit. "manly," *andreie*].

Thesleff, *Texts*, 196.19–23. whenever he eats, craves the delights of delicacies; who, . . . if he does not chew on something, is discontent."
Spartan boys were taught to eat moderately so that their girth would not increase and to persevere with their responsibilities when hungry: Xen. *Sp. Const.* 2.5–6.

Thesleff, *Texts*, 196.25. "children who live licentiously become slaves when they grow to manhood"
Consequently mothers have a grave responsibility: they can raise their children to be virtual slaves or to be harmonious and temperate as adults.

Thesleff, *Texts*, 196, 29–30. "tempering" (*anateinomena e epiteinomena*)
The education of a child is analogous to the tempering of a lute string, being extended or stretched until it is finely tuned. For the application of harmony to human beings, see also Perictione I, "On the Harmonious Woman," above, and Theano II to Callisto, below.

Thesleff, *Texts*, 196, 32–33. "just as vines which have been improperly tended are deficient in fruit—your children produce the evil fruit"
Plutarch (*De Educ.* 3) also uses an analogy between agriculture and education.

Theano II to Euclides, the Doctor

Thesleff, *Texts*, 196–97, Hercher, 607.9, trans. Vicki Lynn Harper, in Waithe, *Women Philosophers*, 53

According to Thesleff this letter is written in an "affected" Attic *koine* and "perhaps intentionally ridiculous."[39]

As in her letter about Cleon (see below), Theano II does not hesitate to write intimately about a man who is not her kinsman and (in the case of Euclides) to communicate with him. This constitutes additional evidence that women in the Hellenistic period enjoyed more social freedom than, say, their counterparts in classical Athens. See further Sarah B. Pomeroy, *Goddesses, Whores, Wives, and Slaves: Women in Classical Antiquity* (New York, 1975, with a new Preface, 1995), chap. 7.

This letter is unique among the Neopythagorean letters in its specificity. It asks the perennial serious, but amusing, question we still ask in the form of: "Why do the children of a psychiatrist need to be treated by a psychiatrist?" Though there is nothing noticeably philosophical about the following letter, the Pythagoreans were very concerned about health: the lack of good health signaled a lack of spiritual and physical balance and harmony. Pythagoras himself made recommendations about diet, exercise, and self-control that were conducive to good health, and various medical theories were attributed to him and to other Pythagoreans.[40] In its teasing tone, the letter suggests a message sent to a good friend to cheer him up. This letter is also further evidence that these Neopythagorean texts were actually written by women, for who would bother to forge a letter like the following?

TRANSLATION

"Yesterday when someone had dislocated his leg and a messenger had gone to summon you (I myself was there, for the injured party was a friend of mine), the messenger came back quickly, declaring that the doctor himself was ailing and physically unwell. And I—I swear it!—cast away all thought of my friend's pain, and thought only of the doctor's. I prayed to Panacea and to Apollo, the Renowned Archer, that nothing grievous should have happened to the doctor! Now, in spite of my despondency, I inscribe this letter to you, anxious to learn how you are: lest, perhaps, your gastric orifice is in ill plight, or your liver has been damaged by fever, or some organic harm has befallen you. Thus—

disregarding the innumerable limbs of my friends—shall I fondly cling to your dear health, my good doctor."

Thesleff, *Texts*, 1975. "Panacea"

Panacea was a warrior daughter of Asclepius, god of healing. Apollo was associated with Asclepius.

Theano II to Eurydice

Thesleff, *Texts*, 197.3, Hercher, 606, nr. 7, trans. Sarah B. Pomeroy

INTRODUCTION

In the two letters that follow and in her letter to Nicostrate (below) Theano II shows herself to be an expert on women's issues, especially on counseling women married to unfaithful husbands. The advice she offers is in keeping with Pythagorean views advocating virtuous and harmonious conduct and suggests that the injured women are Pythagoreans, though they may simply have consulted Theano because of her expertise. The adulterous husbands are certainly not abiding by the conduct prescribed by Pythagoras.

Analogies between music and human emotions are common in the Neopythagorean texts. They indicate that, like other upper-class women in the Hellenistic world, the Neopythagoreans were well educated in the musical arts.[41] Women and their families were proud of this accomplishment: they are portrayed in sculpture, including terra-cotta figurines and grave stelae, with musical instruments, in particular stringed instruments such as lutes and citharas (fig. 10).[42] Wind instruments—flutes and shepherd's pipes—were considered inferior and associated with lower-class women, such as *hetairai*. In the musical education of Neopythagoreans and other elite women, the emphasis was different. As the numerous references to harmony as well as the writings of Ptolemaïs indicate (see below), the Neopythagoreans were steeped in musical theory, for that was traditional among Pythagoreans. Other Hellenistic women were proud of their ability to play music, but, although poetry by Hellenistic women is extant, there is no written evidence that they understood, or cared to understand, the intricacies of esoteric musical theory.

TRANSLATION: THEANO TO EURYDICE

"What grief clutches your soul? Are you disheartened for no other reason than that the man with whom you are united [*sunoikeo*] visits a *hetaira* and gets bodily pleasure with her?

Figure 10. Grave stele of Nico from Alexandria, ca. 250 BC. A slave offers a lyre to an upper-class woman. Cairo. Egyptian Museum, C. G. 9259. Courtesy of the Deutsches Archäologisches Institut, Cairo.

But it ought not to engross you thus, O admirable among women, for don't you see that when the ear is filled with pleasure from the melody of an instrument and song, when it is satiated with this it is well-pleased to hear a flute and shepherd's pipe? What is the connection between the flute and musical chords and the amazing sound of an instrument of the most honeysweet quality? Consider that it is the same with you and with the *hetaira* with whom your husband is united [*sunoikeo*].

"Your husband is thinking of you because of his disposition, nature, and reason. But when he becomes satiated he unites [*sunoikeo*] with a *hetaira* casually. Thus those in whom there is a destructive taste have some desire for sustenance that is not good."

Theano II to Callisto

Thesleff, *Texts*, 197–98, Hercher, 604.5, trans. Vicki Lynn Harper, in Waithe, *Women Philosophers*, 47–48

INTRODUCTION

This long letter was written in the Attic *koine*.[43] The letter or treatise of advice from an older, successful person to a younger person was traditional, normal, and common. Older people do appear to have the habit of offering advice that has not been requested. Thus, for example, Plutarch, in the *Advice to the Bride and Groom,* characterizes himself as a mature husband with wisdom to impart to a new bridegroom. In Xenophon's *Oeconomicus* a mature Ischomachus tells Socrates about his early days of marriage, providing an example and comparison to the thoughtless and wasteful Critobulus. One of the topics Ischomachus covers in detail is the management of slaves in order to keep them productive, cooperative, and loyal. Letters of advice from woman to woman, however, are found in Greek literature only among these Neopythagorean documents. In her opening sentences Theano II asserts that household management is indeed women's business.

A daughter usually learned household management from her mother as she grew up. Then, when she was married and moved into her husband's house, her mother-in-law would instruct her. Demographic factors, including deaths in the older generation and marriage around the age of fifteen, could well leave the young bride in need of advice about managing a large household. Though she will have been familiar with slaves from the day she was born, she might be living far apart from her natal family, in an unfamiliar urban or rustic neighborhood, and in a household with slaves of a different ethnicity and training from those she had known in her parents' home. In Xenophon's *Oeconomicus* the husband himself tells his young bride how he wishes his household to be managed.[44] For a man, Ischomachus seems to have been unusually involved in the details of household organization.[45]

Theano II may have been familiar with Xenophon's treatise. Their conclusions are compatible, but some of their arguments, observations, and emphases differ. Xenophon's treatise is far longer and deals with the economy of a large, wealthy estate, as well as with the relationship between husband and wife. In the *Oeconomicus*, Ischomachus wastes no time in pondering whether slaves are naturally different from free people. He chooses the most trustworthy of the slaves to assume the responsibilities of the mistress and master when the latter are unavailable. Ischomachus's goal in advocating that slaves be treated decently and rewarded for their good work is ultimately to increase the profitability of his estate. In contrast, Theano's goal is to maintain a harmonious, trouble-free household. Moreover, the woman in authority is to manage the slaves rationally, not be influenced by her passions and emotions. Like other Neopythagoreans, Theano II uses an analogy to a stringed instrument: she advises Callisto to keep the slaves "in tune," with neither too much tension nor too much slack.

In this letter Theano II may also be reacting against popular theories, such as Aristotle's views on natural slavery. Like Xenophon, she considers slaves to be intact human beings, different from free people only in their civil status. Both point out that proper treatment of slaves will curb their desire to run away and will render them easier to exploit. Aristotle, in contrast, had argued that slaves were inherently inferior to free males, for slaves (like children and women) lacked the rational element of the mind (*logos*: *Pol.* 1254b.1.2.13). Therefore, although Aristotle views the slaves' tasks as domestic, he can conceive of the master only as male (*despotes*, *Pol.* 1255b. 1.2.23). Aristotle (*Pol.* 1255a.1.2.16–17) also discusses the use of force: is it an incitement to virtue and therefore good, or is it merely a demonstration of the power of the stronger over the weaker?

TRANSLATION

"To you younger women, just as soon as you are married, authority is granted by law to govern the household. But, to do well, instruction about household management is needed from older women, a continual source of advice. It is well to learn what you do not know ahead of time and to deem most proper the advice of older women; in these matters a young soul must be brought up from girlhood. The primary authority of women in the household is authority over the slaves. And the greatest thing, my dear, is good will on the slaves' part. For this possession is not bought along with their bodies; rather, intelligent mistresses bring it about in time. Just usage is the cause of this—seeing to it that they are neither worn out by toil nor incapacitated by deprivation.

"For they are human in nature. There are some women who suppose the profitable to be what is most unprofitable: maltreatment of their slaves, overburdening them with tasks to be done, and depriving them of the things they need. And then, having made much of an obol's profit, they pay the price in enormous damages: ill-will and the worst treacheries. As for you, let there be ready at hand a measure of food that is proportionate to the amount of woolwork produced by a day's work. With respect to the diet of your slaves, this will suffice. As for undisciplined behavior, one must assist to the utmost what is fitting for you, not what is advantageous to them. For it is necessary to estimate one's slaves at their proper worth. On the one hand, cruelty will not bring gratitude to a soul; on the other hand, reasoning, no less than righteous indignation, is an effective means of control. But if there is too much unconquerable vice on the part of the slaves, one must send them away to be sold. Let what is alien to the needs [of the house] as well be estranged from its mistress as well [lit. "Let what is alien to the need be estranged from the (female) proper judge as well"].

"Let proper judgment of this take precedence so that you will determine the true facts of wrongdoing in keeping with the justice of the condemnation, and the magnitude of wrongdoing in proportion to the proper punishment. But sometimes the mistress' forgiveness and kindness towards those who have erred will release them from penalties. In this way, too, you will preserve a fitting and appropriate mode of life. There are some women, my dear, who because they are cruel—brutalized by jealousy or anger—even whip the bodies of their slaves as if they were inscribing the excess of their bitterness as a memorandum. In time, some of these [female slaves] are used up, utterly worked out; others procure safety by escaping; but some stop living, withdrawing into death with their own hands. In the end, the isolation of the mistress, bewailing her lack of domestic consideration, finds desolate repentance. But, my dear, likening yourself to musical instruments, know what sound they make when they are loosened too much, but that they are snapped asunder when stretched too tight. It is the same way for your slaves. Too much license creates dissonance in the matter of obedience, but the stretching of forceful necessity causes the dissolution of nature itself. One must meditate on this: 'Right measure is best in everything.' Farewell."

COMMENTARY

Thesleff, *Texts*, 197.31–32. "in these matters a young soul must be brought up from girlhood."
Myia's letter to Phyllis (below) concerning the employment of a wet nurse indicates that children might well be accustomed to the services of a slave from the day of birth (see chap. 6, below).

Thesleff, *Texts*, 197.31. "The primary authority of women in the household is authority over the slaves [*therapainon*]."

Servants might be free women forced by economic necessity to work outside their homes, but it is far more likely that they were slaves. (See commentary on Myia's letter to Phyllis, below, chap. 6.) Moreover, the specific content of Theano's letter leaves no doubt that the servants she is discussing are slaves. Female slaves, ranging from children to adults, were more likely to work indoors and thus be under the mistress's authority. Their tasks included cleaning, carrying water and firewood, grinding grain, and other food preparation. They also provided personal care for their owner's family, such as nursing, cleaning and folding clothing, assisting at the toilette, and sexual services for the men in the household.

They often produced all the clothing worn by their owners and slaves in the household, and in their spare time they were expected to spin. A comfortable urban Greek household usually employed many more female than male domestics. Male slaves would work outdoors, farming, gardening, doing yard work, delivering messages, and accompanying their master or his sons in their daily routines.[46] Gender roles might be altered in times of need, especially at harvest time, when women could be deployed outdoors. We note that in Xenophon's *Oeconomicus* the husband is the supreme authority in the household, but he delegates command to his wife after he has trained her to manage affairs as he would. In contrast, Theano II assumes that the young wife will take up the reins in the household immediately. Both Xenophon and Theano II emphasize the importance of winning the good will of the slave. Xenophon offers material rewards, such as a share in the profits and better clothing, Theano II simply recommends not using corporal punishments for slaves, as in her letter to Euboule (above), and she does not advise using such harsh measures for disciplining children.

Thesleff, *Texts*, 198.5–6. "a measure of food that is proportionate to the amount of woolwork produced by a day's work."

The reference to woolwork as the means of calculating a slave's food allowance makes it clear that the domestic slaves are female. Papyrus accounts from Hellenistic Egypt show that food rations were allocated according to the age, sex, and intensity of the job performed, while sometimes the quality of the food was gauged according to the status of the slave.[47]

Thesleff, *Texts*, 198.10. "reasoning [*logismos*], no less than righteous indignation, is an effective means of control."

We may contrast Aristotle's view that women possessed the rational part of the soul, but it was dormant, while slaves did not possess it at all (see above).

Thesleff, *Texts*, 198.17–21. "women, my dear, who because they are cruel—brutalized by jealousy or anger—even whip the bodies of their slaves as if they were inscribing the excess of their bitterness as a memorandum. In time, some of these [female slaves] are used up, utterly worked out; others procure safety by escaping; but some stop living, withdrawing into death with their own hands."

Slaves constituted a large capital investment. The prudent owner would keep them healthy, well fed, and willing to work, guarding lest they become ill, malevolent, unsalable, or in other ways prove to be an unprofitable investment. She would not punish them when she herself had lost self-control or was angry. The Pythagorean Archytas of Tarentum also cautioned against punishing slaves in anger. Thus he said in response to the negligence of his steward: "I would have beaten you to death by now, if I were not angry."[48]

Thesleff, *Texts*, 198.23. "musical instruments"
Ta organa may refer to organs of the human body or to musical instruments: *LSJ*, s.v. *organon*.

Thesleff, *Texts*, 198.23–27. "likening yourself to musical instruments, know what sound they make when they are loosened too much.... One must meditate on this: 'Right measure is best in everything.'"

Theano closes with a distinctively Pythagorean *sphragis*, the analogy between the harmonious human being and the well-tempered musical instrument. We may compare the sentiments with those expressed by Perictione I in her treatise "On the Harmonious Woman."

Theano II to Nicostrate

Thesleff, *Texts*, 198, Hercher, 604.5, trans. Vicki Lynn Harper, in Waithe, *Women Philosophers*, 44–46

INTRODUCTION

This letter was written in the Attic *koine*. Much of Theano's advice concerning coping with a philandering husband is similar to that given by Perictione I. The betrayed wife should not demean herself by being jealous or taking revenge. She should not lower herself to the level of her husband, who is enslaved by sexual passion and in thrall to a shameless woman. His madness accentuates, by contrast, the wife's reasonable, noble demeanor. By their behavior such a husband and wife belie Aristotle's view (*Pol.* 1.5.6–7 [1260a]) that, though both women and men possess the deliberative part of the soul, only men can exercise it. In fact, even the courtesans are rational and calculating; though they enslave men, unlike the men they themselves are not slaves to passion and sexual appetites (see below). Theano's advice foreshadows the common statement of psychologists in the modern Western world: You cannot change other people; in coping with difficulties created by others, you must change yourself.

Hetairai advertised their financial success and ability to command high prices by displaying their lucre in the form of gold and precious stones. Of course, they wore cosmetics. Wealthy respectable wives who were not Pythagoreans regularly wore jewelry and cosmetics, too, as we can see in Apulian vase painting (fig. 1, and see chaps. 1 and 2). Nevertheless, Pythagoras preferred that his female disciples distinguish themselves from all other women by eschewing precious jewelry and cosmetics.

The men of Croton in the days of Pythagoras and the philandering husbands of Neopythagoreans did not err merely by occasionally hiring a *porne* (common prostitute). Although Pythagoras did not approve of any infidelity, a few hours with a *porne* in a brothel would have constituted a brief "fling," a one-time expense.[49] Rather, the licentious husbands were supporting or contributing to the support of the entire household of a concubine or *hetaira*, including children, slaves, clothing, the house and its furnishings, religious expenses, in short, all the needs of daily life.[50] Exclusive access to a desirable and expensive *hetaira* or concubine in the highly competitive Greek society increased a man's amour propre. (Among all the available suitors she had chosen *him*.) A woman in the sex trade was not modest, like a respectable wife; thus she served as a display of conspicuous consumption. Perhaps the household of the *hetaira* was less expensive than that of the husband and legitimate wife; perhaps not. In any case, the wife's dowry had contributed to the economic foundation of the marital *oikos*, and her work and management skills assured its continuing prosperity, while the "kept" woman could no longer ply her trade and was dependent on one man for her livelihood.

In the *Dialogues of the Courtesans*, Lucian (born ca. AD 120) offers a realistic dramatic sketch of the lives of classical and Hellenistic courtesans and their swains, one that complements the picture painted in the Neopythagorean letters. The courtesans in Lucian are usually mercenary, though they may accept some lovers because they are handsome or pleasing. If they bear a child they tend to rear a boy and either expose a girl baby or raise her to be a *hetaira* (*DMeretr*. 1.281, 14.320). Most of their clients are unmarried youths, and the women are concerned that they will be deserted when their swains do marry (*DMeretr*.1.281–83). In one case a client is a married man; his wife said the courtesan had driven him crazy by means of drugs, but the only drug was his own jealousy of another lover (*DMeretr*. 8.301). The husband finally paid a talent (a huge price) for the courtesan's exclusive services for eight months. Competition among men for a desirable courtesan is a frequent theme, as well as competition among women for a wealthy lover.[51] Resort to witchcraft (including charms, spells, curses, and magical devices) to attract men is common (*DMeretr*. 1.281, 3.287–89). Courtesans are also available to wealthy female clients for lesbian relationships, although one courtesan terms these liaisons "unusual" (*allokoton*: *DMeretr*. 5.289). Athenaeus (ca. AD 170–230) also portrays *hetairai* as witty, sophisticated, and entertaining.[52] Most of the historical women who are featured in Athenaeus and Lucian lived in the classical and early Hellenistic period and illustrate the authors' belief that human nature does not change over time.[53] Thus the scenarios described in the letters are perennial in the lives of courtesans and do not indicate that the Neopythagorean letters were written in Lucian's day.

Interestingly enough, the wives do not complain about the expenses involved when their husbands support other women. Perhaps they may not have been fully aware of the extravagant sums involved, though Theano points out that the errant husband may perceive the diminution of his livelihood and of his reputation. Rather, they bemoan their husband's sexual infidelity and mental and emotional servitude to another woman.

TRANSLATION

"Greetings. I hear repeatedly about your husband's madness: he has a courtesan; also that you feel jealous anger toward him. My dear, I have known many men with the same malady. It is as if they are hunted down by these women and held fast; it is as if they have lost their minds. But you are dispirited by night and by day, you are sorely troubled and contrive things against him. Don't you, at least, be that way, my dear. For the moral excellence of the wife is not surveillance of her husband but companionable accommodation; it is in the spirit of accommodation to bear his folly.

"If he associates with the courtesan with a view towards pleasure, he associates with his wife with a view towards the beneficial. It is beneficial not to compound evils with evils and not to augment folly with folly. Some faults, dear, are stirred up all the more when they are condemned, but cease when they are passed over in silence, much as they say fire quenches itself if left alone. Besides, though it seems that you wish to escape notice yourself, by condemning him, you will take away the veil that covers your own condition.

"Then you will manifestly err. You are not convinced that love of one's husband resides in conduct that is noble and good. For this is the grace of marital association. Recognize the fact that he goes to the courtesan in order to be frivolous, but that he abides with you in order to share a common life; that he loves you on the basis of good judgment, but her on the basis of passion. The moment for this is brief. It almost coincides with its own satisfaction. In a trice it both arises and ceases. The time for a courtesan is of brief duration for any man who is not excessively corrupt. For what is emptier than desire whose benefit of enjoyment is unrighteousness? Eventually he will see that he is diminishing his life and slandering his good character.

"No one who understands persists in self-chosen harm. Thus, being summoned by his just obligation towards you and perceiving the diminution of his livelihood [he will take notice of you]. Unable to bear the outrage of moral condemnation, he will soon repent. My dear, this is how you must live: not defending yourself against courtesans, but distinguishing yourself from them by your orderly conduct towards your husband, by your careful attention to the house, by the calm way in which you deal with the servants, and by your tender love for your children. You must not be jealous of that woman (for it is good to extend your emulation only to women who are virtuous); rather, you must make yourself fit for reconciliation. Good character brings regard even from enemies, dear, and esteem is the product of nobility and goodness alone. In this way it is even possible for the power of a woman to surpass that of a man. It is possible for her to grow in his esteem instead of having to serve one who is hostile to her.

"If he has been properly prepared for it by you, he will be all the more ashamed; he will wish to be reconciled sooner and, because he is more warmly attached to you, he will love you more tenderly. Conscious of his injustice towards you, he will perceive your attention to his livelihood, and make trial of your affection towards himself. Just as bodily illnesses make their cessations sweeter, so also do differences between friends make their reconciliations more intimate. As for you, do resist the passionate resolutions of your suffering. Because he is not well, he invites you to share in his plight; because he himself misses the mark of decency, he invites you to fail in decorum; having damaged his own life he invites you to harm what is beneficial to you. Consequently you will seem to have conspired against him and, in reproving him, will appear to reprove yourself.

"If you divorce yourself from him and move on, you will change your first husband only to try another and, if he has the same failings, you will resort to another (for the lack of a husband is not bearable for young women). Or else you will abide alone without any husband like a spinster. Do you intend to be negligent of the house and to destroy your husband? Then you will share the spoils of an anguished life. Do you intend to avenge yourself upon the courtesan? Being on her guard, she will circumvent you; but, if she actively wards you off, a woman who has no tendency to blush is formidable in battle. Is it good to fight with your husband day after day? To what advantage? The battles and reproaches will not stop his licentious behavior, but they will increase the dissension between you by their escalations. What, then? Are you plotting something against him? Don't do it, my dear. Tragedy teaches us to conquer jealousy, encompassing a systematic treatise on the actions by which Medea was led to the commission of outrage. Just as it is necessary to keep one's hands away from a disease of the eyes, so must you separate your pretension from your pain. By patiently enduring you will quench your suffering sooner."

COMMENTARY

Thesleff, *Texts*, 198.33. "hunted down by these women"

Courtesans were free to pursue men and choose their sexual partners. Respectable wives, in contrast, were given in marriage to bridegrooms chosen by their parents.

Thesleff, *Texts*, 200.7–8. "if she actively wards you off, a woman who has no tendency to blush is formidable in battle."

A virtuous wife would be ill-equipped to contend with a *hetaira* who has long given up her innocence ("blush").

Thesleff, *Texts*, 200.12. "Medea"

Medea was notorious for the revenge she took on her husband, Jason, when he discarded her in favor of a new wife. In Euripides' *Medea* (431 BC), Medea killed not only the wife but also the two children Medea had borne to Jason. Her speech to the women of Corinth offers a valuable insight into the position of the Greek wife and the reasons why an unfaithful husband causes immeasurable pain:

> My whole life was bound up in him, as he well knows;
> Yet my husband has proved to be the worst of
> of all beings who breathe and have intelligence.
> We women are the most miserable creatures.
> First we have to buy a husband at a steep price,
> then take a master for our bodies.
> This second evil is worse than the first, but
> the greatest struggle turns on whether we get a bad
> husband or a good one. Divorce is not respectable
> for a woman and she cannot deny her husband....
> If we work things out well and the husband
> lives with us without resisting his yoke,
> life is enviable. Otherwise it is better to die.
> A man, when he is tired of being with those inside,
> goes out and relieves his heart of boredom,
> or turns to some friend or contemporary.
> But we have to look to one person only.[54]

In the Hellenistic period, Euripides was the most popular of the classical tragic poets. Although there were variants of the Medea myth, there can be no doubt that Theano II is referring to the story as told by Euripides. Representations of Medea in the visual arts in the fourth century BC portray her murdering her innocent children, a crime that was regarded as much more serious and more grievous to her husband and to herself than killing her husband's new wife.[55] The Stoic Chrysippus (second half of 3rd c. BC) used the example of Medea to illustrate the conflict between reason and anger in the soul, and Medea continued to be cited in discussions of human psychology by later philosophers.[56]

Thesleff, *Texts*, 200.13. "necessary to keep one's hands away from a disease of the eyes"

Theano II shows her knowledge of disease and infection. The Pythagoreans were particularly interested in health (see above on Theano II to Euclides). Eye infections were common and are frequently discussed in the medical papyri from Roman Egypt. See further R. P. J. Jackson, "Eye Medicine in the Roman Empire," in W. Haase, ed., *ANRW* 2.3, vol. 37.2.*Philosophie, Wissenschaften, Technik* (Berlin, 1995), 2228–52, esp. 2228–29.

Theano II to Rhodope the Philosopher

Thesleff, *Texts*, 200, Hercher, 606.8, trans. Vicki Lynn Harper, in Waithe, *Women Philosophers*, 53

INTRODUCTION

This letter was written in an "affected" Attic.[57] The reference to Plato's *Parmenides* makes it clear that the author lived after the mid-fourth century BC. As we have seen above, Perictione I personified the link between Platonism and Pythagoreanism.

It is difficult to believe that this letter was not written by a woman philosopher named Theano II to another female philosopher, who would understand the contents. That it is brief enough to be what we would classify as a "note" adds to the aura of authenticity. Why would a pseudonymous writer even bother to compose it?

It is interesting to observe that Theano does not hesitate to write of her fondness and admiration for a man who is evidently a stranger to her.

TRANSLATION

"Are you dispirited? I myself am dispirited. Are you distressed because I have not yet sent you Plato's book, the one entitled "Ideas or Parmenides"? But I myself am grieved to the greatest extent, because no one has yet met with me to discuss Cleon. I will not send you the book until someone arrives to clarify matters concerning this man. So exceedingly do I love the soul of the man—on the grounds that it is the soul of a philosopher, of one zealous to do good, of one who fears the gods beneath the earth. And do not think the story is otherwise than it has been told. For I am half mortal and cannot bear to look directly on the star that makes day manifest [the sun]."

COMMENTARY

Thesleff, *Texts*, 200.20. "Cleon"
Iamblichus (*VP,* 267) lists a Cleon among the Pythagoreans from Tarentum. Theano may be referring to someone who was named for this man. Of course, Cleon is a common name, occupying some two columns in Fraser and Matthews (*LGPN* III.A, pp. 250–51), who cite Iamblichus, and *FVSI*, p. 446 for Cleon of Tarentum. Diogenes Laertius (10.84) also mentions a Cleon who was a contemporary of Epicurus.

"Ideas or Parmenides"
Plato asserts in the *Parmenides* that the Ideas exist and are unchangeable.[58] Diogenes Laertius (3.58) gives the two names of the *Parmenides*. Thus the title in the Loeb Library edition is "Parmenides [Or on Ideas: Logical] (*Parmenides e peri ideon: logikos*).[59] Though it has been argued that the second title goes back to Plato himself, the scholarly consensus is that it is Hellenistic.[60]

Theano II. Epistle to Timareta

Thesleff, *Texts*, 200.26, Waithe, *Women Philosophers*, 55, Poll. *Onom*. 10.21
This fragment is quoted by Pollux: "'Master of the house' and 'mistress of the house'—I found both these terms in the letter written by Theano the Pythagorean woman to Timareta."

Theano II to Tim(ai)onides

Thesleff, *Texts,* 200.30–35, Hercher 606, 8, trans. Vicki Lynn Harper, in Waithe, *Women Philosophers*, 55
This letter was written in the Attic *koine*. In tradition and in all texts attributed to Theano I and II, the women named Theano are portrayed as wise, moderate, and harmonious. The letter below is an indication that such adulation was not universal. Theano II was the object of scandal. Like other Pythagorean women, however, she restrains herself from taking revenge by behaving as Timaionides did. Instead, she defends herself and humiliates Timaionides by publishing this letter.

TRANSLATION

"What fellowship is there for you and me? Why do you continually slander us? Or do you not know that we praise you before everybody, even if you do the opposite? Then, again, do realize that even though we praise there is no one who believes, and even though you slander there is no one who listens. And I rejoice on this account: this is how the god sees it and the truth most certainly determines it to be."

Ptolemaïs of Cyrene

Thesleff, *Texts*, 242–43, trans. Andrew Barker, *Greek Musical Writings*, vol. 2, *Harmonic and Acoustical Theory* (Cambridge, 1989), 239–40

Neopythagorean women writers often refer to harmony, concord, attunement, and the proper tension of the strings of a lyre or kithara as a means of describing human emotions and relationships. To be sure, as educated Pythagoreans, these women would have understood not only how to tune and play a stringed instrument but also at least some of the musical theory underlying their practice. Ptolemaïs is particularly interesting in this context, for she writes of musical theory per se, rather than using musical concepts metaphorically.

The following passages by Ptolemaïs are quoted by Porphyry (232/33–ca. 305 AD) in his commentary on Claudius Ptolemy's *Harmonics* (*In Ptolemaei Harmonica Commentarium*). Ptolemy (who is better known as an astronomer) wrote in Alexandria during the first half of the second century AD. Porphyry quotes Ptolemaïs as an authority on canonic theory and remarks that the scholar Didymus (1st c. BC) adopted some of Ptolemaïs's views. Knowledge of the canonic theory indicates that Ptolemaïs had a firm grasp of mathematics. "Canonic" refers to straightness: a stretched string may thus be understood as a straight line and music seen as an expression of mathematical ratios and intervals that can be measured. Ptolemaïs's vocabulary shows that she was familiar with other sciences that were studied in the Hellenistic period.[61] For example, she uses such terms as *parapegmata*, a word used by astronomists to denote the movable pegs placed in a stone to indicate astronomical and meteorological events.

The treatise of Ptolemaïs deals with the philosophical issue of reason and perception in Pythagorean harmonics and in the theories Aristoxenus of Tarentum (4th c. BC) discussed in his *Elements of Harmony*.[62] Her detailed discussion of Aristoxenus indicates that she owned copies of his texts or perhaps read them in the great library at Alexandria; in any case, she must have had them unrolled in front of her while she wrote. The argument among commentators in this period may be viewed as the familiar conflict between mind and body fought in the arena of musical theory. Pythagorean musical theory was based on mathematical principles, while other theorists favored using empirical sensory data. Although the title of her treatise seems to suggest otherwise, Ptolemaïs prefers the more moderate position of Aristoxenus, who considered both hearing and reason as the basis of the science of harmonics.[63]

Porphyry, in his *Commentary on Ptolemy's Harmonics*, describes Ptolemaïs's work as an "introduction" (*eisagoge*). He quotes the following passages from her *Pythagorean Doctrine of the Elements of Music*. In his *Commentary* Porphyry states: "A canon measures the attunements among musical notes—those differences which are studied as numerical ratios; these measurements may be used to correct the senses' perceptual deficiencies." But Ptolemaïs of Cyrene also writes about this matter (i.e., the use of the *kanon*) in her *Pythagorean Doctrine of the Elements of Music*, as follows:[64]

> The science of *kanonike* [canonics] of whom is it mainly characteristic? In general, of the Pythagoreans; for what we now call *harmonike* [harmonics] they used to name *kanonike*. From what do we derive the term *kanonike*? Not, as some people think, by transference from the instrument called the *kanon*, but from straightness, on the grounds that it is through this science that reason [*logos*] discovers what is correct, and discovers the *parapegmata* [i.e. "markings on a ruler positioned next to a string," see above] of what is well attuned.
>
> They also call *kanonike* the investigation that employs syrinxes [panpipes] and *auloi* [flutes] and the rest, though these are not strictly canonic; but they call them "canonic" too because the ratios and theorems fit them. Hence it is rather that the instrument was named "*kanon*" by derivation from the science of *kanonike*. A *kanonikos*, in general, is a harmonic theorist [*harmonikos*] who constructs ratios in connection with attunement [*to hermosmenon*]. *Mousikoi* and *kanonikoi* are different; for "*mousikoi*" is the name given to the harmonic theorists who begin from perceptions, while "*kanonikoi*" is that given to the Pythagorean harmonic theorists. But each of the two groups is in the generic sense *mousikoi*.

To this she adds, in the form of question and answers once again:

> The theory that uses the *kanon*—of what does it consist? Of the things postulated by the *mousikoi* and those adopted by the *mathematikoi*. The things

postulated by the *mousikoi* are all those adopted by the *kanonikoi* on the basis of perceptions, for instance that there are concordant and discordant intervals, and that the octave is compounded from the fourth and the fifth, and that the excess of a fifth over a fourth is a tone, and similar things. Those adopted by the *mathematikoi* are all those which the *kanonikoi* study theoretically in their own special way, only beginning from the starting points given by perception, for instance that the intervals are in ratios of numbers, and that a note consists of numbers of collisions, and other things of the same sort. Hence one might define the postulates of *kanonike* as lying both within the science concerned with music, and within that concerned with numbers and geometry.

After quoting Ptolemy, Porphyry continues:[65]

Pythagoras and his successors wish to accept perception as a guide for reason at the outset, to provide reason with a spark, as it were; but they treat reason, when it has set out from these beginnings, as working on its own in separation from perception. Hence if the system [*systema*] discovered by reason in its investigation no longer accords with perception, they do not retrace their steps, but level accusations, saying that perception is going astray, while reason by itself has discovered what is correct, and refutes perception.

An opposite position to this is held by some of the *mousikoi* who follow Aristoxenus, those who applied themselves to a theoretical science based in thought, while nevertheless setting out from expertise on instruments. For they treated perception as authoritative, and reason as attending on it, for use only when needed. According to these people, to be sure, it is only to be expected that the rational postulates of the *kanon* are not always concordant with the perceptions.

Porphyry then introduces his final and longest quotation from Ptolemaïs:[66] "Concerning these matters Ptolemaïs of Cyrene wrote briefly about these subjects in her introductory treatise, and Didymus entered on them at great length in his *On the Difference between the Aristoxenians and the Pythagoreans*. We shall write out what each of them says, altering a few things for the sake of brevity. Ptolemaïs, then, writes as follows:"

What is the difference between those who are distinguished in the field of music? Some preferred reason by itself, some perception, some both together. Reason was preferred by those of the Pythagoreans who were especially keen on disputing with the *mousikoi*, arguing that perception should be thrown out completely, and that reason should be brought in as an autonomous criterion in itself. These people are wholly refuted by their practice of accepting something perceptible at the beginning, and then forgetting that they have done so. The instrumentalists [*organikoi*], on the other hand, preferred perception: they gave no thought at all, or only feeble thought, to theory.

What is the distinction between those who prefer the combination of both? Some accepted both perception and reason in the same way, as being of equal power, while others accepted the one as the leader, the other as the follower. Aristoxenus of Tarentum accepted both in the same way. For what is perceived cannot be constituted by itself apart from reason, and neither is reason strong enough to establish anything without taking its starting points from perception, and delivering the conclusion of its theorizing [*theorema*] in agreement with perception once again. In what way does he want perception to be in the lead of reason? In order [*taxis*], not in power [*dynamis*]. For when the perceptible thing, whatever it may be, has been reviewed by perception, then, he says, we must put reason in the lead, for the theoretical study of this precept. Who are those who treat both together alike? Pythagoras and his successors. For[67] they wish to accept perception as a guide for reason at the outset, to provide reason with a spark, as it were; but they treat reason, when it has set out from these beginnings, as working on its own in separation from perception. Hence if the system [*systema*] discovered by reason in its investigation no longer accords with perception, they do not retrace their steps, but level accusations, saying that perception is going astray, while reason by itself has discovered what is correct, and refutes perception. Who are in opposition to these? Some of the *mousikoi* who follow Aristoxenus, those who applied themselves to a theoretical science based in thought, while nevertheless setting out from expertise on instruments. For they treated perception as authoritative, and reason as attending on it, for use only when needed.

The Letters and Treatises of Neopythagorean Women in the West

Aesara on Human Nature

Thesleff, *Texts*, s.v. Aresas, pp. 48–50, Stob. 1.49.27, pp. 355–57, trans. Vicki Lynn Harper, in Waithe, *Women Philosophers*, 20

INTRODUCTION

Stobaeus, the only source, identifies the author as Aesara, a Pythagorean of Lucania. According to some biographical traditions, Pythagoras had a daughter named Aisara; hence this name would be a likely one for a Neopythagorean woman. Thesleff places the author in the third century BC and identifies the dialect as Doric. He argues that the author is a man, Aresas of Lucania (who is mentioned by Iamblichus (*VP* 266), noting his ties to the school of Archytas, though he reports other scholarly views about the attribution.[1] This Aresas was a contemporary of Gorgias and therefore dates to the late fifth century BC.[2] It is difficult to follow Thesleff's arguments because they are presented in the highly condensed style appropriate to an apparatus criticus. He seems to base his identification of the author as male on two emendations.[3] Thesleff is not persuasive here: Mary Ellen Waithe with Vicki Harper,[4] Sister Prudence Allen,[5] and Ian Plant[6] take Stobaeus at face value and identify the author as Aesara of Lucania, as I do.

A long fragment of the text is preserved. It is a philosophical treatise that offers no clues about the author's gender. As all Greek philosophers do, Aesara uses masculine pronouns and words when writing about human beings in general and about concepts, like the soul, that apply to both women and men. Like Perictione's treatise *On Wisdom*, Aesara's text is written for both women and men.

Aesara discusses natural law as it concerns individual morality, the family,

---

[1] See the introductory paragraph of Chapter 5.

and society.[7] The tripartite soul, comprising mind, spirit, and desire, is Platonic, and common to both women and men.[8] The sphere of mind is thought and judgment; spirit encompasses courage and strength; and friendship, love, and kindness correspond to the third of the soul that is desire. All three components need to be in balance and to work together in harmony. Understanding human nature is essential for understanding law and morality.[9] As Harper and Waithe explain, law and justice are analogous to the spirited element of the soul. Finally, mind (*noos*) creates harmony between such dissimilar things as sweetness and seriousness and pleasure and virtue.

TRANSLATION

"Human nature seems to me to provide a standard of law and justice both for the home and for the city. By following the tracks within himself whoever seeks will make a discovery: law is in him and justice, which is the orderly arrangement of the soul. Being threefold, it is organized in accordance with triple functions: that which effects judgment and thoughtfulness is [the mind], that which effects strength and ability is [high spirit], and all that effects love and kindliness is desire. These are all so disposed relatively to one other, that the best part is in command, the most inferior is governed, and the one in between holds a middle place; it both governs and is governed.

"The god thus contrived these things according to principle in both the outline and completion of the human dwelling place, because he intended man alone to become a recipient of law and justice, and none other of mortal animals. A composite unity of association could not come about from a single thing, nor indeed from several which are all alike. (For it is necessary, since the things to be done are different, that the parts of the soul also be different, just as in the case of the body [the organs of touch and] sight and hearing and taste and smell differ, for these do not all have the same affinity with everything.)

"Nor could such a unity come from several dissimilar things at random, but rather, from parts formed in accordance with the completion and organization and fitting together of the entire composite whole. Not only is the soul composed from several dissimilar parts, these being fashioned in conformity with the whole and complete, but in addition these are not arranged haphazardly and at random, but in accordance with rational attention.

"For if they had an equal share of power and honor, though being themselves unequal – some inferior, some better, some in between—the association of parts throughout the soul could not have been fitted together. Or, even if they did have an unequal share, but the worse rather than the better had the greater share, there would be great folly and disorder in the soul. And even if the better had the greater, and the worse the lesser, but each of these had not the proper proportion, there could not be unanimity and friendship and justice throughout the soul, since when one is arranged in accordance with the suitable proportion, this sort of arrangement I assert to be justice.

"And indeed a certain unanimity and agreement in sentiment accompanies such an arrangement. This sort would justly be called good order of the soul, whichever, due to the better part's ruling and the inferior's being ruled, should add the strength of virtue to itself. Friendship and love and kindliness, cognate and kindred, will sprout from these parts. For a closely-inspecting mind persuades, love desires, and high spirit is filled with strength; once seething with hatred, it becomes friendly to desire.

"Mind having fitted the pleasant together with the painful, mingling also the tense and robust with the slight and relaxed portion of the soul, each part is distributed in accordance with its kindred and suitable concern for each thing: mind closely inspecting and tracking out things, high spirit adding impetuosity and strength to what is closely inspected, and desire, being akin to affection, adapts to the mind, preserving the pleasant as its own, and giving up the thoughtful to the thoughtful part of the soul. By virtue of these things the best life for man seems to me to be whenever the pleasant should be mixed with the earnest and pleasure with virtue. Mind is able to fix these things to itself, becoming lovely through systematic education and virtue."

COMMENTARY

Thesleff, *Texts*, 49.1. "both for the home and for the city."
Like Pythagoras himself, Aesara sees the *oikos* not merely as a component of the city but as a realm equal to the city. Although Aesara does not mention that *oikoi* function under the authority of a woman (see below, on Myia to Phyllis), the Hellenistic reader will have understood that the sphere of women is here considered to be equal to men's sphere.[10]

Thesleff, *Texts*, 49.9. "*The* god"
Waithe, *Women Philosophers*, and Plante translate *ho theos* as "god," but "the god" is not only a more accurate translation but also more appropriate to a polytheistic religion.

Thesleff, *Texts*, 49.21–23. "For if they had an equal share of power and honor, though being themselves unequal—some inferior, some better, some in between—the association of parts throughout the soul could not have been fitted together."

Here too is a reflection of the Platonic doctrine that justice is the harmonious and equal balance of the components of the tripartite soul and likewise of law and justice. Like Plato, Aesara does not differentiate between the souls of women and men.

Melissa to Cleareta

Thesleff, *Texts*, 115–16, Hercher, 607, *P. Haun.* (3rd c. AD, no provenance, where the letter is paraphrased from Doric into the Attic *koine*), trans. Sarah B. Pomeroy.

According to Thesleff, Melissa's letter should be dated to the third century BC.[11]

INTRODUCTION

Melissa's letter is consistent with the views on women's wisdom and virtues expressed by Perictione I, Theano II, and Phintys. Melissa differs from Pythagoras in that she believes respectable women may wear some cosmetics, whereas Pythagoras banished them entirely.

Melissa's name, a common women's name, means "honey bee." In Greek thought, the woman who is like a bee is virtuous, industrious, clean, and a good housekeeper.[12]

TRANSLATION

"You appear to have the majority of virtues all by yourself. Your enthusiastic wish to hear about women's adornment offers good hope that you will perfect yourself as far as virtue is concerned. It is necessary for the woman who is chaste and free to live with her lawful husband, quiet, having made her face beautiful inexpensively, wearing clean white simple clothing, but not overly costly or elaborate. She must avoid sheer, gold, or purple clothing. These are useful for *hetairai* ensnaring more men. Her character, not her dresses, is the adornment of a woman who is pleasing to her own husband, not to her neighbors.

"She should wear the red blush of modesty instead of rouge on her face, and honor, decorum, and chastity instead of gold and emerald. She must direct her love of beauty not toward expensive clothing but toward chastity, household management, and pleasing her own husband, by accomplishing what he wants. For to a woman of decorum the wishes of her husband are an unwritten law by which she must live her life.

"She must consider that the most beautiful and greatest dowry she has brought with her is orderliness. She should trust in the beauty and treasure of her soul, rather than in that of her face and possessions. Jealousy and sickness take away the latter, but for the woman who has them the former are possessions until death."

COMMENTARY

Thesleff, *Texts*, 115. "white simple clothing."
The original Pythagoreans also wore white: see chap. 1, above.

Thesleff, *Texts*, 115.27–116.1. "It is necessary for the woman who is chaste and free . . . but not overly costly or elaborate."

In *Advice to the Bride and Groom* (29), Plutarch gives similar instructions concerning the moderate use of adornment and the need for a wife to deploy enough charms, both artificial and natural, to please her husband, without resorting to the meretricious and ostentatious displays deployed by courtesans.

Thesleff, *Texts*, 116. "the red blush of modesty"
Cf. Theano II to Nicostrate (chap. 5) who describes a *hetaira* as a woman who has no tendency to blush.

Thesleff, *Texts*, 116.3–4. "She must avoid sheer, gold, or purple clothing. These are useful for *hetairai* ensnaring more men."

As the remarks of Theano I about not baring her arm in public and about nudity in the husband's presence makes clear, Pythagorean women approved of seductive dress and behavior, but only in private and only to enhance their relationship with their husband.[13]

Thesleff, *Texts*, 116.13. "For to a woman of decorum the wishes of her husband are an unwritten law by which she must live her life."

The unwritten law may be seen as higher and more immutable and universal than written laws (see, inter alia, Xen., *Mem.* 4.4.19).

Phintys of Sparta. "On the Moderation of Women," Fragment I

Thesleff, *Texts*, 151, Stob. 4.23.61, pp. 588–91, trans. Vicki Harper, in Waithe, *Women Philosophers*, 26–28

INTRODUCTION

There are several possibilities for the date, lineage, and even the name of Phintys. Thesleff suggests that she is the same as the Philtys, daughter of Theophris of Croton, mentioned in Iamblichus's catalogue.[14] He also suggests that her father was Callicratidas, who died in 406 BC at the battle of Arginusae.[15] This genealogy would place Phintys in the last quarter of the fifth century BC and beginning of the fourth. Stobaeus (4.23.61, p. 588), however, who preserves her writings, states that Phintys is the daughter of Callicrates.[16] The name Callicrates is attested in fourth-third century Tarentum, where a Callicrates was a mint official or some sort of administrator in 235–238 BC.[17] Therefore it seems most likely that Phintys was a Neopythagorean in Tarentum in the third to second century BC, and of Spartan descent, like other Tarentines.[18] The use of names from classical Sparta was characteristic of the Spartan revival in the Hellenistic period.[19] Phintys writes in Doric. The title of her essay is *Peri gynaikos sophrosynas*. *Sophrosyne* is translated here as "moderation." It may also be construed as "self-control," a virtue traditionally ascribed to women in Greek thought (see chap. 3). Phintys goes on to define the virtues suitable to women and men, respectively, and the virtues that are appropriate to both. Both women and men should study philosophy in order to understand their specific virtues. Though much of her advice is conventional, her view that women should philosophize is found in other texts of Pythagorean women, and it was decidedly not the opinion of most Greeks. In fact, Aristotle thought women were innately incapable of rational thinking (see chap. 5, above).

Phintys writes in hyperbole. Whereas other Neopythagorean women are concerned about adultery of both husbands and wives, Phintys fulminates only about the consequences of adultery in women. She warns that it is worse than crimes that merit the death penalty, that it is an offence not only to the family, but to gods, ancestors, and country. True to Spartan tradition she thinks in absolutes—no nuances, no extenuating circumstances—advocates stringent ethical standards, and contemplates the most drastic penalties for moral transgressions.

TRANSLATION

"A woman must be altogether good and orderly; without excellence [*arête*] she would never become so. The excellence appropriate to each thing makes superior that which is receptive of it: the excellence appropriate to the eyes makes the eyes so; that appropriate to hearing, the faculty of hearing; that appropriate to a horse, a horse; that appropriate to a man, a man. So too the excellence appropriate to a woman makes a woman excellent. The excellence most appropriate to a woman is moderation [*sophrosyne*]. For, on account of this virtue, she will be able to honor and love her husband.

"Now, perhaps many think that it is not fitting for a woman to philosophize, just as it is not fitting for her to ride horses or speak in public. But I think that some things are peculiar to a man, some to a woman, some are common to both, some belong more to a man than a woman, some more to a woman than a man. Peculiar to a man are serving in battle, political activity, and public speaking; peculiar to a woman are staying at home and indoors, and welcoming and serving her husband. But I say that courage [*andreia*] and justice and wisdom are common to both. Excellences of the body are appropriate for both a man and a woman, likewise those of the soul. And just as it is beneficial for the body of each to be healthy, so too, it is beneficial for the soul to be healthy. The excellences of the body are health, strength, keenness of perception, and beauty. Some of these are more fitting for a man to cultivate and possess, some more for a woman. For courage and wisdom are more appropriate for a man, both because of the constitution of his body and because of his strength of soul, while moderation is more appropriate for a woman.

"Therefore one must discover the nature of the woman who is trained in moderation, and make known the number and kinds of things which confer this good upon a woman. I say this comes from five things: first, from piety and reverence concerning her marriage bed; second, from decency with respect to her body; third, from the processions of those from her own household; fourth, from not indulging in mystery rites and celebrations of Cybele; and fifth, from being devout and correct in her sacrifices to the divine.

"Of these, that which most of all causes and preserves moderation is being incorruptible in respect to her marriage, and not getting mixed up with a strange man. For, first, a woman who thus transgresses does an injustice to the gods of her race, providing not genuine, but spurious, allies to her house and family. She does an injustice to the natural gods by whom she swore, along with her ancestors and kin, to share in a common life and the lawful procreation of children. She also does an injustice to her fatherland, by not abiding among those who were duly appointed for her. Then she is wont to err over and above those for whom death, the greatest of penalties, is determined. On account of the magnitude of injustice to do wrong and commit outrages for the sake of pleasure is unlawful and least deserving of mercy. The issue of all outrage is destruction."

Phintys of Sparta, "On the Moderation of Women," Fragment 2

Thesleff, *Texts*, 153, Stob. 4.23.61a, p. 591–93, Waithe, *Women Philosophers*, 30

TRANSLATION

"One must consider this too, that she will find no purifying remedy for this fault, so as to be chaste and loved by the gods when approaching their temples and altars. For in the case of this injustice most of all, even the divine spirit is merciless. The noblest honor and the chief glory of a married woman is to bring witness of her virtue with respect to her husband through her own children, if, haply, they should bear the stamp of likeness to the father who sired them. This sums up the subject of moderation with respect to marriage.

"My thoughts on moderation with respect to bodily decency are as follows: The woman of moderation must be clad in white, simply and plainly dressed. She will be thus if, indeed, she does not wear transparent or embroidered robes, or those woven from silk, but, rather, garments that are decent and plain white. The main thing is that she be decent and avoid luxury and display; then she will not arouse ignominious envy in other women. As for gold and emeralds, she simply will not deck herself out in them, for then she would display characteristics of wealth and arrogance towards ordinary women.

"But the well-regulated city, arranged throughout with a view to the whole, must be based on sympathy and unanimity. One must even debar from the city the craftsmen, who make such ornaments. The woman of moderation must embellish her appearance not with imported and alien ornaments, but with the natural beauty of the body; washing clean with water, she must adorn herself with modesty rather than these. Thus she will bring honor to the man with whom she shares her life, and to herself.

"Next, women must make public processions from the house in order to sacrifice to the founder-god of the city on behalf of themselves and their husbands, and entire households. Moreover, it is not when the evening star has risen, nor in darkness, that a woman must make her expeditions to attend the theatre or to purchase wares for the house, but rather, as market-time approaches, just so long as it is light. This she must do guided by one handmaid, or at the most, two.

"Next, she must offer prayers of sacrifice to the gods to the extent to which she is authorized to do so, but must refrain from secret rites at home, and celebrations of Cybele. The common law prevents women from celebrating these rites, because among other things, such religious practices lead to drunkenness and derangement. But the mistress of the house, even presiding at home, must be temperate and untouched in the face of everything."

COMMENTARY

Thesleff, *Texts*, 152.2, 6. "it is not fitting for her to ride horses"
Since the archaic period Spartan women were familiar with horses and drove chariots. Figurines excavated in Sparta depict female divinities as riders. Agesilaus II used to play "pony on a stick" with his son and two daughters (Plut. *Ages*. 25.6, *Sayings of Spartans*, 213.70). This report is further indication that girls played at riding astride. In 220/219 BC the heroic wife of Panteus fled on a gal-

loping horse (Plut. *Cleom.* 38). The Spartans Cynisca and Euryleonis were the first women whose chariots were victorious at Olympia.[20] Sparta was not the only city where an equestrienne might be seen. In central Rome, at the eastern end of the Forum, a statue honoring the heroine Cloelia riding a horse had been on display probably since the fourth century BC.[21] Since riding and owning horses were also a means of displaying wealth, Phintys may have been advising women to be more modest.

Thesleff, *Texts*, 152.2, 6. "it is not fitting for her to . . . speak in public."

Spartan women played a role in politics by praising the brave and jeering at cowards and bachelors. When a member of the Gerousia (Council of Elders) was elected, he was followed by throngs of young men who praised him and many women who sang of his excellence and congratulated him on his good fortune.[22] Phintys, however, does not approve of these practices of her countrywomen, which were unique in the Greek world.

Thesleff, *Texts*, 152.11. "courage" (*andreia*).

See Perictione I, chap. 5, above. Compare Thesleff, *Texts*, 142.20. "courageous" [lit. "manly," *andreie*] on courage as a virtue of women as well as of men.

Thesleff, *Texts*, 152, 1.12–15. "Excellences of the body are appropriate for both a man and a woman. . . . It is beneficial for the soul to be healthy."

Attention to the physical welfare of women as well as of men was part of the Spartan tradition, widely attested in literature including Xenophon, *The Spartan Constitution*, the poetry of Alcman and Aristophanes, Plutarch, *Life of Lycurgus*, as well as in sculpture.[23] Pythagoras included a private morning walk and an afternoon walk with fellow disciples as part of the recommended daily regimen (Iambl. *VP* 96–97).

Thesleff, *Texts*, 152–53, 25–28, 1–2. "and not getting mixed up with a strange man. . . . By not abiding among those who were duly appointed for her."

Phintys here reflects the well-known Spartan xenophobia. Spartans were concerned not so much about adultery per se but rather about liaisons with a non-Spartan. The Spartans practiced husband-doubling and wife-lending for the purposes of reproduction, but the wives were permitted to have intercourse only with another Spartan, never with a foreigner.[24]

Thesleff, *Texts*, 153, fr. 2.16–19. "white, simply and plainly dressed. She will be thus if, indeed, she does not wear transparent or embroidered robes, or those woven from silk, but, rather, garments that are decent and plain white."

Pythagoras himself had urged the women of Croton to dedicate their elaborate clothing to Hera Lacinia, to dress simply, and to come to hear his homily without an entourage of slaves (see chap. 2). Such advice, echoed through the letters of women writers beginning with Perictione I, is a continuing reminder not only of the wealth of the Pythagoreans but also of their constant desire to avoid conspicuous consumption (see below).

Thesleff, *Texts*, 153.13–14. "they should bear the stamp of likeness to the father who sired them."

This statement concerns the legitimacy of the child, but it is interesting also to discuss why Phintys does not note that, of course, the child may resemble the mother, or both parents, as well. Children belonged to the family (*oikos*) of their father and remained with him in case of divorce or with the father's family in case of the father's death.[25] As a result of these legal arrangements and the more private lives of women, the child was seen more frequently with his or her father and paternal relatives than with the mother and maternal relatives. Therefore the observer was more likely to perceive resemblances (or the lack thereof) on the father's side. Nossis (ca. 300 BC) states that it is also good for a girl to resemble her mother.[26]

Thesleff, *Texts*, 153.27. "washing clean with water."

See chap. 5, Perictione I, on bathing.

Thesleff, *Texts*, 153.26–28. "The woman of moderation must embellish her appearance not with imported and alien ornament, but with the natural beauty of the body; washing clean with water, she must adorn herself with modesty rather than these."

Pythagoras had advised women not to wear cosmetics. Doubtless he was influenced by the prohibition on the wearing of cosmetics attributed to Lycurgus. In Sparta cosmetics, perfumes, and other bodily adornments were banished, and the legendary beauty of Spartan women was a natural result of good health and exercise.[27] With the exception of Ovid, no male Greek or Roman author approves of cosmetics. They are variously described as deceptive, condemned as a needless expense, associated with drugs and magic, and suitable only for prostitutes and other women seeking adulterous relationships.[28] A treatise on cosmetics, however, is attributed to a Cleopatra who probably lived in the first century BC. Her work includes medical remedies as well as advice on improving one's appearance with hair dyes, etc.[29] Xenophon, who admired much about the Spartan way of life, preferred that his wife not wear cosmetics because they were deceptive.[30] Nevertheless, the visual arts in the Greek world as early as Bronze Age frescoes from Cnossus and Thera indicate that most respectable women—even those of the highest rank, including priestesses—used cosmetics liberally, with no attempt to render their appearance as natural. They dyed their eyebrows, applied rouge made of alkanet, and exaggerated the pallor of their skin with white lead carbonate (which is nowadays known to be toxic).[31] Melissa and Perictione I also advise women against using cosmetics (see above and chap. 5).

Thesleff, *Texts*, 154.1–3. "Next, women must make public processions from the house in order to sacrifice to the founder-god of the city on behalf of themselves and their husbands, and entire households."

Pythagoras believed women were especially pious. Here Phintys states that a woman is responsible for sacrificing not only on behalf of herself but also for her husband and entire *oikos*. Throughout antiquity, even when their public role was otherwise diminished, women always played an important role in religion. Their participation was essential to the religious well-being of the polis. The citizenry celebrated the cult of the founder each year. In Tarentum (known as Taras to the Greeks), Phintys celebrated the cult of Taras. Taras, originally a river, became anthropomorphized into Taras, son of Poseidon and a local nymph, Satyrion. According to other mythological traditions, Satyrion was a son of Poseidon.[32] Tarentum also had a human founder named Phalanthos, who was heroized. By the time of Phintys the cult of Taras overshadowed the cult of Phalanthos. See further Irad Malkin, *Myth and Territory in the Spartan Mediterranean* (Cambridge, 1994), 127, 129.

Thesleff, *Texts*, 154.5–6. "guided by one handmaid, or at the most, two."

The female slaves would both carry packages and serve as chaperones and bodyguards; they were a means of advertising and preserving a woman's respectability. Slaves embodied a capital investment; thus, they were also used to display the owner's wealth. Consistent with the lack of ostentation favored by the Pythagoreans and Neopythagoreans, the number of slaves visible in public was limited to one or two. Thus this recommendation echoes the earlier advice to avoid luxury and display in order not to arouse envy in other women. Such envy would cause a lack of harmony in society.

Thesleff, *Texts*, 154, 6–8. "Next, she must offer prayers of sacrifice to the gods to the extent to which she is authorized to do so, but must refrain from secret rites at home, and celebrations of Cybele. The common law prevents women from celebrating these rites, because among other things, such religious practices lead to drunkenness and derangement."

Among the Asian cults and mystery religions that spread through the Greek world in the Hellenistic period, the cult of Cybele was one of the most popular.[33] Women were attracted to the cult and were particularly visible in the cult ceremonies. Critics railed against the frenzied orgiastic state, the uninhibited dancing, the wild tossing of the head, the percussive Asian music, and the nocturnal setting of many of the cult ceremonies. In a word, the cult of Cybele was totally anathema to the Pythagorean ideal of decorum, moderation, and temperance.

Perictione II. "On Wisdom"

Thesleff, *Texts*, 146, Stob. 3.1.120, pp. 85–87, trans. Vicki Harper in Waithe, *Women Philosophers*, 55–56

INTRODUCTION

Perictione II bears the same name as Plato's mother. Her text has some affinities with Platonism, especially in its emphasis on geometry and arithmetic. She writes in an "affected" Doric and is therefore discussed in this chapter, whereas Perictione I, who writes in Ionic, is discussed in chapter 5.[34] Thesleff points out similarities between this treatise and another *On Wisdom* attributed to Archytas II, but these similarities are not close and are largely confined to one paragraph of Archytas.[35]

Perictione II recommends philosophizing as a goal for both women and men because it brings human beings closer to the divine. That the soul has no sex is also a Platonic concept and appropriate to a woman who bears the name of Plato's mother and who is herself an example of a female philosopher.

TRANSLATION

"Humanity came into being and exists in order to contemplate the principle of the nature of the whole. The function of wisdom is to gain possession of this very thing, and to contemplate the purpose of the things that are.

"Geometry, therefore, and arithmetic, and the other theoretical studies and sciences are also concerned with the things that are, but wisdom is concerned with all the genera of these. Wisdom is concerned with all that is, just as sight is concerned with all that is visible, and hearing with all that is audible. As for the attributes of things, some belong universally to all, some to most things, some to individual things as such.

"It is appropriate to wisdom to be able to see and to contemplate those attributes which belong universally to all things; those that belong to most things are the business of natural science, while separate sciences are concerned with the more individual and particular. On account of this, wisdom searches for the basic principles of all the things that are, natural science for the principles of natural things, while geometry and arithmetic and music are concerned with quantity and the harmonious.

"Therefore, whoever is able to analyze all the kinds of being by reference to one and the same basic principle, and, in turn, from this principle to synthesize and enumerate the different kinds, this person seems to be the wisest and most true, and, moreover, to have discovered a noble height from which he will be able to catch sight of the god and all the things separated from him [the god] in seried rank and order."

COMMENTARY

Thesleff, *Texts*, 146.17. "the harmonious" (*to emmeles*)

Thesleff, *Texts*, 146.18. "one and the same basic principle"

As we have seen, according to the Pythagoreans, *harmonia* is the principle of everything, including (as Perictione II states here) geometry, arithmetic, and the musical arts.[36]

Myia to Phyllis

Thesleff, *Texts*, 123–24, Hercher, 608, trans. Vicki Harper, in Waithe, *Women Philosophers*, 15–16

INTRODUCTION

The name Myia appears in Iamblichus's catalogue of Pythagorean women (*VP* 267). Myia was the name of one of the daughters of Pythagoras and Theano I. She became the wife of Milo of Croton.[37] This treatise was written in the third or second century BC by a woman named for the original Myia, who was (like her mother Theano I) a paragon among women. Like Theano II, in her letter to Euboule, this Neopythagorean Myia gives advice on childrearing. Myia means "carrion fly, bluebottle."[38] The name Phyllis refers to greenery and is common in bucolic literature (e.g., Verg., *Ecl.* 3.76, 78, 5.10, 7.14, 10.37). Thus the two women are naturally well matched.

Myia was also the name of a Spartan poet who wrote hymns.[39] Thesleff determined that this letter was written "in an inconsistent Doric."[40] He therefore classifies Myia among the western authors and dates her to the third or second century BC.[41] Like Theano, in her letters to wives married to philandering husbands and in her writing on childcare, Myia offers useful, practical advice. Her present subject is baby care and the choice of a wet nurse, but she ends by promising to give more advice when the child is older.

Myia directs her advice on the selection of a wet nurse to Phyllis alone, rather than to both the mother and the father. Though the mother was not going to nurse her infant, mothers were in charge of young children. The sexual division of labor was thought to be natural. As Xenophon (*Oec.* 7.24–25) writes: "The god was aware that he had both implanted in the woman and assigned to her the nurture of newborn children, he had measured out to her a greater affection for newborn babies than he gave to the man."[42] Plato (*Laws* 7.806 A, E) also considers the nurturing of children a basic function of women. Aristotle (*Gen. an.* 3.759b7) formulates the same thought negatively: "No male creatures customarily trouble themselves about children."[43]

In a well-to-do household, wet nurses were considered a normal part of a baby's retinue of caretakers. Wet nurses are discussed in papyrus letters found in Egypt.[44] According to Plutarch (*Eroticus*, 9) nurses are part of the natural hierarchy: the nurse rules the child. Plutarch may have written a treatise titled "The Wetnurse."[45] His own wife, Timoxena, nursed some of her children herself, and employed a wet nurse for the others.[46]

In the first and second centuries AD, male moralists—for example Tacitus, Frontinus, Plutarch, and Pseudo-Plutarch—urged mothers to nurse their own babies, though they recognized that, despite the presence of breasts, nursing was not always possible (e.g., Ps. Plut. *On the Education of Children*, 2c, 3c, d). Therefore it is important to observe that here, in the only extant ancient text on nursing by a woman to a woman, the possibility of the mother nursing her baby is not even raised. This was not yet the La Leche League era, when women supported and instructed nursing mothers in their efforts to feed their babies themselves. Myia has no doubt that Phyllis will not nurse her baby herself but will employ a wet nurse.

Numerous reasons for a postpartum woman to prefer a wet nurse come to mind: the obvious one is that the new mother does not want the responsibility and inconvenience of nursing. Fifty percent of infants of all classes in antiquity died in their first year; the mother who employed a wet nurse would bond less with her baby than a mother who nursed her baby herself. Moreover, in this era of high infant mortality the nonlactating new mother could become pregnant again more quickly. Furthermore, if she had given birth to a girl, she might produce a boy sooner. As we can see from Myia's letter, the woman who nursed was advised to avoid sexual contact with her husband. Therefore we may conjecture that the baby's father would have supported his wife's decision not to nurse. Wet nurses were ubiquitous conveniences for those who could afford them.

Soranus of Ephesus, who was the leading gynecologist in Rome during the reign of Hadrian (AD 117–138), also prefers that babies be fed mother's milk, but he nevertheless gives much more extensive advice concerning the selection of a wet nurse and her care of the baby. Myia's advice, though more concise, is consistent with that given by Soranus.[47] The general belief that the nursing infant would imbibe the personal characteristics of the nurse along with her milk permeates the thinking of both Myia and Soranus. The nurse must be orderly and temperate herself in order to transmit these virtues to the nursling. We therefore deduce that these virtues are not confined to the freeborn but may be found in lower-class women.

There was no Dr. Spock to change childcare in classical antiquity. The uniformity of views on childrearing found in literature and in documents from classical Athens to Roman Egypt and imperial Rome makes it impossible to draw any conclusion based only on the content about when and where Myia wrote her letter to Phyllis.

TRANSLATION

"Greetings. Because you have become a mother of children, I offer you this advice. Choose a nurse who is well disposed and clean, one who is modest and not given to excessive sleep or drink. Such a woman will be best able to judge how to bring up your children in a manner appropriate to their free-born station— provided, of course, that she has enough milk to nourish a child, and is not easily overcome by her husband's entreaties to share his bed. A nurse has a great part in this which is first and prefatory to a child's whole life, i.e., nurturing with a view to raising a child well. For she will do all things well at the appropriate time. Let her offer the nipple and breast and nourishment, not on the spur of the moment, but according to due consideration. Thus will she guide the baby to health. She should not give in whenever she herself desires to sleep, but when the newborn desires to rest. She will be no small comfort to the child. Let her not be irascible or loquacious or indiscriminate in the taking of food, but orderly and temperate and, if at all possible, not foreign, but Greek.

"It is best to put the newborn to sleep when it has been suitably filled with milk, for then rest is sweet to the young, and such nourishment is easy to digest. If there is any other nourishment, one must give food that is as plain as possible. Hold off altogether from wine, because of its strong effect, or add it sparingly in a mixture to the evening milk. Don't continually give the child baths. A practice of infrequent baths, at a mild temperature, is better. In addition, the air should have a suitable balance of heat and cold, and the house should not be too drafty or too closed in. The water should be neither hard nor soft, and the bedclothes should be not rough but falling agreeably on the skin. In all these things nature yearns for what is fitting, not what is extravagant. These are the things it seems useful to write to you for the present: my hopes based on nursing according to plan. With the help of the god, we shall provide feasible and fitting reminders concerning the child's upbringing again at a later time."

COMMENTARY

Thesleff, *Texts*, 123.12–13. "a mother of children"
If Phyllis is already a mother and has not yet hired a wet nurse, she must have begun by nursing her babies herself. Thus the newborns would have received the colostrum that is now recognized to be especially beneficial. On the other hand, the opening sentence may merely be a device Myia adopted to open her discussion of wet-nursing.

Thesleff, *Texts*, 123.13–16. "Such a woman will be best able to judge how to bring up your children in a manner appropriate to their free-born station"

The civic status of the wet nurse varied. She was ideally a slave in the infant's household who had given birth and was still lactating. A lactating slave might be available within Phyllis's household. A relative might lend a lactating slave when needed.[48] Otherwise a lactating slave could be rented from another owner or purchased for this purpose. A freedwoman or a freeborn woman, compelled by economic circumstances to wean her own baby and work outside her own home, might seek this job as a source of income.

The nurse's own baby would usually be abruptly weaned from its own mother's milk. Perhaps the slave infant would be passed to another lactating slave in the household, who would nurse the infant along with her own baby. Otherwise a crude cup with a spout would be used to give babies their nourishment. A wet nurse often continued to be a member of the household and to look after the child even after weaning. Hence it was important to choose a nurse whose characteristics were consistent with the educational ideals of the parents.

When the duties of the wet nurse continued even after the baby was weaned, she cared for the child until, in the case of a boy, he went to school. In the case of a girl, the nurse might become part of the dowry and accompany her to her husband's home. A grateful nursling might manumit a faithful nurse.

Thesleff, *Texts*, 123.15. "and not given to excessive . . . drink." See below on Thesleff, *Texts*, 123.29.

Thesleff, *Texts*, 123.17–18. "is not easily overcome by her husband's entreaties to share his bed."

Thus Soranus advises that the wet nurse be "self-controlled" so as to abstain from coitus, "for coitus cools the affection toward [the] nursling by the diversion of sexual pleasure and moreover spoils and diminishes the milk or suppresses it entirely by stimulating menstrual catharsis through the uterus or by bringing about conception."[49] Lactation does not inevitably cease in a pregnant woman, but it may, and eventually the wet nurse would have to be replaced. The celibacy restriction is common in wet-nursing contracts from Roman Egypt.[50] Such contracts stipulate a period of one to three years, most usually two—a long time for a husband and wife to abstain from intercourse. Both partners or the woman's owner, however, would have been concerned about losing the income accruing from wet-nursing. That Myia refers to the nurse's male partner as her "husband" does not necessarily indicate her social status. Even though slaves could not contract a legal marriage, they often informally referred to their commitment to another person as a "marriage" and called their partner "husband" or "wife."

Thesleff, *Texts*, 123.20–22. "Let her offer the nipple and breast and nourishment, not on the spur of the moment, but according to due consideration."

Similarly, Soranus (38 [107]) warns the nurse not to offer the breast at all times or just because the child cries (39 [108]). The Pythagorean character of this piece of advice appears in Myia's admonition that the nurse be thoughtful.

Thesleff, *Texts*, 123.22. "She should not give in whenever she herself desires to sleep"

The nurse must adhere to the Pythagorean ideal of self-control, subordinating her natural appetites for sex, sleep, and wine, and thinking instead about what is good for the baby.

Thesleff, *Texts*, 123.25–26. "not foreign, but Greek."

This criterion, in addition to the reference to "free-born station" in line 16, above, draws attention to the civic status of the wet nurse: freeborn, slave, or freedwoman. A barbarian was likely to be a slave, a Greek more likely to be a free working woman. Greek slaves, however, were also available from time to time. Greeks were thought to be the best baby-tenders because they were considered civilized and could speak to the baby in Greek without an accent. Thus Soranus recommends that the wet nurse "should be self-controlled, sympathetic, and not have a bad temper, a Greek, and neat."[51] Ps.-Plutarch insists that nurses be Greek, neither barbarians nor prisoners of war (*Education of Children*, 3d–e, 7a).

Thesleff, *Texts*, 123.29. "Hold off altogether from wine"

Soranus writes that at first the nurse should abstain from drink because the wine passes to the milk, and the nursling becomes sleepy.[52] Soranus does allow the nurse to drink a little white wine later on as the baby grows older.[53] Here we see that a nurse might be tempted to go further and mix some wine into the baby's evening milk in order to ensure a restful night for herself.

Thesleff, *Texts*, 123.31–32. "Don't continually give the child baths. A practice of infrequent baths, at a mild temperature, is better."

Soranus also cautions against frequent bathing of the newborn, who becomes weak and vulnerable to illness and head injury.[54] Nurses, however, are tempted to bathe infants too often so that they will become sleepy.

Thesleff, *Texts*, 123.31–124.5. "balance of heat and cold, and the house should not be too drafty or too closed in. The water should be neither hard nor soft. . . . What is fitting, not what is extravagant."

The rearing of a baby should be consistent with the Pythagorean doctrine of harmony, seeking balance and avoiding excess.[55]

CHAPTER SEVEN

The Neopythagorean Women as Philosophers

VICKI LYNN HARPER

The extant works of Neopythagorean women comprise both treatises and letters of advice. How should one characterize these disparate works? There is good reason to conclude that many of the letters, as well as treatises, count as philosophy. In this chapter I analyze a number of these writings as philosophical works, comparable to canonical texts by philosophers such as Plato and Aristotle. I explain why these works should be classified as philosophy and in what respects it seems appropriate to apply the term *Pythagorean* to them. I do not directly address the question of whether these works are really written by women, though I do believe this to be plausible.[1]

My commentary is selective in the following way: first, I do not comment on the works I regard as not having philosophical import. In this category I put the letters by Theano II to Euclides, Rhodope, and Tim(ai)monides. Second, some works clearly allude to Plato's dialogs and may be more Platonic than Pythagorean. As an example, I comment briefly on similarities between Aesara's "On Human Nature" and Plato's *Republic*, though I also point out two intriguing differences between these texts. Perictione II ("On Wisdom"), part of which overlaps with the fragments of "On Wisdom" attributed to Archytas (Thesleff, *Texts*, 43–45), would be another example in this category, and I do not discuss it here. I also see Platonic elements in Phyntis ("On the Moderation of Women"), though this treatise's specific applications of the norm of moderation to the social conditions of women's lives sets it apart from the other two; I comment on that aspect of Phyntis's work later. Third, I comment briefly on Theano I's "On Piety" insofar as it relates to interpretations of the role of number in Pythagorean philosophy. My main focus, however, is on the following group, where I comment in detail on some works, and only briefly on others, on the grounds of similarity with respect to philosophical import: Perictione I ("On the Harmonious Woman") and Theano II (letters to Euboule, Euridice, Callisto, and Nicostrate). I consider this group to embody an original and distinctive contribution to Western philosophy. (Melissa's letter to Cleareta and Myia's to Phyllis offer advice on moderation and the care of infants that is consonant with the more subtle and philosophically reflective works by Perictione I and Theano II.) Finally, I comment on Ptolemaïs in the context of the general legacy of Pythagorean philosophy, relating my discussion to my main point about the philosophical import of the works I analyze in detail.

Aesara, "On Human Nature"

Thesleff, *Texts*, 48–50[2]

This work reflects a familiarity with ideas and even some textual details of Plato's *Republic*. Not only is there the analogy between justice in the soul of the individual and justice in the state, but the tripartite analysis of the soul (mind, high spirit, and desire) explicitly differentiates each part by its function (*erga, pragmata*). The just soul is characterized by proper hierarchical order (the better ruling the inferior), and there is unanimity (*homonoia*) and agreement (*homophrosyna*) among the parts as to which should rule; friendship (*philia*), love (*eros*), and kindliness (*philophrosyna*) grow among them. These points all correspond to Plato's analysis of the soul in *Republic*, book 4, and his characterization of the just individual as one in whom the several parts each perform their own function (*ta hautou pratton*, 441 E). The just individual is also temperate (*sophron*). The virtue of temperance or moderation (*sophrosyne*) in the individual is specifically characterized by friendship (*philia*) and concord (*symphonia*) among the parts because they all agree that the reasoning part should rule (442 C–D). The Aesara fragment parallels the ideas of the *Republic* passage, using similar, if not identical, language. In its second sentence it even echoes the analogy to hunting and the metaphor of "tracking down" justice that Plato uses in 432 B–D. However, there is a pleasing reversal about the order of discovery in Aesara's fragment: Aesara analyzes justice in the soul as the model for justice in the state (and the household), while Plato first hunts for justice in the state as an instructive model for justice in the individual, on the grounds that justice "writ large" must be easier to discern (368 D–369 A, 434 E). Aesara's claim is that "by following the tracks within himself whoever seeks will make a discovery: law is in him and justice, which is the orderly arrangement of soul," and this provides the model for discerning justice in larger, external contexts. According to Aesara, one starts by reflecting upon what is most familiar from one's own experience. (Is it too fanciful possibly even to hear an echo of Heraclitus [DK 101]: "I searched myself"?)

The second twist is Aesara's introduction of the household into the analogy. Justice in the soul is analogous to both justice in the household and justice in the state. It is probably pointless to speculate as to how the analogy might progress, if pressed. Should the orderly household, as well as the just soul, provide a model for the orderly state? If so, how could the analogy go? If the wife is to be thought of as ruler of the household, who has the role of the high-spirited element? On the other hand, if we think of the husband as ruler of the household and the wife as his natural ally (as well as the locus of emotion?), then would courage be the distinctive virtue of wives? Usually, as in the selection from Phintys, it is moderation that is thought to be most appropriate for women. It seems better not to press the analogies, but simply to think in terms of a well-functioning whole with concordant parts. Finally, is there an analogy between microcosm and macrocosm such that the well-ordered soul reflects cosmic order? Aesara's fragment does not address this question.[3]

In contrast to the rather Platonic Aesara fragment, the group of texts upon which I wish to focus can be analyzed as applications of a Pythagorean principle of *harmonia* to the social conditions of women's lives. I shall elucidate this claim in what follows.

It is not surprising that these texts should be somewhat eclectic. None of them dates back to the time of Pythagoras himself,[4] but they are consonant with a philosophical viewpoint that is appropriately called Pythagorean. Reliable evidence may be too scanty for confidence about Pythagoras and the earliest Pythagoreans, though even with respect to these, some points seem well supported.[5] There is also good evidence to support information about developments in Pythagoreanism in the fifth and early fourth centuries BC, including the work of Philolaus and Archytas.[6] Iamblichus reports a distinction between two kinds of Pythagoreans, the *akousmatikoi* and the *mathematikoi*.[7] Although Iamblichus is a late source, his contention that there was such a division is corroborated by earlier sources, and it is plausible that this was true by the fifth century BC, well before Plato.[8] According to Iamblichus, "the philosophy of the *akousmatikoi* comprises undemonstrated akousmata (precepts, things heard), without reasoning, that one should act in such a way."[9] Examples of Pythagorean *akousmata* include such tokens as "do not overstep the balance beam" and "do not stir the fire with a knife."[10] Of course, as Diogenes Laertius notes, one need not be overly literal; many of these *akousmata* seem to invite metaphorical interpretation.[11] Though Iamblichus's testimony may be unjustifiably deflationary, apparently the *akousmatikoi* did not give a reasoned account connecting precepts to basic principles or to a distinctly Pythagorean worldview.

In contrast to the *akousmatikoi*, the *mathematikoi* focus on number theory and mathematics.[12] Exactly what this means is, however, far from clear. The term could even apply to different groups and different projects. Related issues concern the connection between mathematics and Pythagorean views of the cosmos, as well as the relation between the analysis of musical concords in terms of ratios of whole numbers and normative, as well as descriptive, views of the cosmos.

In *Metaphysics* 986 a 22 Aristotle reports on a table of opposites that includes limit and unlimited, odd and even, unity and plurality, right and left, male and female, rest and motion, straight and crooked, light and darkness, good and bad, square and oblong. This involves a normative contrast (good in one column, bad in the other) and also terminology that can be related to numbers and the representation of numbers by figures comprising patterns of dots that characterize odd numbers as square and even numbers as oblong.[13] But it is not at all clear from this how or whether numbers might have an explanatory role to play in the analysis of cosmic order.

In his groundbreaking work, which separated the historical Pythagoras from the fabricated persona attributed to him by later sources, Walter Burkert concluded that the historical Pythagoras was not engaged in the projects of rational cosmology or mathematics at all.[14] Other scholars argue that Burkert went too far and that it is plausible to believe that Pythagoras shared at least some of the interests of the philosophers who flourished in nearby Miletus somewhat before and at roughly the same time that Pythagoras was growing up on Samos.[15] Without assuming that Pythagoras articulated a detailed cosmology, it does not seem unreasonable to hypothesize that he believed in the existence of an orderly cosmos and that he connected his religious and moral beliefs with the idea of cosmic order in some way. Of course, it might have been a minimal understanding of cosmic order, one in which moral purpose was the main point of cosmology, rather than a rational cosmology in the spirit of Anaximander or Anaximenes. But even the *akousmata* support the idea that Pythagoras's cosmos must exhibit some mathematical relationships.[16]

Another connection with numbers concerns the Pythagorean idea of harmonia. The four numbers that constitute the sacred *tetractys* (and add up to the perfect number ten) also serve to specify the ratios that define the basic concords of harmonia: the fourth (4:3), the fifth (3:2), and the octave (2:1).[17] *Akousmata* not only characterize *harmonia* as the finest (*kalliston*) thing but also support the relation between musical concords and the *tetractys*: Iamblichus connects the *tetractys* to the Delphic oracle and characterizes it as the harmonia in which the sirens sing.[18] Without claiming that early Pythagoreans were able to construct adequate proofs for the correlation between musical concords and fixed ratios of whole numbers, it seems clear that harmonia is a central Pythagorean concept, with normative import, and that it is connected with number in a definitive way.

For a well-articulated model of cosmic order one must wait for Philolaus. The term *Pythagorean* is also properly applied to Philolaus of Croton, and his ideas can be seen as at least in part a development of an earlier Pythagorean belief in the significance of cosmic order. In the case of Philolaus, it is clear that mathematics plays an important role in the explanation of cosmic order, and Huffman relates his ideas to harmonia in a unique way.[19] The contrast with earlier Pythagorean philosophy can be highlighted by noting an important difference between the terminology of Philolaus and the table of opposites reported by Aristotle in *Metaphysics* 986 a. The table of opposites includes the terms *limit* and *unlimited*, but Philolaus speaks in the plural of *limiters* and *unlimiteds*.[20] The importance of this can be seen by reflecting that simply thinking in terms of the imposition of some limit on an unlimited range of possibility is not enough to account for a normative concept of order. Definite ratios may define beautiful musical concords, but equally definite ratios of randomly selected pitches could define dissonances. Harmonia was assumed to exclude random dissonances all along, as the *akousmata* suggest. But the concept of limit presented in the table of opposites cannot account for this. Thus, Huffman suggests, Philolaus presents harmonia as a separate normative principle of order, one that also serves to solve the problem of Parmenides' challenge to the intelligibility of the sensible world.[21] (Huffman also shows that Philolaus develops an original view of the relation of number to harmonia and to cosmic order, but I do not pursue that here.) For the purpose at hand, I merely want to establish that harmonia is a fundamental Pythagorean concept and that it has normative force. The importance of cosmic order and its normative implications for a disciplined way of life is another basic Pythagorean idea, though it need not entail elaborate mathematical analysis or be driven by a specific project of rational cosmology.

In any case, Aristotle's testimony in the *Metaphysics* suggests that Pythagoreans (or so-called Pythagoreans) may have connected number with things in more than one way.

In the first book of the *Metaphysics*, Aristotle offers at least two interpretations of the relation between things and numbers in Pythagorean philosophy: things resemble numbers (985 b 28–33; DK 58 B4), and the elements of numbers are the elements of all the things that are (986 a 1–2; DK 58 B4). In the fourteenth book, he offers one or two more: things are numbers or are composed out of numbers (1090 a 32–35). The fragment from Theano I, "On Piety" (Thesleff, *Texts*, 195.10–

17) can be related to Aristotle's critical presentation of Pythagorean views of the relation between numbers and things. It ridicules the idea that everything is created from number, asserting instead that what Pythagoras said was "everything is generated according to number, that the primary order is in number."[22] The fragment is perhaps best understood as a polemical reply to Aristotle's criticism of the view that things are composed of numbers.

The aspects of Pythagorean philosophy I wish to pursue here, however, are those that can be related to the letters and treatises that can be interpreted as applying a Pythagorean principle of harmonia to the social conditions of women's lives. At first sight, the letters of advice may seem unphilosophical, not because of their literary format, but because a hasty reader might think they are merely prudential, or worse, that they are nothing more than dogmatic precepts for behavior, unsupported by reasons or principles. But if one thinks of harmonia as a normative concept and explores the idea that a commitment to a principle of harmonia has normative implications for the way one should live one's life, these letters and treatises become philosophically quite interesting. The point is that actual social conditions do not conform to the ideal; there is a collision between ideal theory and the conditions for actual practice.

The harmonious order of the cosmos is regarded as beautiful and good; it is the finest thing. It is something that one should try to emulate by the discipline of living an orderly life. Ideally, one's every enterprise should be in tune with the order of the harmonious whole. Thus, an ethical implication of accepting the Pythagorean way of life would be that one ought to accept limitations for oneself in the interest of the harmonious order of the whole. Needless to say, there could be some strains of commitment to this principle. A belief in the immortality of the soul and reincarnation, as attested for the early Pythagoreans,[23] may have mitigated some of the strain: one's future lives provide an opportunity for long-term justice. But it is not at all clear that later Pythagoreans or Neopythagoreans had to accept the doctrine of reincarnation, nor is reincarnation mentioned in any of the works analyzed here. What is important, though, is that the Pythagorean belief in cosmic harmony does not require that any existing social order here and now be ideal. Even in less than ideal social positions or settings, however, a concern for social stability and order should outweigh a desire for revolt. From a Pythagorean point of view, the disorder of anarchy would be the worst possible outcome.[24] This is not to deny that some reform of existing social conditions might be appropriate: Pythagoras's undermining of the double standard for men and women is a striking example.[25] Such reform was aimed at strengthening, rather than weakening, social bonds and marital commitment.[26] But the burden of bearing the constraints of a less than ideal social order falls on those in subordinate positions, those with less power than those to whom they are subordinated. Although women were relatively well respected in Pythagorean communities, the Neopythagorean authors of the works I analyze in detail address social conditions that are far from ideal; even well-born women suffer the strain of their subordination. This provides an opportunity for their readers to view commitment to the normative principle of harmonia from the perspective of those "below," who are constrained by their social circumstances.

I now turn to my argument that the treatises and letters of advice by Neopythagorean women count as philosophy and that they are comparable to canonical works of Greek philosophy in significant and specific ways. I draw some comparisons to Plato, but, for a variety of reasons, I wish to focus on similarities to Aristotle, especially with respect to Aristotle's methodology in the *Nicomachean Ethics*. My overall aim in making these comparisons concerns the consistency of criteria for including specific texts or bodies of work in a canon of philosophical works or excluding them on the grounds that they do not count as philosophy. My point is that, if one classifies Aristotle's *Nicomachean Ethics* as philosophy, consistency requires that one classify writings by Neopythagorean women as philosophy too. I am not claiming that the Neopythagorean women whose work I discuss below read Aristotle's *Nicomachean Ethics*.[27] (I have argued that the text of Perictione I's "The Harmonious Woman" shows a familiarity with Plato's *Republic*.)[28] If we assume that a Neopythagorean woman such as Theano II was not familiar with Aristotle's views about methodology in ethics, her contributions are all the more remarkable. At this point, in order to explain why I focus on a comparison of works by Neopythagorean women with Aristotle, rather than Plato, it is necessary to state in exactly what respects I wish to compare them. Despite their most likely disparate worldviews, I see four points of similarity between works of Neopythagorean women (especially those by Perictione I and the Neopythagorean Theano II) and Aristotle's approach to ethics in the *Nicomachean Ethics*.[29] Similarities include (1) reflection upon human experience and its relevance to the application of philosophical insight to practice; (2) a concern with moral psychology as essential for ethical practicability; (3) an emphasis on the role of character and a practical concern for the development of character; and (4) the importance of flexibility and context in the application of principle to practice.

In some of these respects, for example, the importance of moral psychology and the development of character, there are obvious parallels to Plato's philosophy as well, especially to a work such as the *Republic*, in which such topics are discussed at length. Otherwise, the writings by Neopythagorean women are particularly comparable to Aristotle's approach. I argue that this is so with respect to the emphasis on practicability and the importance of flexibility in the application of principle to practice. In my discussion of Ptolemaïs at the end of this chapter, I point out a further similarity between some basic Pythagorean presuppositions and Aristotle's philosophical stance. Whether or not they were familiar with Aristotle's views, in emphasizing practicability and in adopting a methodology similar to Aristotle's approach to ethics, Neopythagorean women were innovative with respect to Pythagorean philosophy, while remaining true to its basic tenets. Finally, there is the issue of Aristotle's comments on women. Indeed, Aristotle expresses some sexist views on women.[30] These views are consonant with those of many of his male contemporaries and may be inconsistent with Aristotle's own views elsewhere, as in *Categories* 3b 33–37, where he asserts that primary substances do not admit of degrees and that one human being cannot be more a human than another. But my comparisons concern Aristotle's general views on methodology and on ethical theory and its practicability, not his specific views on women or political and social structures. His general views on ethical theory, methodology, and practicability do not entail a sexist view of women. However, the fact that Aristotle is writing from a position of privilege with respect to gender (as well as social class) not only constitutes a significant difference between Aristotle and the Neopythagorean women but also points to something that is truly original in their contribution to Greek philosophy generally. In this respect, there is an illuminating contrast.

There are at least two significant differences between Aristotle and the Neopythagorean women. First, the metaphysical assumptions that shape their distinct worldviews may be different: as far as we know, the Neopythagorean women may or may not believe in the immortality of the soul. But we do know that Aristotle does not accept a doctrine of reincarnation and does not endorse the immortality of the soul in any personal sense.[31] His normative view of the human good addresses the topic of *eudaimonia*, flourishing or doing well, in this life. Second—and perhaps most interestingly—there is the fact that Aristotle speaks from a position of class and gender privilege, while the Neopythagorean women speak from the standpoint of their subordinate social position as women. Though the Neopythagorean women who had the leisure to write philosophy were from an elite class, their actual experience as women gave them greater insight into the burdens of the less privileged. These women show a keen appreciation of the strains of commitment to a philosophy that places primary importance upon the Pythagorean principle of *harmonia* despite less than ideal social conditions.[32]

The writings of Neopythagorean women bring an original perspective and new insight to ancient Greek philosophy.

Practical Reasoning: The Application of Principle to Practice

The Neopythagorean women share a conviction that theoretical normative principles should be applicable in practice. Practicability is a criterion of adequacy for ethical principles. As Aristotle insists in the second book of the *Nicomachean Ethics* (1103 b), the point of his ethical inquiry is not theoretical knowledge of what virtue is, but to become good—otherwise inquiry would be useless.[33] Similarly, the Neopythagorean women writers are concerned to work out the normative implications of Pythagorean principles for the actual contexts of human life, including the realities of less than ideal social conditions. Pythagoras may have succeeded in persuading early Pythagorean men to give up their concubines, but social practice in the Hellenistic times of Neopythagorean women included a double standard for men and women and restricted social roles for women. From this perspective, I would like to examine works by Theano II and Perictione I, with respect to the first two points of similarity to Aristotle's approach to ethics articulated above: reflection upon human experience as relevant for the application of philosophical insight to practice and a practical concern for moral psychology as it applies to actual human beings.

Both Theano II and Perictione I address the issue of the double standard and marital infidelity. I begin with Theano II's Letter to Nicostrate, because of its particularly careful attention to moral psychology.

Theano's letter, addressed to the wife of a philandering husband, is aimed at possibilities for reconciliation, healing, and the preservation of a beneficial and meaningful marital relationship. Without minimizing the pain and anger felt by Nicostrate, it appeals to the whole gamut of her tangled emotions in the best possible way. It suggests a genuine concern for the well-being of both husband and wife and pays shrewd attention to psychology as it focuses on practical ways to facilitate marital reconciliation and moral amendment.

The letter's opening reference to the husband's "madness" immediately sets the scene for a way of seeing the situation that offers hope for both husband and wife. The suggestion that he is not currently in his right mind leaves open the possibility that he is not a bad person when he is himself. Perhaps he is not incurably wicked. It could be a temporary case of weakness because he was "hunted down" by that woman and now is "held fast" by the immediacy of his own unruly passion, a passion that, at a deeper level and in the long run, he does not really desire to have. Thus immediate first-order desires can conflict with a more fundamental desire for goodness. Such frivolity is not consonant with what he really wants: a good life. This line of thought is also a balm to Nicostrate's injured self-esteem, which Theano proceeds to fortify: "If he associates with the courtesan with a view towards pleasure, he associates with his wife with a view towards the beneficial." The wife is associated with goodness and reason ("he loves you on the basis of good judgment, but her on the basis of passion.") This encourages the wife to adopt a positive self-image. Theano also endorses the view that "no one who understands persists in self-chosen harm."[34] This psychological principle applies to both wife and husband. The letter emphasizes the point that attempts at jealous retribution on the wife's part would cause self-inflicted harm to herself, not to mention a malicious sense of satisfaction to the husband, as long as his current state of madness persists: "Because he is not well, he invites you to share in his plight." This appeal acknowledges the reality of Nicostrate's anger (Don't give him that satisfaction!) but channels it in a constructive direction. How much better to act nobly, thus paving the way for his recovery, and—as an exemplar of "nobility and goodness"—to rise in his esteem as he returns to his right mind: "If he has been properly prepared for it by you, he will be all the more ashamed; he will wish to be reconciled sooner . . . he will love you more tenderly." Theano not only cultivates Nicostrate's sense of self-esteem and her desire to be a good person but also fortifies her sense of agency in a positive way. And from the tangled skein of Nicostrate's emotions, she pulls out the thread of love. If Nicostrate loves her husband, she will want him to be well, and she will want to be esteemed and loved by him. Theano also highlights the idea that, far from gaining unmerited advantage, wrongdoers harm themselves and everything they love. The closing reminder of the tragic excesses of Medea urges Nicostrate to view her own jealousy and anger with horror.

Theano's advice to Nicostrate can also be compared to Aristotle's thoughts about disillusionment in the context of friendship: "But if we accept another person as good, and he turns out to be an obvious villain, should we continue to love him?" (*Eth. Nic.* 1165 b). Aristotle's answer to this question is yes, as long as the person is not incurably wicked. We have an obligation to aid in the redemption of his character, as long as this is possible. In her letter to Nicostrate, Theano seems optimistic about the possibility of her husband's reformation. Theano focuses on ways to mend the fabric of a relationship that may be basically sound.[35] It is not surprising that someone who is committed to a Pythagorean principle of harmonia would suggest possibilities for reconciliation in such a case. But what about less promising cases? What if an errant friend or spouse does seem to be incurably wicked or incapable of reformation?

In the first fragment of "On the Harmonious Woman," Perictione is not always optimistic about the possibility of mutuality in marital reconciliation:

> A woman must bear everything on the part of her husband, even if he should be unfortunate, or fail on account of ignorance or illness or drink, or cohabit with other women. For this error is forgiven in the case of men; for women, never. Rather, retribution is imposed. Therefore she must keep the law and not be envious. She must bear anger and stinginess, fault-finding, jealousy and abuse, and any other trait in his nature. (trans. VLH)

Perictione starkly acknowledges a double standard for men and women and the subordinate position of wives in relation to their husbands. Infidelity may be a fault (*hamartia*), but it is forgiven (*epichoreetai*) in the case of a man, but never for a woman.

Positive law or established convention (*nomos*) may not coincide with the ideal. Pythagoras advocated fidelity for both sexes alike, but here the double standard is a social reality, and any practical application of the principle of harmonia must acknowledge it. That *nomos* may diverge from the ideal is underscored by the evaluative language of fault: not just by the use of word *hamartia* but also by the terminology in the catalog of faults and abuse that a woman may have to bear on the part of her husband. For example, the word I have translated as "abuse" (*kakegorie*) connotes evil-speaking, calumny, or slander, as opposed to justified chastisement. The language acknowledges that the husband is at fault, that his character is flawed. Nevertheless, by *nomos*, the wife must bear it. The accommodation seems wholly one-sided; there is no suggestion that the husband might reform. The faults are a part of his nature now.[36]

Perictione's text does, however, offer a thin ray of hope for the wife, even given the brute facts of her current situation. (Even if she does believe in reincarnation, she need not be consoled solely by the thought of better luck in future reincarnations.) There is a subtle suggestion that she can handle it; with discretion she can manage the effects of her husband's recalcitrant character: "Being discreet, she will deal with all of his characteristics in a way pleasing to him." The participle from the verb *sophroneo*, here translated as "being discreet," connotes moderation or self-control, a virtue thought to be especially appropriate to women among the Greeks.[37] This is consonant with part of Theano's advice to Nicostrate; rather than lashing out, reacting furiously to her husband's error, she should concentrate on the probity of her own conduct and character. But the Greek for the verbal expression translated above as "will deal with" comes from a verb (*tithemi*) that may connote active disposal or management. By her own agency, by the nobility of her own disposition, she can minimize the negative impact of her husband's flaws. There is still a possibility for some kind of harmony—even love—even though all of the accommodation must be on her side. Thus, although social reality (which may be less than ideal) and circumstances may restrict the ways in which a woman can satisfy the normative principle of harmonia, in limited ways this is not humanly impossible.

Melissa's Letter to Cleareta also acknowledges inequality between husband and wife: "For to a woman of decorum the wishes of her husband are an unwritten law by which she must live her life."[38] But Melissa's language is neutral as to the propriety and quality of the husband's wishes. This is in contrast to the evaluative language used by Perictione, language that underlines the fact that her husband is morally flawed.

Perictione confronts another brute fact of human experience in fragment 2 of "On the Harmonious Woman": parents can be flawed too. Parents were traditionally accorded great respect in Greek society.[39] But how far does parental reverence require us to go? "Thus, whether living or departed, it is necessary to revere them and never to murmur against them; even if they should act wrongly because of disease or deception, one should exhort and instruct, but in no way hate them. There could be no greater human error and injustice than to sin against one's parents" (trans. VLH). Here Perictione focuses on our inward emotional response: one should love one's parents unconditionally, in no way hate them. But she leaves room for intervention too, by exhortation and instruction: "Even if they should act wrongly because of disease or deception, one should exhort and instruct, but in no way hate them."[40] Unfortunately, sometimes (through illness, especially) parents become irrational and thus incapable of responding to reasonable instruction or exhortation. This is a fact of human experience. Perictione's text asserts, "Even in madness one must well-nigh obey them." (Notice that this does not say, flat out, that one must.) Aristotle seriously considers whether devotion to one's parents can be excessive, foolish, or morally base in the seventh book of the *Nicomachean Ethics* (1148 a 22–b 5). What can we note in Perictione's text that might indicate her probable response to this human dilemma? Perhaps the term I have translated as "exhortation" (*paregorein*) does not presuppose the rationality of the person to whom it is addressed. A secondary meaning of the word is "to console, comfort, soothe." In such circumstances, piety may not require obedience, but rather, love and care.

Perictione—and Phintys as well—are also notable for their attention to human psychology when they urge women to eschew luxury and ostentation. Phintys notes that an ostentatious display of luxury not only shows an arrogant disregard for other, less wealthy, women but also arouses their envy.[41] It is bad for the ostentatious woman herself, and it insidiously undermines the character of other women as well. Obviously, this does not promote social harmony, and it is not surprising that Pythagoras insisted on simplicity of dress and manner for early Pythagorean women. Perhaps Perictione goes overboard in her claims about the relation between extravagance and the feminine psyche: "Women who eat and drink every costly thing, who dress extravagantly and wear the things that women wear, are ready for the error of every vice, both with respect to the marriage bed and the rest of wrongdoing."[42] But we might interpret this in terms of symptoms, rather than as a simple causal claim. The description could apply to a woman of unbridled desires, someone without regard for anyone else, or anything that really matters. Extravagance of dress and behavior could be a symptom of arrogant disregard of all that is good and noble and fine.

The Role of Character and Character Development

The third point of significant comparison between the writings of Neopythagorean women and Aristotle's (and Plato's) approach to ethics concerns their attention to the role of moral character and practical consideration of how character is to be developed. They share the belief that moral excellence concerns feelings and emotions as well as action. Though right action is important, it is not enough to act in accordance with stipulated rules; one should be disposed to act rightly because of one's character. Virtuous character requires appropriate feelings, with respect to both appetite and emotion.[43] This means that one should take pleasure in what is good and feel pain or disgust at what is bad. What one takes pleasure in is an indication of one's character.[44] A basic assumption is that it is possible to shape one's desires and emotional responses through a process of appropriate habituation. Aristotle and Neopythagorean women agree that one cannot begin the process of habituation soon enough, especially with respect to pleasure. Theano's Letter to Euboule is a good example to illustrate this.[45]

As Theano remarks near the beginning of her letter, "When pleasure and children are brought up together, it makes the children undisciplined. What is sweeter to the young than familiar pleasure?" This does not mean that one can altogether avoid bringing up children with pleasure. As Aristotle notes, to some extent, this is the case with all of us: "Again, pleasure has grown up with all of us since infancy and is consequently a feeling difficult to eradicate, ingrained as it is in our lives. And, to a greater or lesser extent, we regulate our actions by pleasure and pain."[46] But it does mean that one must encourage restraint from an early age, in order to shape our desires aright. Once again, the avoidance of luxury is a must. Only in this way can we become truly free (*eleutheros*). Theano and Aristotle agree that being free is not a matter of being able to do anything one happens to want. One can be enslaved even without being subjected to external constraint. Theano urges Euboule to train and discipline her children "so that they shall not become slaves of their feelings, greedy for pleasure and shrinking from pain." This chimes well with Aristotle's characterization of a life driven by the pursuit of pleasure as "utter slavishness."[47] Human beings have the capacity for self-reflection and deliberate choice; the marks of agency. We have a capacity for second-order, as well as first-order, desires. That is, we can desire to have desires we do not yet possess or desire not to have some we do. In her letter to Nicostrate, Theano endorses the principle that "no one who understands persists in self-chosen harm." Thus one would wish to have desires that are not harmful, and anyone who truly recognizes that some of his or her desires are harmful will be motivated to eradicate them. The trouble is, such recognition is not automatic. As Plato stresses in book 4 of the *Republic*, the development of firm convictions about what is truly to be sought or feared is no easy process; hence the rigorous system of education decreed for future guardians. Theano counsels Euboule not only to avoid luxury for her children but also to "exercise her charges in the things they dread—even if this causes them some pain and distress." Only in this way will Euboule be able to cultivate true freedom, rather than slavery, for her children, so that they "shall honor virtue above everything and be able both to abstain from pleasure and to withstand pain." The inner compulsion of uncontrollable desires constitutes slavery every bit as much as external constraint. True freedom lies in self-control.

Flexibility in Contextual Ethics

The final point of comparison concerns the flexibility of a contextual approach to ethics. Theano's letter to Callisto is consonant with the flexibility of Aristotle's doctrine of the mean as explained in book 2 of the *Nicomachean Ethics*.[48] But I argue that there is also a significant difference because Theano is writing from a standpoint that gives her greater insight into the burdens of those who occupy the less privileged strata of society. She shows a sympathetic understanding of the lives of servants and slaves that goes beyond anything in Aristotle's writings.

In her letter to Callisto, Theano recommends flexible guidelines for assessing human character and action, emphasizing "right measure" and proper judgment as appropriately proportionate to context. She cautions Callisto to "determine the true facts of wrongdoing in keeping with the justice of the condemnation" and to avoid excessive punishment. She reminds her that "reasoning no less than righteous indignation is an effective means of control," and she adds that sometimes it is appropriate to override strict justice in favor of kindness and forgiveness. Thus Theano shares with Aristotle an appreciation of flexibility and context in the application of principle to practice.

But subtleties of the text suggest an extra dimension, one that may reflect distinctively Pythagorean views. Theano's musical analogy and her understanding of "right measure" are illuminated by an appeal to the principle of harmonia, which is central to Pythagorean thought. As we noted earlier, this principle applies not just to music but also to the entire cosmos and everything in it. According to Pythagoreans, a cosmos is an ordered world system, and all order is defined by the delineation of limit in the unlimited, or, definition of what was indefinite. (This may not be a sufficient condition for good order, but it is a necessary one.) For example, the Pythagoreans noted that in a range of sound rising in pitch, the limits imposed by the musical intervals of the octave, the fifth, and the fourth are defined by the specific rations of 2:1, 4:3, and 3:2, respectively. That is, if the strings of a musical instrument are tightened to the same tension, then if one string is twice as long as another, the notes they sound will be precisely an octave apart. From measured (limited) intervals, harmonious music is produced.

Pythagoreans often use analogies to music in discussing ethical concerns. All coherent structure, whether it is musical, ethical, social, or cosmological, is preserved by the delineation of differences. Order is a relation among things which are distinct from one another; without the definition of different entities, there is only an indefinite, undifferentiated mass. What is indefinite is "unlimited" (*apeiron*), or "without boundary." The word is probably formed from an alpha privative *a*, meaning "without," plus *peiras*, "limit" or "boundary." (An alternative etymology for the word suggests the root of the verb *perao*, "to traverse," rather than the noun *peiras*.) But all differences are a part of the same coherent whole. Thus, according to the Pythagoreans, all nature is akin, even though there are differences within nature.

Early Pythagorean doctrines of reincarnation and the transmigration of souls reflect the idea that "all things that come to be alive must be considered akin."[49] The same soul that is incarnated as an animal in one life can reappear as a human being in another. For individual souls, hierarchy is not immutably fixed, and the manner in which one leads one's current life can affect one's future reincarnations. In this respect, a sincere belief in the doctrine of reincarnation might very well have extended early Pythagoreans' imaginative appreciation of other living creatures and people. We do not know whether or not Theano accepts the doctrine of reincarnation, but this could possibly be true for Theano, too, if she also accepts the doctrine. The thought that "I" could be a different kind of animal, or a human being of an opposite gender, or of a different social status should alter one's perspective on social justice or the exploitation of animals.[50] I pursue this theme in the following section.[51]

Subjects and Objects

On the eve of Callisto's marriage, Theano's letter to the prospective bride does not mention the bridegroom at all. Instead, it focuses on Callisto's new job as mistress of the household, especially its attendant role of authority in relation to the household slaves. There is no doubt that these are slaves, for Theano does not mince words as she stresses the importance of "good will on the slaves' part, for this possession is not bought along with their bodies." Not only the reference to the buying of their bodies but also the use of an unambiguous word for slavery (*douleia*) makes this clear. In fact, here Theano even uses the singular collective term for slaves. The word does not even acknowledge that the group over whom Callisto must exercise her authority is made up of a number of individuals. Indeed, the whole phrase "good will on the slaves' part" strikes modern readers as an offensive oxymoron: at the very least, it is a category mistake to expect good will from a bunch of tools. So how can anyone claim that Theano's letter shows any kind of sympathetic awareness of the slaves' plights?

In my analysis, Theano is attempting to influence Callisto's attitude, to move her away from an attitude of commodification in which slaves are seen as objects or commodities to be used and bought and sold, to a sympathetic awareness of the slaves' subjectivity and an acknowledgment that, despite their current social status, these are women significantly like herself. (Not to mention the Pythagorean possibility that in future reincarnations social positions may be reversed.) This does not mean Theano must be an abolitionist, far less an advocate of radical social revolution. As noted above, the Pythagorean doctrine of reincarnation provides a different perspective and even allows for long-term rectification of injustice in ways that are not open to different worldviews. But it is precisely the thought that "I" could be someone or something else that should affect one's attitude toward others. I believe Theano's terminology is intentional, in subtle ways, down to the last detail. The collective term for slave (*douleia*) is one of three different terms she uses to refer to the slaves under Callisto's authority; she also uses the inclusive term *oiketai*, "household inmates," which could apply to everyone living in the household, regardless of status, and the term *therapainai* (maidservants), a more neutral term than *douleia*, which could apply to freedwomen as well as slaves. In line 30 of Thesleff's text of the letter, when she says that the primary responsibility of the mistress is "authority over the maidservants," the term used is the genitive of *therapainai*. No doubt the maidservants are slaves. But this particular term, while making social hierarchy explicit and emphasizing the authority of the mistress, does not refer to the slaves by a term that explicitly designates them, collectively, as slaves. The exact connotations of words can have extensive import and may influence attitude in subtle, or even unsubtle, ways. Surely it would be more difficult to achieve a sympathetic awareness of the slaves' plight if one thought of them in terms of the collective designation for slaves, *douleia*. The letter opens with the inclusive term *oiketai* and, as I now argue, ends with a simile that, by the logical principle of transitivity, articulates a significant likeness between the mistress and the women who are her slaves.

In most of the first part of the letter, Theano talks as if responsibility to one's slaves is simply analogous to cost-effective maintenance of inanimate tools by keeping them in good working order; at most, the mistress of the household should control potentially recalcitrant slaves just as one would draft animals. This would be to treat them as objects, rather than as subjects, whose desires, needs, and interests are worthy of consideration in their own right. Theano does not question the justice of the slaves' subordinate role, insisting that, if they display "unconquerable vice," one must "send them away to be sold." Nor does Theano question the idea that individuals should be subordinated to the welfare of the community. In this respect, she shares antiquity's most prevalent attitude toward "enemies of the house." As noted above, the relevant question here is not whether Theano is an abolitionist, but whether her letter to Callisto urges any kind of sympathetic acknowledgment of the slaves' humanity and subjectivity; I think the answer is yes.

The tale of the brutal mistresses, which builds up to the crescendo and finale of the letter, deserves close study. There are several textual details that may bear on the answer to our question. At first there is a plurality of brutal mistresses: the passage begins with "some women." So when the reader comes to the feminine plural article "some (females)" at the beginning of the next sentence, one expects to hear more about the mistresses. Yet, without using any noun to mark the shift, the author has turned her attention from mistresses to slaves. Her shift of attention to the abused slaves is especially poignant here because it suggests an increasingly sympathetic awareness of the slaves' feelings: "Some are used up, utterly worked out." Although this sentence could be compatible with a narrow concern for the cost-effectiveness of mere objects, the Greek verbs for "used up" (*analisko*) and "worked out" (*diaponeo*) here can also apply to people. When Theano writes, "Others procure safety by escaping," is this merely analogous to noting that a valuable draft horse may bolt? Or does it convey a sense of the slaves' desperate desire for safety? And finally, when Theano writes, "but some stop living, withdrawing into death by their own hands," could she be suggesting that suicide, as an individual and deliberate act, is distinctively human, thereby acknowledging the slaves' humanity? I think there is an intentional progression here.

At this point in the text, the discussion returns to the mistresses, but with a subtle shift in focus. Not only is the term *mistress* now in the singular, but grammatically, the subject of the sentence is not the mistress herself but the isolation of the mistress. The syntactical construction no longer presents the mistress directly to us as a subject. It is as if Theano is arguing that, by denying the subjectivity of her servants, the brutal mistress has erased her own.

The finale is the simile to musical instruments: "Likening yourself to musical instruments, know what sounds they make when they are loosened too much, but that they are snapped asunder when stretched too tight. It is the same way for your servants (*therapainai*)." But, if I am like something in some respect, and if my servant is like the same thing in the same respect, it follows that I am like my servant in that respect. (Since resemblance is a symmetrical relationship, if my servant resembles a lyre in being breakable under too much tension, then a lyre resembles my servant in this respect. Thus, by the logical principle of transitivity, since I resemble a lyre in this respect, and a lyre resembles my servant in the same respect, it follows that I resemble my servant: we are both vulnerable; both of us can be strained past the breaking point.) The analogy suggests a significant likeness between the mistress and her servants. The subordination of the servants' role is mirrored in the subordination of the social role of the mistress, for the mistress of a household is subordinate to its master; both servant and mistress are instrumental to the maintenance of social order. Both must stay in tune; but in both cases the ultimate concern is that, if the string is stretched too tightly, it will snap. If the strings are broken, it is difficult to see just what kind of harmony—the desired social end—is possible. Thus, although Theano does not reject the institution of slavery as such or question the subordination of women, the nuances of the text suggest a sympathetic awareness of the slaves' humanity and subjectivity, inviting Callisto to compare the women who are her slaves to herself.

Experiential Knowledge: Reason and Perception in Neopythagorean Epistemology

In my discussion of writings by Neopythagorean women, I have drawn several comparisons to the philosophy of Aristotle, especially to Aristotle's approach to ethics and practical reasoning. Of course the idea that, from a practical point of view, the application of moral principles would require experiential knowledge is not so surprising. This is not the same thing at all as claiming that ethics must be based upon philosophical anthropology or that moral philosophy must be grounded in human nature and an understanding of the specifically human good. In the *Nicomachean Ethics*, Aristotle makes this stronger claim: in arguing against Plato's conception of an absolute Good and his metaphysical theory of Forms, Aristotle stresses the idea that he is seeking the human good, that the point of moral philosophy is not to gain theoretical knowledge, and that, unlike areas of inquiry such as mathematics, there can be no exact science of ethics.[52] But even in the case of theoretical knowledge within the province of an exact science, experience and perception are not irrelevant for Aristotle. The deductive structure and universal premises of an exact science may be modeled after an axiomatic system such as geometry,[53] but for Aristotle, experience and perception are still relevant in two important ways: they have an essential inductive role to play in the acquisition of the first premises of a science,[54] and science should not only be consistent with our experience but also explain what we see.[55] Given the importance of experience and perception in Aristotelian philosophy, could my comparisons of Neopythagorean writings to Aristotle be seriously misleading? In epistemological debates about the foundations of knowledge, aren't the Pythagoreans among the champions of reason, as opposed to perception? I would like to address this point in the context of a discussion of the extant fragments of Ptolemaïs's "The Pythagorean Doctrine of the Elements of Music."

Reason and Perception: Ptolemaïs on the Role of Perception in "The Pythagorean Doctrine of the Elements of Music"

Many of our Neopythagorean female writers have invoked the Pythagorean principle of harmonia by musical analogies and vivid imagery (e.g., Theano's unforgettable image, in the Letter to Callisto, of broken strings that have been stretched too tight). As Pomeroy notes in chapter 5, above, it is particularly interesting to consider Ptolemaïs because she is not speaking metaphorically, but rather addressing the topic of music theory directly. She is not merely a "cultivated woman" but a musicologist with a detailed understanding of harmonic theory and mathematics.[56] Her specific topic, in quotations preserved by Porphyry, concerns the issue of the role of reason (*logos*) and perception (*aesthesis*) in harmonic theory.[57] ("What is the difference between those who are distinguished in the field of music? Some prefer reason by itself, some perception, some both together.")[58] In these passages, Ptolemaïs distinguishes among several groups (and subgroups) that take a stand on this issue: those that favor reason, whom she identifies as Pythagoreans; those that favor perception, whom she calls "instrumentalists" (*organikoi*); and finally, those like Aristoxenus, who accepts both perception and reason as equal in power (*dynamis*). Ptolemaïs herself seems to favor the position of Aristoxenus.[59] It is interesting to note that Aristoxenus of Tarentum, a Peripatetic philosopher who studied with Aristotle and Theophrastus, first studied with Xenophilus, a Pythagorean pupil of Philolaus.[60] Ptolemaïs distinguishes between two groups of Pythagoreans. In the second selection (9.11 in Barker, *Greek Musical Writings*, vol. 2; the text is also included in chapter 5 of this volume), Ptolemaïs characterizes "Pythagoras and his successors" in the following way:

> Pythagoras and his successors wish to accept perception as a guide for reason at the outset, to provide reason with a spark, as it were; but they treat reason, when it has set out from these beginnings, as working on its own in separation from perception. Hence if the system [*systema*] discovered by reason in its investigation no longer accords with perception, they do not retrace their steps, but level accusations, saying that perception is going astray, while reason itself has discovered what is correct, and refutes perception.

Notice that this is different from the way she characterizes the subgroup of Pythagoreans, of whom she is particularly critical, in the third selection (9.12 in Barker's *Greek Musical Writings*, vol. 2; the text is also included in chapter 5 of this volume):

> Reason was preferred by those of the Pythagoreans who were especially keen in disputing with the *mousikoi*, arguing that perception should be thrown out completely, and that reason should be brought in as an autonomous criterion

in itself. These people are wholly refuted by their practice of accepting something perceptible at the beginning, and then forgetting that they have done so.

I would characterize the difference in the following way: the second group forgets altogether that perception is a starting point and that the systematic accounts they discover by reason should have explanatory import for what we do or do not perceive.

To say that reason is authoritative when there is a discrepancy between theory and perception is not the same as saying that theory has nothing to do with what we perceive and so is irrelevant to our experience. The Pythagoreans (unlike the Eleatics, whom Aristotle criticizes in *Physics* 2.2) believe there really is a cosmos, an orderly world system, and that mathematical analysis can help us to understand this order. Sometimes this entails having to explain what we don't see. A wonderful example is the reported postulation by Philolaus and other Pythagoreans of the existence of counter-earth as a tenth planet moving around the central fire.[61] According to the theory of the *tetractys*, the number of planets should equal the sacred number ten. Our experiential observations account for only nine (counting the circle of the fixed stars as one of these, along with the earth, moon, sun, Mercury, Venus, Mars, Jupiter, and Saturn). So, although there must be a tenth (reason tells us so), we need to explain why we don't see it: it is always on the opposite side of the central fire.

Ptolemaïs characterizes the subgroup of Pythagoreans she discusses in the third extract as departing from the position of Pythagoras and his true successors. Perception and experience have a relevant place in Pythagorean epistemology; theory has import for how we are to explain our experience.

If this is so, why might Ptolemaïs nevertheless go a step farther and prefer the Peripatetic theory of Aristoxenus? Perhaps because, in the Pythagorean theory of harmonics, there are theoretical limitations that make it impossible to build a systematic account of perception in music. I do not discuss in any detail the specific conflicts between perception and Pythagorean theory,[62] but it is notable that the Pythagorean approach to harmonics works in terms of ratios of whole numbers in defining the different concords such as octave, fifth, and fourth. What Pythagorean theory cannot handle is anything that cannot be explained in terms of ratios of whole numbers because the account would involve irrational numbers. But if musical sound presupposes a continuum, we do face this problem. Aristoxenus's theory could circumvent this problem by a new and innovative approach that better reconciles theory with musical perception and experience,[63]

Pythagoras is not Aristoxenus, but, as Ptolemaïs clarifies for us, perception does have a role to play in Pythagorean theory. My analysis of the Neopythagorean fragments is consistent with the role of perception and experience in Pythagorean epistemology. But, in addition to their overall fidelity to Pythagorean principles, Neopythagorean women writers were innovative as well. While adhering to the basic tenets of Pythagorean theory, the writings of Neopythagorean women develop the philosophy with new theory, especially with respect to methodology, as well as providing original insights and practical applications to Greek philosophy generally.

Introduction

1. There were three major groups of Greeks, distinguished by their dialects: Dorians, Ionians, and Aeolians.
2. P. Haun.
3. Alfonso Mele (*Magna Grecia. Colonie acheé e Pitagorismo* [Naples, 2007], passim), however, finds connections between traditions related about Theano and Achaean myth.
4. Thesleff, *Texts*, 210.
5. Some Athenian literature portrays learned or philosophical women, including Aspasia (in Socratic dialogues) and Melanippe the Wise (*Sophe*, in Euripides: R. Kannicht, *Tragicorum Graecorum Fragmenta* [Göttingen, 2004], 5.1: 537–53, and C. Collard and M. Cropp, *Euripides: Fragments. Aegeus-Meleager* [Cambridge, MA, 2005], 572–611).
6. Sarah B. Pomeroy, *Spartan Women* (New York, 2002).
7. Joseph Coleman Carter, ed., *The Chora of Metaponto: The Necropoleis*, 2 vols. (Austin, 1998).
8. Joseph Coleman Carter, *Discovering the Greek Countryside at Metaponto* (Ann Arbor, 2006).
9. Carter, *Discovering the Greek Countryside at Metaponto*, 80.
10. On the grid, the distribution of equal shares of land, and the influence of Pythagoreanism, see ibid., 206, where Carter cites P. Lévêque and P. Vidal-Naquet, *Cleisthenes the Athenian*, trans. D. A. Curtis (Atlantic Highlands, NJ, 1996), 63–72.
11. In 1991 A. De Siena organized an exhibit of women's ornaments from the Iron Age to Late Antiquity, displaying coiffures and ornamental objects: *Femminili in Basilicata dall'età del ferro al tardo antico: La documentazione archeologica*, Museo Archeologico Nazionale di Metaponto, Jan. 14–June 30, 1991. There was no catalog, but there was a *dépliant*. I am grateful to A. De Siena for supplying this information in an e-mail, Jan. 18, 2010, and to Francesca Silvestri for supplying the *dépliant*.
12. E.g., tomb 71 in Carter, *Discovering the Greek Countryside at Metaponto*, 177–78, and figs. 4.51–53.

13. For cooking equipment and storage vessels, see Joseph Coleman Carter, ed., *Living Off the Chora: Diet and Nutrition at Metaponto* (Austin, 2003), 25–28.

14. See further Sarah B. Pomeroy, *Xenophon Oeconomicus: A Social and Historical Commentary* (Oxford, 1994), esp. 42–43.

15. E.g., Sarah B. Pomeroy, *Women in Hellenistic Egypt, from Alexander to Cleopatra* (New York, 1984; pbk., with new foreword, Detroit, 1990; ACLS History E-Book, 2004), 61–71, and Jane Rowlandson, ed., *Women and Society in Greek and Roman Egypt: A Sourcebook* (Cambridge, 1998).

16. See further Riedweg, *Pythagoras*, x. For early Pythagoreanism, see also Carl Huffmann, *Pythagoras,* first published Feb. 23, 2005; substantive revision Nov. 13, 2009. http://plato.stanford.edu/entries/pythagoras/.

17. *FGrH* B328, Fr. 91, nos. 25–26.

18. Thus F. Jacoby in *FGrH* IIIb, vol. 1 (Leiden, 1954), 380.

19. Iambl. *VP* 267.

20. On the complex and controversial subject of one of the major sources for the biography of Pythagoras and early Pythagoreanism, see, e.g., John Dillon and Jackson Hershbell, *Iamblichus: On the Pythagorean Way of Life*, Society of Biblical Literature Texts and Translations, vol. 29. *Graeco-Roman Religion,* ser. 11 (Atlanta, 1991), 6–14. Scholars have determined that the sources of Iamblichus range from reliable to conjectural. On Iamblichus's catalog, see chap. 1, below.

21. P. Von der Mühll, "Was Diogenes Laertios der Dame, der er sein Buch widmen will, ankündigt," *Philologus* 109 (1965): 313–15.

22. See further Riedweg, *Pythagoras*, x–xi and chap. 1.

23. Iambl. *VP* 267, and passim; Diog. Laert. 8.42–43; Porph. *Plot.* 4.19.

24. Diog. Laert. 8.41–43.

25. Diog. Laert. 8.85. The sentence in DL is incomplete: *biblia kai epigrapsai* (and to publish books) is an editorial insertion.

26. Richard Bentley, *Dissertation upon the Epistles of Phalaris, 1699* (London, 1816), 304.

27. B. L. van der Waerden, *Die Pythagoreer: Religiöse Bruderschaft und Schule der Wissenschaft* (Zurich, 1979). Theano is not cited in the index.

28. W. Burkert, "Craft versus Sect: The Problem of Orphics and Pythagoreans," in *Jewish and Christian Self-Definition*, ed. B. F. Meyer and E. P. Sanders, vol. 3 (London, 1982), 1–22, 183–89, and esp. 17–18.

29. C. J. de Vogel, *Pythagoras and Early Pythagoreanism* (Assen, 1966), 138 and passim.

30. Peter Kingsley, *Ancient Philosophy, Mystery, and Magic: Empedocles and Pythagorean Tradition* (Oxford, 1995), chap. 12.

31. Nancy Demand, "Plato, Aristophanes, and the Speeches of Pythagoras," *GRBS* 23 (1982): 179–84.

32. Burkert, *Lore and Science*, 115n38) notes that Dicaearchus (*ap.* Porph. *Plot.* 19) states that the content of Pythagoras's speeches was unknown, but he is imprecise, for Dicaearchus does present some dogmas.

33. E.g., Sarah B. Pomeroy, "*Technikai kai Mousikai*: The Education of Women

in the Fourth Century and in the Hellenistic Period," *AJAH* 2 (1977): 51–68; Susan Guettel Cole, "Could Greek Women Read and Write?" *Women's Studies* 8 (1981): 129–55, reprinted in *Reflections of Women in Antiquity*, ed. Helen Foley (London, 1981), 219–45; Rowlandson, *Women and Society in Greek and Roman Egypt,* 14, 119, 225, 281, 285; and see chap. 4, below.

Chapter 1 · Who Were the Pythagorean Women?

1. See further Sarah B. Pomeroy, *Spartan Women* (New York, 2002), 10–11.
2. Iambl. *VP* 31, 143, Timaeus, *FGrH* 566 Fr. 131.
3. Alfonso Mele, "Il pitagorismo e le popolazioni anelleniche di Italia," *Annali del Istituto Orientale di Napoli. Archeologia e Storia Antica* (Naples, 1981), 3: 61–96, esp. 64–65.
4. Ibid., 76.
5. Iambl. *VP* 267.31, 61, 192–94. See also Porph. *VPyth.* 61, Paul Poralla, *A Prosopography of Lacedaemonians from the Earliest Times to the Death of Alexander the Great (X–323 B.C.)*, 2nd ed., with an Intro., Addenda, and Corrigenda by A. S. Bradford (Chicago, 1985), no. 702, cited herein as *Poralla²*, and *LGPN* 3A s.v. Due to the constraints of brevity in a lexicon, the basis on which *LGPN* 3A assigns dates to the various women Pythagoreans is not always clear.
6. *LGPN* 3A s.v.
7. *LGPN* 3A s.v.v.
8. See *Poralla²*, no. 760. See further Conrad M. Stibbe, *Das Andere Sparta* (Mainz, 1996), 211.
9. *LGPN* 3A s.v. 6th century BC. *Poralla²*, nos. 423 and 454, identifies Cratesicleia and Cleanor as Pythagoreans of an unknown time.
10. Plut. *Cleom.* 2.2, 11.2.
11. See further Pomeroy, *Spartan Women*, esp. 11, 88–89, 92–93, 152, and 155.
12. *LGPN* 3A s.v. 6th to 5th century BC.
13. Iambl. *VP*, 132.
14. For traditions concerning an additional daughter, Aesara, see chap. 6, below.
15. Iambl. *VP*, 265. A magician named Aristeas is the subject of a story about Metaponto that can be associated with the altar of Apollo and the enclosure called the *manteion*. See further Joseph Coleman Carter, *Discovering the Greek Countryside at Metaponto* (Ann Arbor, 2006), 216–17, and Burkert, *Lore and Science*, 147–49. Thesleff, *Intro.*, states that Aristeus is Aristaios [i.e., Aristaeus], 121n1, and see 74n6.
16. See further on widows and children in the families of Demosthenes and of Phormio and Pasio: Sarah B. Pomeroy, *Families in Classical and Hellenistic Greece: Representations and Realities* (Oxford, 1997), esp. chap. 5.
17. Clem. *Strom.* 1.80.4, p. 52, and 4.7.44, p. 268, and Thesleff, *Texts*, 201.
18. 1.8, see further Joseph Russo, "The Poetics of the Ancient Greek Proverb," *Journal of Folklore Research* 20 (1983): 121–30, esp. 127.
19. I am grateful to Dorothy Helly for this observation. Diogenes Laertius often attributes sayings to philosophers. He culled these quotations from various secondary sources. They may or may not have been authentic, but like, e.g., Plutarch's *Say-*

ings of Spartan Women, their ancient audience will have found them believable and worth repeating.

20. *LGPN* 3A s.v. Sparta? Archaic?

21. Iambl. *VP*, 4, Porph., *VPyth*. 4.

22. The tale about the house of Theano being converted into the temple of Demeter entered through a sanctuary of the Muses sounds like the story about the house of Pythagoras at Metaponto. I am grateful to Joseph Carter for this observation. See also G. Vallet, "Stenopos of the Muses," in *Mélanges de philosophie, de littérature et d'histoire ancienne offerts à Pierre Boyancé* (Rome, 1974), 749–59.

23. Diog. Laert. 3.47, *LGPN* 3A s.v. 4th century BC.

24. See above on Cratesicleia.

25. *LGPN* 3A s.v. 4th century BC.

26. See further Carl Huffmann, "Aristoxenus' *Pythagorean Precepts*: A Rational Pythagorean Ethics," in *La construzione del discorso filosofico nell'età dei Presocratici* (The Construction of Philosophical Discourse in the Age of the Presocratics), ed. M. M. Sassi (Pisa, 2006), 103–21, esp. 107.

27. *LGPN* 3A s.v. 4th century BC.

28. *LGPN* 3A s.v. 5th century BC?

29. *LGPN* 3A s.v. 6th century BC.

30. *LGPN* 3A s.v. 5th–4th century BC. Nistheadousa—*Poralla*², no. 552: Pythagorean of unknown time.

31. Manuscripts vary. Nistheadousa is listed with a question mark in Diels-Kranz (Berlin, 1951), vol. 1, p. 448, nr. 58A, "Pythagoreische Schule: A. Katalog des Iamblichos," but not cited in *Poralla*² or in *LGPN* 3A. John Dillon and Jackson Hershbell (*Iamblichus: On the Pythagorean Way of Life*, Society of Biblical Literature Texts and Translations, vol. 29, *Graeco-Roman Religion*, ser. 11 [Atlanta, 1991], 269) do not include her.

32. *LGPN* 3A s.v. 5th–4th century BC.

33. *LGPN* 3A s.v. 5th–4th century BC.

34. *LGPN* 3A s.v. 6th century BC, but s.v. Autocharidas 5th century. *Poralla*², nos. 419, 172: a Pythagorean of unknown time.

35. In addition, a certain Deino was variously said to be the wife of Pythagoras and/or Brontinus: see chap. 2, below.

36. Diog. Laert. 8.41. The historical sources for this episode all mention his mother: see chap. 2, below. On the name of Pythagoras's mother, see Riedweg, *Pythagoras*, 6. J. Bollansée (*Hermippos of Smyrna and His Biographical Writings: A Reappraisal* [Leuven, 1999], 49) argues that Pythagoras's mother colluded in a "shameless sham" to convince people that her son could visit Hades and return.

37. The story sounds like a scene from Comedy, inspired by Dionysus's descent in Aristophanes' *Frogs*.

38. For the hallucinatory state of consciousness and "inner vision" induced by a sojourn in a cave, see Y. Ustinova, *Caves and the Ancient Greek Mind: Descending Underground in the Search for the Ultimate Truth* (Oxford, 2009), chap. 1 and pas-

sim. Ustinova (191, 242) argues that the repetition of *catabasis* in the biographies of Pythagoras and the early sources serves to authenticate the stories.

39. *Pace* Burkert, *Lore and Science*, 159, who asserts that it is "highly unlikely that Pythagoras brought his mother with him to Croton."

40. See note 48, below.

41. William V. Harris, *Ancient Literacy* (Cambridge, MA, 1989), 65–67. E.g., recently, Carl Huffmann, "Pythagoreanism" and *"Pythagoras,"* Stanford Encyclopedia of Philosophy, online, first published Feb. 23, 2005; substantive revision Nov. 13, 2009. http://plato.stanford.edu/entries/pythagoras/.

FGrH B328, Fr. 91, nos. 25–26, fails to discuss literacy, although it is relevant in establishing the reliability of the sources for early Pythagoreanism. See further below, chap. 3.

42. Harris, *Ancient Literacy*, 65–66.

43. See further Stephen A. White, *"Principes Sapientiae*: Dicaearchus' Biography of Philosophy," in *Dicaearchus of Messana: Text, Translation, and Discussion*, ed. William W. Fortenbaugh (New Brunswick, NJ, 2001), 195–236, esp. 210, 218n49. Burkert, *Lore and Science*, 239–40, is anachronistic in his evaluation of wisdom reproduced through oral transmission as lacking "logical foundation or systematic and conceptual coherence" (240). Of course Burkert wrote in the mid-twentieth century, before scholars had generally come to view the oral tradition with the respect it enjoyed in archaic and classical Greece.

44. Diog. Laert. (8.36) refers to Pythagorean memoranda.

45. Cornelius Agrippa von Nettesheim, *Declamation on the Nobility and Preeminence of the Female Sex* (*De nobilitate et praecellentia foeminei sexus*) (Antwerp, 1532), trans. and ed. Albert Rabil Jr. (Chicago, 1996), 81, and see further Christiane L. Joost-Gaugier, *Pythagoras and Renaissance Europe* (Cambridge, 2009), 45, 56.

46. See Intro., above.

47. Burkert, *Lore and Science*, 117n50, see also 115n42, commenting on Dicaearchus, fr. 34, sees oral tradition as inferior to written history, but his assessment is anachronistic. See chap. 2, below.

48. According to Dicaearchus in Aul. Gell. 4.11.14. Dillon and Hershbell, *Iamblichus: On the Pythagorean Way of Life*, 7, see this report as a caricature, and Burkert, *Pythagoreanism*, 106n48, 139, hypothesizes that Dicaearchus is being sarcastic and ironical. There are other traditions as well about Pythagoras's reincarnations: see, e.g., Heraclides in Diog. Laert. 8.4, who does not mention Alco.

49. Diog. Laert. 8.8, 21 calls her Themistoclea, citing Aristoxenus = Aristoxenus fr. 15 (Wehrli). Porph. *VPyth*. 41 calls her Aristocleia. The *Suda* s.v. Pythagoras, refers to her as Thecleia.

50. Arist. *Metaph*. 986a.

51. See Kathleen Freeman, *The Pre-Socratic Philosophers: A Companion to Diels, Fragmente der Vorsokratiker*, 2nd ed. (Cambridge, MA, 1959), 244–45.

52. See further Pomeroy, *Spartan Women*, 10–11, and passim.

53. See P. Cartledge, "Sparta and Samos: A Special Relationship," *CQ* 32 (1982):

243–65, and recently Maria Pipili, "The Clients of Laconian Black-Figure Vases," 75–83, 201–7, in *Les clients de la céramique grecque, Actes du colloque de l'Académie des Inscriptions et Belles-Lettres, 30–31 janvier 2004*, ed. J. de la Genière (Paris, 2006), for ceramic evidence for commercial links between Laconia and Samos.

54. Iambl., *VP* 267. Similarly on women's attraction to Epicureanism, Bernard Frischer, *The Sculpted Word: Epicureanism and Philosophical Recruitment in Ancient Greece* (Berkeley, 1982), 62, wrote: "It would be hard to overemphasize the appeal of a school that was willing to grant females full rights of participation in all of its activities."

55. Leonid Zhmud, *Wissenschaft, Philosophie und Religion im früühen Pythagoreismus* (Berlin, 1997), 67–69; Burkert, *Lore and Science*, 105n40; and Dillon and Hershbell, *Iamblichus: On the Pythagorean Way of Life*, note that Iamblichus is a valuable source (p. 3) and draw attention to the earlier sources that he used (p. 60).

56. Iambl. *VP*, 110.

57. Joseph Coleman Carter, ed., *Living Off the Chora: Diet and Nutrition at Metaponto* (Austin, 2003), 20, 22, fig. 10.

58. Iambl. *VP* 241; Pl. *Resp.* 398E–399C, *Lach.* 188D, 193D, *Epistle* 7.336C; Arist. *Pol.* 1342b12.

59. See chap. 2, below, and see also Burkert, *Lore and Science*, 185. Marilyn B. Skinner (*Sexuality in Greek and Roman Culture* [Malden, ME, 2005], 154) suggests these restrictions were prompted by Pythagoras's interest in physical health.

60. Iambl. *VP*, 21, 96–97, Diog. Laert. 8.19.

61. See further Carter, *Living Off the Chora*, 6–7.

62. Eating meat that had been sacrificed in behalf of the community was permitted in some cases, for those who were allowed to eat [meat] could consume only those animals that could be sacrificed (Porph., *VPyth.* 43).

63. Carter, *Living Off the Chora*, 33–35.

64. Iambl. *VP*, 106, 187.

65. Iambl. *VP*, 193.

66. Arist. fr. 157–58, 177 (Gigon); Iambl. *Protr.* 21, no 31.

67. Iambl. *VP* 150, Arist. fr. 157 Gigon, Porph. *Pyth.* 44, and see further Riedweg, *Pythagoras*, 31–33, 37, 67–71, 75.

68. Carter, *Living Off the Chora*, 32.

69. Iambl. *VP*, 98, and see chap. 2, below.

70. Iambl. *VP*, 100, 149. "Researchers found that you fall asleep faster, sleep deeper, and wake up in a better mood after sleeping on linen! And linen offers these great benefits: Exceptional natural strength, Superior luster and durability, Absorbent, Lint-free." www.cuddledown.com/shopping/product/detailmain.jsp?itemID=656&itemType=PRODUCT&RS=1&keyword=linen.

71. According to Diog. Laert. 8.19, Pythagoras wore white wool.

72. Plut., *Isis and Osiris*, 4.

73. Iambl. *VP*, 187. The Pythagorean women may have been permitted to wear less valuable jewelry. Beth Cohen, in a private communication, Nov. 30, 2009, points out that very little Greek jewelry is preserved, particularly from the Archaic Period. In the Classical Period, gold was the predominant material employed for jewelry. It is

thought that, earlier, other materials were also employed, some of which must have been ephemeral. There is evidence that bronze (and gilded bronze) were used for jewelry, especially bracelets. (The metal earrings attached to marble statues must have been bronze.) And it is believed that ivory (which could be painted) must also have been employed, particularly for earrings: there are no preserved examples, however.

74. See further Sarah B. Pomeroy, *Xenophon Oeconomicus: A Social and Historical Commentary* (Oxford, 1994), chap. 5.

75. Iambl. *VP* 54. Cf. Fritz Graf, "Dionysian and Orphic Eschatology," in *Masks of Dionysus*, ed. T. H. Carpenter and C. A. Faraone (Ithaca, 1993), 239–58, esp. 256, on the women in the Greek world whose wealth offered them some freedom to become members of Bacchic groups.

76. The father of Pythagoras, however, had been a merchant (Iambl. *VP* 5) or a stone carver: Hermipp. fr. 19 (Wehrli), and see now Bollansée, *Hermippos of Smyrna and His Biographical Writings*, 49.

77. I am grateful to Joseph Carter for sending a copy of his talk "Metaponto in 500 BC (more exactly the 50 years around 500 BC): Pythagoras and Bonifica of the Chora," before publication. The following summary is based largely on Professor Carter's archaeological analyses both in this talk and in *Discovering the Greek Countryside at Metaponto*.

78. Carter, *Discovering the Greek Countryside at Metaponto*. I am grateful to Joseph Carter for this comment.

79. Ibid., 78, and Carter, *Living off the Chora*, 15–16.

80. Carter, *Discovering the Greek Countryside at Metaponto*, 79.

81. Ibid., 150.

82. Justin, *Epitome of the Philippic History of Pompeius Trogus*, trans., with notes, by the Rev. John Selby Watson (London, 1853), adapted. www.forumromanum.org/literature/justin/english/trans20.html#4.

83. 20.4. 11 " . . .ut matronae auratas uestes ceteraque dignitatis suae ornamenta uelut instrumenta luxuriae deponerent eaque omnia delata in Iunonis aedem ipsi deae consecrarent, 12 prae se ferentes uera ornamenta matronarum pudicitiam, non uestes esse 13 In iuuentute quoque quantum profligatum sit, victim feminarum contumaces animi manifestant."

84. Trans. A. MacGregor, in *Justin: Epitome of the Philippic History of Pompeius Trogus*, trans. J. C. Yardley (Atlanta, 1994), 166n9.

85. See further Andrew Dalby, "Levels of Concealment: The Dress of *hetairai* and *pornai* in Greek Texts," in *Women's Dress in the Ancient Greek World*, ed. Lloyd Llewellyn-Jones (London, 2002), 111–124, esp. 113. Dalby does not mention Pythagoras or the Neopythagorean texts. See also Daniel Ogden, "Controlling Women's Dress: *Gynaikonomoi*," in ibid., 203–25, esp. 209.

86. Plut. *Sol.* 20.4, and see further Pomeroy, *Families in Classical and Hellenistic Greece*, 100–104.

87. K. R. Moore, "Was Pythagoras Ever Really in Sparta?" *Rosetta* 6: 1–25. http://www.rosetta.bham.ac.uk/issue6/pythagoras-sparta/ finds the traditions about Pythagoras's interest in Sparta and visit there credible, though not provable.

88. Timaeus: *FGrH* Fr. 13; Iambl. *VP* 72, 74, and see further Mele, "Il pitagorismo e le popolazioni anelleniche di Italia," 62, 69, 76, 83.

89. Iambl. *VP* 174–75, and Stob. *Flor*.15.45 = Aristox. frgs. 33 and 34 (Wehrli); and Mele, "Il pitagorismo e le popolazioni anelleniche di Italia," 86.

90. Sarah B. Pomeroy, *Goddesses, Whores, Wives, and Slaves: Women in Classical Antiquity* (1975; New York, 1995), 131.

91. Joseph Coleman Carter, ed., *The Chora of Metaponto: The Necropoleis*, 2 vols. (Austin, 1998), 2: 532.

92. Carter, *Discovering the Greek Countryside at Metaponto*, 41.

Chapter 2 · Wives, Mothers, Sisters, Daughters

1. See further Sarah B. Pomeroy, *Families in Classical and Hellenistic Greece: Representations and Realities* (Oxford, 1997), 37, 62, 100–105, 141.

2. Iambl. *VP* 48, 84. Much of the information about the life of Pythagoras related here is drawn from Iamblichus. See Introduction, above. T. M. Robinson ("The Pythagorean Way of Life," in *Pythagorean Philosophy*, ed. K. I. Boudouris [Athens, 1992], 171–81, esp. 179) notes that the respect shown for the wife in this passage is evidence of progress in marital relations.

3. John H. Oakley and Rebecca H. Sinos, *The Wedding in Ancient Athens* (Madison, WI, 1993), 34.

4. Cf. Xen. *Oec.* 7.14, and see further Sarah B. Pomeroy, *Xenophon Oeconomicus: A Social and Historical Commentary* (Oxford, 1994), 275.

5. On the biographical traditions concerning Pythagoras, see, inter alia, Charles Kahn, *Pythagoras and the Pythagoreans* (Indianapolis, IN, 2001), chaps. 1 and 2, and Carl Huffmann, "Pythagoras," *Stanford Encyclopedia of Philosophy*, online, first published Wed., Feb 23, 2005; substantive revision Fri., Nov. 13, 2009. http://plato.stanford.edu/entries/pythagoras/.

6. Wife of the Pythagorean Brontinus, or according to some sources, Pythagoras's wife: see chap. 1, above.

7. See further Pomeroy, *Goddesses, Whores, Wives, and Slaves: Women in Classical Antiquity* (1975; New York, 1995), 91, and chap. 4, below.

8. E.g., Jan Hoffman, "Public Infidelity, Private Debate: Not My Husband (Right?)," *New York Times*, Mar. 16, 2008, Styles, 1, 8.

9. Cf. Solon's view that the husband of an heiress should be physically able to have intercourse with her three times a month: Plut. *Sol*. 20.2–3.

10. Hieronymus of Rhodes fr. 42 (Wehrli), Diog. Laert. 8.21, and see further I. Lévy, *Recherches sur les sources de la legend de Pythagore* (Paris, 1926), 36–39, and Stephen A. White, "Hieronymus of Rhodes: The Sources, Text, and Translation," 79–276, in *Lyco of Troas and Hieronymus of Rhodes*, ed. William W. Fortenbaugh and Stephen A. White (New Brunswick, NJ, 2004), 202, fr. 50. On the visit to the underworld, see also chap. 1, above.

11. Iambl. *VP* 56, Diog. Laert. 8.10.

12. Iambl. *VP* 202, Stob. *Ecl*. 4.1.49.

13. Plut. *Advice to the Bride and Groom*, 31, and see further *Plutarch's "Advice to the Bride and Groom" and "A Consolation to His Wife,"* ed. Sarah B. Pomeroy (New York, 1999), 48, 56.

14. Cf. the debate about Michelle Obama's sleeveless dresses: Maureen Dowd, "Should Michelle Cover Up?" *New York Times*, Mar. 8, 2009, www.nytimes.com/2009/03/08/opinion/08dowd.html.

15. E.g., Diog. Laert. 8. 6; Diod. Sic. 10.9.3–4.

16. Cic. *De Inv.* 2.1–3.

17. See further C. J. de Vogel, *Pythagoras and Pythagoreanism: An Interpretation of the Neglected Evidence on the Philosopher Pythagoras* (Assen, 1966), 179–81, and Kathy L. Gaca, "The Reproductive Technology of the Pythagoreans," *CP* 95 (2000): 113–32, and Gaca, *The Making of Fornication. Eros, Ethics, and Political Reform in Greek Philosophy and Early Christianity* (Berkeley, 2003), 107–9.

18. See further Sarah B. Pomeroy, *Spartan Women* (Oxford, 2002), 64 and passim.

19. Iambl. *VP* 213; Occellus, *de Univ. Nat.* 51–53: Thesleff, *Texts*, 136–37.

20. Xen., *Sp. Const.* 1.3, and see further Pomeroy, *Spartan Women*, 33, 106, 109, 110, 125, 133–34, 150.

21. Plut. *Lyc.* 15 and see further Pomeroy, *Spartan Women*, 41–44, 54, 56.

22. D. W. Amunmdsen and C. J. Diers, "The Age of Menarche in Classical Greece and Rome," *Human Biology* 41 (1969): 125–32.

23. Ibid.

24. See further Pomeroy, *Goddesses, Whores, Wives, and Slaves*, 85–86.

25. Joseph Coleman Carter, *Discovering the Greek Countryside at Metaponto* (Ann Arbor, 2006), 41–42, and see chap. 1, above.

26. J. Lawrence Angel, "Paleoecology, Paleodemography, and Health," in *Population, Ecology, and Social Evolution*, ed. S. Polgar (The Hague, 1975), 167–90, esp. 176, and in a personal letter, and Thomas J. Gallant, *Risk and Survival in Ancient Greece* (Stanford, CA, 1991), 20–21.

27. Carter, *Discovering the Greek Countryside at Metaponto*, 42, 223–24.

28. See further Pomeroy, *Goddesses, Whores, Wives, and Slaves*, 227–28, and passim.

29. See Pomeroy, *Spartan Women*, 34–37, 39, 47–49, 68, 102, and see further below.

30. Keith Hopkins ("On the Probable Age Structure of the Roman Population," *Population Studies* 20 [1966]: 245–64, esp. 260–63) argued that women dying between fifteen and twenty-nine were more likely to be commemorated because their husbands were still alive to erect tombstones.

31. Xen. *Oec.* 10.12–13, see further Pomeroy, *Xenophon Oeconomicus*, 308–9.

32. Thus Sarah B. Pomeroy, *The Murder of Regilla: A Case of Domestic Violence in Antiquity* (Cambridge, MA, 2007), 121.

33. Diehl, fr. 7, trans. Marylin Arthur, in Pomeroy, *Goddesses, Whores, Wives, and Slaves*, 49.

34. Sarah B. Pomeroy, "The Relationship of the Married Woman to Her Blood Relatives in Rome," *Ancient Society* 7 (1976): 215–27.

35. Val. Max. *Memorable Deeds and Words*, 6.3.9.

36. Philostr. *VS* 555, and see further Pomeroy, *The Murder of Regilla*, passim.

37. *plagarum vestigia*: August. *Confessions* 9.9.

38. Plut. *Quaest. Rom.* 108.

39. On traditions concerning the death of Pythagoras see, inter alia, John Dillon and Jackson Hershbell, *Iamblichus: On the Pythagorean Way of Life*, Society of Biblical Literature Texts and Translations, vol. 29. *Graeco-Roman Religion*, ser. 11 (Atlanta, 1991) 191–92.

40. Iambl. *VP* 209–10; Stob. *Ecl.* 4.37.4 = Aristoxenus fr. 39 (Wehrli).

41. See further Sarah B. Pomeroy, "*Technikai kai Mousikai*: The Education of Women in the Fourth Century and in the Hellenistic Period," *AJAH* 2 (1977): 51–68, esp. 52–53.

42. De Vogel, *Pythagoras and Pythagoreanism*, 125, thinks probably only the boys are meant.

43. See further Pomeroy, *Spartan Women*, chap. 1.

44. Iambl. *VP* 4, Porph. *VPyth.* 4, Timaeus *FGrH* 566 Fr. 131.

45. See further Pomeroy, *Spartan Women*, 6–8.

46. *Pythagorean Precepts*, fr. 34 = Stob. *Ecl.* 4.25.45. See further Carl A. Huffman, "The *Pythagorean Precepts* of Aristoxenus," *CQ* 58 (2008): 104–20, and Huffman, "Aristoxenus' *Pythagorean Precepts*: A Rational Pythagorean Ethics," in *La construzione del discorso filosofico nell'età dei Presocratici* (The Construction of Philosophical Discourse in the Age of the Presocratics), ed. M. M. Sassi (Pisa, 2006), 103–21, esp. 113n7, where Huffman does not consider Iamblichus's reports about the speeches at Croton as reliable evidence for original Pythagoreanism, but he does trust the *Precepts*. The *Precepts*, however, are consistent with Iamblichus's reports about the Pythagorean way of life.

47. See further de Vogel, *Pythagoras and Pythagoreanism*, 140–41, quoting Antisthenes.

48. Iambl. *VP* 41–42; Aristoxenus, fr. 39 (Wehrli) = Stob. *Ecl.* 4.37.4, also advises that sexual activity for *paides* should not begin until age twenty and should be engaged in rarely and not when sated with food and drink.

49. De Vogel, *Pythagoras and Pythagoreanism*, 85–89.

50. Lycoph. *Alex.* 1141–73.

51. Fritz Graf, "The Locrian Maidens," in *Oxford Readings in Greek Religion*, ed. Richard Buxton, trans. H. and D. Harvey (1978; Oxford, 2000), 250–70, and James M. Redfield, *The Locrian Maidens* (Princeton, 2003), 85–92 and passim.

52. Carter, *Discovering the Greek Countryside at Metaponto*, 175, 177, 223–24.

53. Pomeroy, *Spartan Women*, 34–37, 39, 47–49, 68, 102.

54. See further Riedweg, *Pythagoras*, 16, and for the site of the temple, see below, on Calypso.

55. Roberto Spadea, "Santuari di Hera a Crotone," in *Héra: Images, espaces, cultes*, Actes du Colloque International du Centre de Recherches Archéologiques de l'Université de Lille III et de l'Association P.R.A.C., novembre 1993, ed. J. de La Genière (Naples, 1997), 235–59, esp. 253–55, 258.

56. Strabo 6.3.4.c 280; Livy 24.3; Serv. *ad Aen.* iii.552.

57. See further Mary Jaeger, "Livy, Hannibal's Monument, and the Temple of Juno at Croton," *TAPhA* 136 (2006): 389–414, esp. 399–400.

58. http://etext.virginia.edu/etcbin/toccer-new2?id=Liv3His.sgm&images=images/modeng&data=/texts/english/modeng/parsed&tag=public&part=176&division=div2.

59. E.g., A. S. F. Gow and D. L. Page, *The Greek Anthology: Hellenistic Epigrams* (Cambridge, 1965), no. 3 = *Anth. Pal.* 6.265, and see below.

60. See further Roberto Spadea, *Ricerche nel Santuario di Hera Lacinia a Capo Colona di Crotone* (Rome, 2006), 31–49.

61. Polyb. 3.33.18, Livy 28. 46.16.

62. Iambl. *VP* 54.

63. For the Nuragic ship: Spadea, *Santuario di Hera Lacinia a Crotone*, 27.

64. See J. G. Frazer, *Pausanias's Description of Greece*, 6 vols. (London, 1898), 3: 184, on Paus. 2. 17.4 for other images of Hera wearing floral crowns.

65. Spadea, "Santuari di Hera a Crotone," 246.

66. Ibid. See Roberto Spadea, "Il Tesoro di Hera," *BA* 88 (1994): 1–34, esp. 26.

67. According to Herod. 2.81 the Egyptians used linen and abstained from using wool for burials and in temples, and see chap. 1, above.

68. According to Diog. Laert. 8.19 Pythagoras himself wore white wool because the use of linen had not yet reached Magna Graecia.

69. Iambl. *VP* 100, 149, Diog. Laert. 8.19,33.

70. Iambl. *VP* 56; Just. *Epit.* 20.4.10–12; Diod. Sic.10.9.6.

71. Thus Pomeroy, *Xenophon Oeconomicus*, 61–65.

72. Xen. *Oec.* 9.3.6.

73. *IG* [2] 1514–29, and see Tullia Linders, *Studies in the Treasure Records of Artemis Brauronia Found in Athens*. Skrifter utgivna av Svenska institutet i Athen. 40; 19 (Stockholm, 1972).

74. See further Pomeroy, *Xenophon Oeconomicus*, 61–64.

75. See further Tullia Linders, *Studies in the Treasure Records of Artemis Brauronia found in Athens*.

76. Pomeroy, *The Murder of Regilla*, 144, 161–62.

77. See further Joan Breton Connelly, *Portrait of a Priestess* (Princeton, 2007), 198–202.

78. Maurizio Giangiulio, "Per la storia dei culti di Crotone antica. Il santuario di Hera lacinia. Strutture e funzioni cultuali, origini storiche e mitiche." *Archivio storico per la Calabria e la Lucania* (1982), 49: 5–69, esp. 41.

79. See John Pedley, *Sanctuaries and the Sacred in the Ancient World* (Cambridge, 2005), 113.

80. Giangiulio, "Per la storia dei culti di Crotone antica," 15–16, 39.

81. See further ibid., 26–27.

82. Ibid., 7–8.

83. G. Pugliese-Carratelli, "Il dibattito e le conclusion," in *Crotone*: Atti del XXIII Convegno di studi sulla Magna Grecia, Taranto, ottobre 7–10, 1983, ed. G. Pugliese-

Carratelli (Taranto 1984), 610-14, esp. 613. Giangiulio, "Per la storia dei culti di Crotone antica," and G. Maddoli, "I Culti di Crotone," *Crotone: Atti del XXIII Convegno di studi sulla Magna Grecia, Taranto, ottobre 7-10, 1983* (Taranto, 1984), 312-43, esp. 323-24.

84. Paus. 3.13.9, Maddoli, "I Culti di Crotone," 323-25, draws attention to connections between the cult of Hera Lacinia and that of Aphrodite in Crete, and see Pomeroy, *Spartan Women*, 122.

85. Giangiulio, "Per la storia dei culti di Crotone antica," 11, 34-35.

86. Juliette de La Genière, "Note sur une muserolle disparue," in La Genière, *Héra: Images, espaces, cultes*, 261-65.

87. Giangiulio, "Per la storia dei culti di Crotone antica," 59.

88. Maddoli, "I Culti di Crotone," 318-20.

89. In the "Severe Style" with thick long hair folded up behind her neck: Madeleine Mertens-Horn, "La scultura di marmo," in *Metaponto: Archeologia di una colonia greca*, ed. A. De Siena (Taranto, 2001), 71-88, esp. fig. 75, and 76-79.

90. Spadea, "Santuari di Hera a Crotone," in La Genière, *Héra: Images, espaces, cultes*, 235-59, esp. 253-55, 258; and see further Roberto Spadea, *Il Tesoro di Hera: Scoperte nel santuario di Hera lacinia a Capo Colona di Crotone*, Museo Barracco, marzo 28-giugno 30, 1996 (Milan, 1996), passim.

91. On the motifs and find spots of these reliefs, see recently Torben Melander, "The Import of Attic Pottery to Locri Epizephyrii: A Case of Reinterpretation," in *Pots for the Living, Pots for the Dead*, Acta Hyperborea 9, ed. A. Rathje, M. Nielsen, and B. B. Rasmussen (Copenhagen, 2002), 59-82. The corpus has now been published as *I pinakes di Locri Epizefiri: Musei di Reggio Calabria e di Locri*, ed. E. L. Caronna et al., 15 vols. (Rome, 1999-2007).

92. See further Pedley, *Sanctuaries and the Sacred in the Ancient Greek World*, 113-14.

93. Polyb. 12.4.5-16, Schol. On Dion. Per. 366 = GGM II 445.30. I am grateful to Walter Penrose for sending a copy of his unpublished paper "From Bastards to Aristocrats: Illegitimacy, Colonization, and Matrilineal Ancestry in Lokroi Epizifyrioi?" See further Simon Pembroke, "Locres et Tarante, le role des femmes dans la foundation de deux colonies grecques," *Annales: Économies, Sociétés, Civilisations* 5 (1970): 1240-70, esp. 1253.

94. *Anth. Pal.* 6.265, trans. Marilyn B. Skinner, "Nossis Thêlyglossos," in *Women's History and Ancient History*, ed. Sarah B. Pomeroy (Chapel Hill, NC, 1991), 20-47, esp. 22.

Chapter 3 · Who Were the Neopythagorean Women Authors?

1. See further Thesleff, *Intro.*, and Thesleff, *Texts*. For interpretation, see also M. Meunier, *Femmes pythagoriennnes: Fragments et letters de Théano, Perictioné, Mélissa, et Myia* (Paris, 1932).

2. Thesleff, *Intro.*, 113-15, and see chaps. 5 and 6, below.

3. Flora R. Levin, *Greek Reflections on the Nature of Music* (Cambridge, 2009).

4. Ibid., 58n22.

5. Thesleff, *Intro.*, 7n2, describing her as "an antiquarian," and Thesleff, *Texts*, 242–43. E. Zeller (*Die Philosophie der Griechen in ihrer geschichtlichen Entwicklung dargestellt*, ed. W. Nestle [Leipzig, 1923, repr. Hildesheim, 1963], vol. 3, pt. 2, pp. 125–26n2) considers her a Neopythagorean.

6. Levin, *Greek Reflections on the Nature of Music*, 231–37, 242n4, 246, fig. 8. Andrew Barker (*Greek Musical Writings: Harmonic and Acoustic Theory* [Cambridge, 1986], 230) dates Ptolemaïs third century BC to first century AD, preferring the later date (following Düring, see chap. 5, below).

7. Zeller, *Philosophie der Griechen*, 3.2, 4th ed. (Leipzig, 1902), 79: see the complete survey in Thesleff, *Intro.*, 30–41.

8. W. Burkert, e.g., review of H. Thesleff, *An Introduction to the Pythagorean Writings of the Hellenistic Period*, Gnomon 34 (1962): 763–68, and Burkert, "Zur Geistesgeschichtlichen Einordnung einiger Pseudopythagorica," in *Pseudepigrapha*, vol. 1, *Pseudopythagorica*, ed. Kurt von Fritz. Entretiens sur l'Antiquité Classique. Publieés par Olivier Reverdin, 18 (Vandoeuvres and Geneva, 1972), 25–55.

9. "On the Problem of the Doric Pseudo-Pythagorica: An alternative Theory of Date and Purpose," in von Fritz, *Pseudopythagorica*, 59–87, esp. 72.

10. Burkert, *Lore and Science*, 95.

11. P. M Fraser, *Ptolemaic Alexandria* (Oxford, 1972), 1: 493.

12. Alfons Städele, *Die Briefe des Pythagoras und der Pythagoreer*, vol. 15, Beiträge zur Klassischen Philologie (Meisenheim am Glan, 1980), 352–53.

13. Charles H. Kahn, *Pythagoras and the Pythagoreans: A Brief History* (Indianapolis, IN, 2001), 74. Bruno Centrone, "Platonism and Pythagoreanism in the Early Empire," in *The Cambridge History of Greek and Roman Political Thought*, ed. C. Rowe and M. Schofield (Cambridge, 2000), 559–83, esp. 567, also dates some of the writings to the third or second century BC, although in *Pseudopythagorica Ethica: I trattati morali di Archita, Metopo, Teage, Eurifamo*, Elenchos, Collana di testi e studi sul pensiero antico, 17 (Naples, 1990), 44, he had concluded that the texts should be dated to the first century BC. See also the undogmatic discussion in Peter Kingsley, *Ancient Philosophy, Mystery, and Magic: Empedocles and Pythagorean Tradition* (Oxford, 1995), chap. 20, esp. 323–24.

14. Waithe, *Women Philosophers*, 26 and passim.

15. An example is Carl Huffmann (*Pythagoreanism*, first published March 29, 2006, with substantive revision June 14, 2010), who (4.2), cites only Centrone's publications of 1990 and 1994 to support his statement: "most scholars (e.g. Burkert 1972b, 40–44; Centrone 1990, 30–34, 41–44 and 1994) have chosen Rome or Alexandria between 150 BCE and 100 CE as the most likely time and place."

16. For example, the publications of Vicki Harper, Flora Levin, Sarah B. Pomeroy, and Mary Ellen Waithe: see notes below.

17. Thesleff, *Texts*, s.v. Arignote, 1 page; Aesara s.v. Aresas, 2 pages; s.v. Myia, 1 page; s.v. Melissa, 1 page; s.v. Perictione, 41/2 pages; s.v. Phintys, 3 pages; s.v. Ptolemaïs, 2 pages; s.v. Theano, 8 pages.

18. For the Neopythagorean women as philosophers, see chap. 7, below.

19. Centrone, *Pseudopythagorica Ethica*, 17, also does not cite any of the female authors. He does mention the texts of Aesara, referring to the author only by the male name Aresas (159, 203, 208, 219). On these names, see chap. 6, below.

20. As in Pomeroy, "*Technikai kai Mousikai*: The Education of Women in the Fourth Century and in the Hellenistic Period," *AJAH* 2 (1977), and *Women in Hellenistic Egypt*, 61, and n122.

21. See chap. 5 below for Ptolemaïs and for the letter of Theano II to Rhodope.

22. Thesleff, *Texts*, 200.

23. For these see Thomas McGinn, *Prostitution, Sexuality, and the Law in Ancient Rome* (New York, 1998).

24. Cratinus the Elder (490–420 BC) of Athens is also said to have written *The Female Pythagorean*. The extant fragment mocks Pythagorean pseudo-learned mumbo-jumbo about debate, opposites, limits, fallacies, and so on. This tradition is probably due to confusion with Cratinus the Younger. See Burkert, *Lore and Science*, 198n25.

25. Sarah B. Pomeroy, *Goddesses, Whores, Wives, and Slaves: Women in Classical Antiquity* (1975; New York, 1995), 119.

26. Frs. 222 and 296–97 = Ath. 4.161c–d; fr. 198 = Ath. 3.122f; Meineke, *FCG* 3.376, *The Tarentines*; and W. Geoffrey Arnott, *Alexis: The Fragments. A Commentary* (Cambridge, 1996), 15, 579–82, 585.

27. Arnott, *Alexis*, 625.

28. Thus Sarah B. Pomeroy, *Women in Hellenistic Egypt, from Alexander to Cleopatra* (New York, 1984; pbk., with new foreword, Detroit, 1990; ACLS History E-Book, 2004), 59–65.

29. Cover image of R. W. V. Catling and F. Marchand, eds., *Onomatologos: Studies in Greek Personal Names, Presented to Elaine Matthews* (Oxford, 2010). Photo by Claudia Wagner. I am grateful to David Harvey for this reference. Claudia Wagner, in a private communication (Aug. 17, 2010) has kindly sent me the description: Garnet ringstone (shape B1). 22x15x3. Unpublished. A woman with rolled hair, necklace, and bracelets, wearing a belted sleeveless chiton with *himation* around her legs, stands with one foot upon a box, writing on a diptych. The box (presumably for scrolls) is rectangular, with a recess in the near side. Ground line. An early gem, still quite Classical in treatment of head and dress. The woman may be a poetess. Third century BC. As usual, the engraving is in mirror image. © Beazley Archive, Oxford University.

30. See further Thesleff, *Intro.*, 7n2, and Thesleff, *Texts*, 242–43, app. 1: Antiquarian Accounts.

31. Porph. *VPyth*. 54–57, and see Christoph Riedweg, *Pythagoras: His Life, Teaching, and Influence* (Ithaca, 2005), 104–6, trans. Steven Rendall, in collaboration with Christoph Riedweg and Andreas Schatzmann, from *Pythagoras: Leben, Lehre, Nachwirkung eine Einführung* (Munich, 2002). Riedweg, *Pythagoras*, 104–6.

32. Lysis in Thesleff, *Texts*, 114.4.

33. Burkert, *Lore and Science*, 199–200, and Riedweg, *Pythagoras*, 108. T. M. Robinson ("The Pythagorean Way of Life," in *Pythagorean Philosophy*, ed. K. I. Boudouris

[Athens, 1992], 171–81, esp.174) sees this impoverishment as a conscious move in the direction of Cynicism.

34. Fraser, *Ptolemaic Alexandria*, 1: 485, 493, and Kahn, *Pythagoras and the Pythagoreans*, chaps. 6 and 8. Neither Fraser nor Kahn discusses Neopythagorean women.

35. Quint. *Inst.* 1.1.6, and see further Suzanne Dixon, *Cornelia: Mother of the Gracchi* (Abingdon, UK, 2007), esp. 26–28.

36. See further Pomeroy, *Women in Hellenistic Egypt*, passim.

37. E.g., Theoc., *Id.* 15, 16–17, 19–20, 35–37.

38. See Thesleff, *Intro.*, 113–16 and passim. *P. Haun.* was published after Thesleff's *Introduction* and *Texts*.

39. Thesleff, *Intro.*, 7n2, and *Texts*, 229, 242–43. Thesleff does not assign a date to Ptolemaïs of Cyrene. See further chap. 5.

40. For these arguments, see Pomeroy, *Women in Hellenistic Egypt*, 59–72, and Intro., above.

41. See, e.g., Susan Guettel Cole, "Could Greek Women Read?" in *Reflections of Women in Antiquity*, ed. Helene P. Foley (London, 1981), 219–45, esp. 229, and K. von Fritz, s.v. "Periktione (2)" P.W., *RE* 19, cols. 794–95.

42. Pomeroy, "*Technikai kai Mousikai*," 57–58. See also Nagy, "The Naming of Athenian Girls: A Case in Point," *CJ* 74(1979) 360–64, for the tendency to give the name Theano to girls who might become priestesses, naming them after a literary model—the priestess in the *Iliad*.

43. Diog. Laert. 5.12–13; Marinus, *Vita Procli*, 29.

44. Diog. Laert. 6.94, 96–98.

45. Pomeroy, "*Technikai kai Mousikai*," 57–58; Bernard Frischer, *The Sculpted Word*," 54, 62, 206; and Catherine J. Castner, "Epicurean Hetairai as Dedicants to Healing Deities?" *GRBS* 23 (1982): 51–57.

46. E.g., for women in the circle of Jerome, see J. N. D. Kelly, *Jerome* (London, 1975), esp. chaps. 10 and 23. The wife of Iamblichus was a pupil of Plotinus. Several other women are mentioned in Porph. *Plot.* 9.11, and in later Neoplatonic circles. See also Intro., above.

47. See, inter alia, P. Wilson-Kastner et al., *A Lost Tradition: Women Writers of the Early Church* (Lanham, MD, 1981).

48. Diog. Laert. 6.94, 96–98.

49. *IGRom* IV 125. See also M. Tod, "Sidelights on Greek Philosophers," *JHS* 77 (1957): 132–41, esp. 140, for inscriptions honoring other women philosophers in the Imperial period.

50. J. Charbonneaux, R. Martin, and F. Villard, *Hellenistic Art*, trans. Peter Green (New York, 1973), 134–35. The precise identification of the characters is not secure since the names are not written on the painting, but it is clear that a woman is listening to a philosopher.

51. See Pomeroy, *Women in Hellenistic Egypt*, 61.

52. See Kingsley, *Ancient Philosophy, Mystery, and Magic*, 320–22, for persuasive

arguments against referring to the Neopythagorean texts as "pseudepigrapha," "literary fictions," and "forgeries."

53. The *scholia* on Callimachus *Aetia* indicate that he consulted her poem: R. Pfeiffer, *Callimachus*, 2. vols. (Oxford, 1949, 1953), 1: 118–19, 2: 115–16.

54. The Neopythagorean Arignote also apparently wrote about numbers. For both Theano I and Arignote, see chap. 5, below.

55. See Cole, "Could Greek Women Read?"

56. On the manuals of Philaenis and Elephantis, see E. W. Thomson Vessey, "Philaenis," *RBPh* 54 (1976): 78–83, and Pomeroy, *Women in Hellenistic Egypt*, 80.

57. M. West, "Erinna," *ZPE* 25 (1977): 116–19.

58. "Supplementary Notes on Erinna," *ZPE* 32 (1978):17–22, esp. 19–21, and see Introduction, above. D. L. Page, *Further Greek Epigrams* (Oxford, 1981), 344n1, also disagrees with West.

Chapter 4 · Introduction to the Prose Writings of Neopythagorean Women

1. Roger S. Bagnall and Raffaella Cribiore, *Women's Letters from Ancient Egypt, 300 BC–AD 800* (Ann Arbor, MI, 2006).

2. Ibid., 16.

3. *P. Haun.* and see p. 1. The Neopythagorean letters are not included in Bagnall and Cribiore, *Women's Letters from Ancient Egypt*.

4. *P. Haun.* and see chap. 5.

5. Thus also Bagnall and Cribiore, *Women's Letters from Ancient Egypt*, 16.

6. Gilles Ménage, *A History of Women Philosophers*, trans. Beatrice H Zedler (Lanham, MD, 1984), 93–95. Originally published as *Historia Mulierum Philosopharum* (Amsterdam, 1692).

7. Thus *Plutarch's "Advice to the Bride and Groom" and "A Consolation to His Wife": English translations, Commentary, Interpretive Essays, and Bibliography*, ed. Sarah B. Pomeroy (New York, 1999), 40–41.

8. *Advice*, 145, 138b.

9. Theano II to Nikostrate = Thesleff, *Texts*, 200.2–5, *Plutarch's "Advice,"* 41.

10. See further Sarah B. Pomeroy, *Women in Hellenistic Egypt, from Alexander to Cleopatra* (1984; Detroit, 1990; ACLS History E-Book, 2004), 94–95.

11. See further C. J. de Vogel, *Pythagoras and Pythagoreanism: An Interpretation of the Neglected Evidence on the Philosopher Pythagoras* (Assen, 1966), 179–81, and Kathy L. Gaca, *The Making of Fornication: Eros, Ethics, and Political Reform in Greek Philosophy and Early Christianity* (Berkeley, 2003), 107–9.

12. Thesleff, *Texts*, 62.30–33.

13. Thesleff, *Texts*, 137.21–25.

14. Thesleff, *Texts*, 136.4–6.

15. Thesleff, *Texts*, 116.1, 2.

16. Kathleen Freeman, *The Pre-Socratic Philosophers: A Companion to Diels, Fragmente der Vorsokratiker*, 2nd ed. (Cambridge, MA, 1959), 259.

17. Abraham J. Malherbe, *Ancient Epistolary Theorists* (Atlanta, 1988), 2, 4.

18. Demetr., *Eloc.* 231.

19. On the continuity between Pythagoreanism and Neopythagoreanism, see Peter Kingsley, *Ancient Philosophy, Mystery, and Magic: Empedocles and Pythagorean Tradition* (Oxford, 1995), chap. 20.

20. Thesleff, *Texts,* 197–98, and see chap. 5, below.

21. Thesleff, *Texts,* 142–45.

22. Thesleff, *Texts,* 199.16.

23. Ath. 13.568a–d describes the subterfuge and camouflage used by prostitutes to improve their appearance.

24. E.g., the laws of Solon stated that children were obliged to look after their parents, but the children of *hetairai* were exempt from this duty: Plut. *Sol.* 22.4.

25. See further Maggie Scarf, *Secrets, Lies, Betrayals: The Body/Mind Connection* (New York, 2004), esp. 185–86.

26. Iambl. *VP* 132, and see chap. 2, above.

27. Thesleff, *Texts,* 197.14, 198.30, 199.1, 9, 12, etc.

28. Philemon, *Adelphoi,* fr. 3 (Kassel-Austin, 4th c. BC), cf. Ath. 569d, and see Susan Lape, "Solon and the Institution of the 'Democratic' Family Form," *CJ* 98 (2002–3): 117–39, esp. 134–35.

29. Robert F. Sutton Jr., *The Interaction between Men and Women Portrayed on Attic Red-Figured Vases* (PhD diss., University of North Carolina, 1981), 290–97.

30. See further Pomeroy, *Women in Hellenistic Egypt,* 50–55, 74–76.

31. Paus. 5.8.11, *P. Oxy.* XIV 2082, Ath. 13.596e, and see further Pomeroy, *Women in Hellenistic Egypt,* 54.

32. Pomeroy, *Women in Hellenistic Egypt,* 86, 88, 95–96.

33. Thomas A. J. McGinn, *Prostitution, Sexuality, and the Law in Ancient Rome* (New York, 1998).

34. Thesleff, *Texts,* 144.12–13.

35. Thesleff, *Texts,* 152.24–153.3.

36. Thesleff, *Texts,* 153.12–14; Iambl. *VP* 48.

37. Thesleff, *Texts,* 142–45.

38. Thesleff, *Texts,* 142–45.

39. Sarah Blaffer Hrdy, *Mothers and Others: The Evolutionary Origins of Mutual Understanding* (Cambridge, MA), 2009, esp. chap. 8, "Grandmothers among Others."

40. See Xen. *Oec.* 7.42, and see further Sarah B. Pomeroy, *Xenophon Oeconomicus: A Social and Historical Commentary* (Oxford, 1994), 39, 60, 223, 285.

Chapter 5 · The Letters and Treatises of Neopythagorean Women in the East

1. R. Hercher, *Epistolographi Graeci* (Paris, 1873, repr. Amsterdam, 1965), esp. pp. 602–8, including Greek texts and Latin translations.

2. Alfons Städele, *Die Briefe des Pythagoras und der Pythagoreer. Beiträge zur Klassischen Philologie,* Heft 115 (Meisenheim am Glan, 1980). Städele discusses the manuscripts in detail, but for criticism, see *P. Haun.* pp. 8–9.

3. Thesleff, *Intro.,* 113–15, and see chap. 3, above.

4. Melissa is not mentioned in Waithe, *Women Philosophers*.

5. C. Wachsmuth and O. Hense, *Ioannis Stobaei: Anthologium*, 5 vols. (Berlin, 1884–1912).

6. Thesleff, *Intro.*, 113, and see chap. 3, above.

7. Thesleff, *Intro.*, 100–102, 106; Thesleff, *Texts*, 194–95, mentions quotations in Lucian, *Amor.* 30, *Imag.* 18–19; *Schol. in Lucian*, p. 124 (Rabe); and Euseb. *Praep. evang.* 10.14.14.

8. It is always possible that Diogenes Laertius was thinking of Theano II, but see chap. 1. Burkert, *Lore and Science*, describes "On Piety" in his index (535) as an "apocryphal letter," though it is a treatise not a letter, and (61), as "a curious document, attributed to Theano, who was usually known as the wife of Pythagoras." But he goes on to argue that it was written after Aristotle as a polemic. "And who is qualified to offer authentic exegesis, if not Pythagoras' wife and student herself?" Thus Burkert undermines his argument for the use of the name Theano as a pseudonym by referring to Theano I as a philosopher whom later philosophers considered an authority on Pythagoreanism. Waithe, *Women Philosophers*, 12–15, accepts Theano I as the author of the texts published under her name.

9. Diog. Laert. 1.89, 91, and see chap. 1, above.

10. See, e.g., the quotations from Gorgo in Herod. 5.51, and Plut., *Sayings of Spartan Women*, and see further Pomeroy, *Spartan Women*, 52–53, 153, and passim.

11. Arignote also discussed number: see chap. 6, below.

12. W. Emmanuel Abraham, "Did the Pythagoreans Use Recursive Definitions and Functions?" in *Pythagorean Philosophy*, ed., K. I. Boudouris (Athens, 1992), 11–21, esp. 15.

13. Arist. *Metaph.* 1.5, trans. W. D. Ross. http://classics.mit.edu/Aristotle/metaphysics.1.i.html. Carl Huffman ("The Pythgorean Tradition," in *The Cambridge Companion to Early Greek Philosophy*, ed. A. A. Long [Cambridge, 1999], 66–87, esp. 82) argues that in this passage Aristotle misinterprets the views expressed by the Pythagorean Philolaus (latter half of the 5th c. BC) on numbers.

14. Burkert, *Lore and Science*, 61n52, incorrectly cites the Greek text as line 12.

15. Clem. Al. *Strom.* iv.7 = Thesleff, *Texts*, 201.6–9. For other apophthegms of Theano I, see chap. 1 and Thesleff, *Texts*, 194–95.

16. Meunier, fr. 3, p. 41, from A. Meineke, ed., *Stobaeus*, vol. 4, *Florilegium Monacense* (Leipzig, 1856), 289, nr. 269.

17. Stob. (Meineke), 4: 289, nr. 268. It is not beyond the realm of possibility that Theano herself had experienced riding a runaway horse. Cloelia, a legendary heroine of early Rome, who had been taken hostage by the Etruscans in the seventh or sixth century BC, was depicted in historical times on horseback as a special form of honor: Livy, 2.13. For women driving carriages, see chap. 2, above.

18. Stob. (Meineke), 4: 290, nr. 270.

19. LP 130.

20. Page, *PMG* 428, trans. Anne Carson, *Eros: The Bittersweet* (Princeton, 1986), 8.

21. Originally published in Pomeroy, *Goddesses, Whores, Wives, and Slaves*, 134–36.

22. Thesleff, *Intro.*, 17, 29, 77, 87.

23. Ibid., 111, 113, 115, and see chap. 6, below, for Perictione II, "On Wisdom."
24. See chap. 3, above, and Waithe, *Women Philosophers*, 111.
25. See Carl A. Huffman, *Archytas of Tarentum: Pythagorean, Philosopher, and Mathematician King* (Cambridge, 2005).
26. See further Pomeroy, *Xenophon Oeconomicus*, 283.
27. Prudence Allen, *The Concept of Woman* (Grand Rapids, MI, 1997), 142.
28. *LSJ*, s.v. *harmodzo* and *harmonia*, and see further Vicki Lynn Harper, "Aristotle and the Late Pythagorean Women Periktione and Theano," in *An Unconventional History of Western Philosophy*, ed. Karen J. Warren (Lanham, MD, 2009), 63–91, esp. 88.
29. See further Helen North, *Sophrosyne: Self-Knowledge and Self-Restraint in Greek Literature* (Ithaca, NY, 1966), 235–37.
30. See Xen. *Oec.* 7.13, and see further Pomeroy, *Xenophon Oeconomicus*, 275.
31. Diehl, fr. 7.
32. Fikret Yegül, *Bathing in the Roman World* (Cambridge, 2010), 43.
33. René Ginouvès, *Balaneutiké* (Paris, 1962), 179–80, and J. Delaine, "Some Observations on the Transition from Greek to Roman Baths in Hellenistic Italy," *Mediterranean Archaeology* 2 (1989): 111–25, esp. 115, 121, 125.
34. See further Keith Thomas, "The Double Standard," *Journal of the History of Ideas* 20: (1959): 195–216.
35. See further Marcel Detienne, *The Gardens of Adonis: Spices in Greek Mythology*, trans. Janet Lloyd (Highlands, NJ, 1977), chap. 1. Originally published as *Les Jardins d'Adonis* (Paris, 1972).
36. Pomeroy, *Families in Classical and Hellenistic Greece*, 126.
37. See further ibid., 12, 39, 118, 166, 184.
38. See Mark Golden, "*Pais*, 'Child,' and 'Slave,'" *AntClass* 54 (1985): 91–104.
39. Thesleff, *Intro.*, 22.
40. On Pythagoras and medicine see, inter alia, C. J. de Vogel, *Pythagoras and Early Pythagoreanism* (Assen, 1966), chap. 10, and Burkert, *Lore and Science*, 88, 272.
41. See Sarah B. Pomeroy, *Women in Hellenistic Egypt, from Alexander to Cleopatra* (1984; Detroit, 1990; ACLS History E-Book, 2004), 560.
42. See J. G. Milne, *Cairo Cat. Gr. Inscrs.*, p. 46, nr. 9259. I. Noshy (*The Arts in Ptolemaic Egypt: A Study of Greek and Egyptian Influences in Ptolemaic Architecture and Sculpture* [London, 1937], 106–7, and plate 12.2) points out that the stele shown in figure 10 is carved in a purely Attic style. Both the lyre and cithara motifs appear as well in Caranis, on the funerary monument of a girl who died at age twenty: see Bernand, *Inscr. métriques*, no. 83, p. 331n10.
43. Thesleff, *Intro.*, 22.
44. See further Pomeroy, *Xenophon Oeconomicus*, passim.
45. In any case, even now women of comfortable means often discuss how to manage their domestic "help," and bestselling books are written by and about nannies.
46. See further Pomeroy, *Xenophon Oeconomicus*, 43–44.
47. Pomeroy, *Women in Hellenistic Egypt*, 139–41.
48. Val. Max. *Memorable Deeds and Sayings*, iv. 1. ext. 1, St. Jerome, *Letter* 79.9, and see further Huffman, *Archytas of Tarentum*, 286–88.

49. See chap. 4, above. On the terminology for women in the sex trade, see Laura K. McClure, *Courtesans at Table* (New York, 2003), 4, 9–26, and Leslie Kurke, "Inventing the Hetaira: Sex, Politics, and Discursive Conflict in Archaic Greece," *ClAnt* 16 (1997): 106–50, esp. 107–10. Neither McClure nor Kurke discusses the Neopythagorean literature.

50. On the expenses involved in keeping a *hetaira* or hiring a prostitute in Athens, see Edward E. Cohen, "Free and Unfree Sexual Work: An Economic Analysis of Prostitution," in *Prostitutes and Courtesans in the Ancient World*, ed. Christopher A. Faraone and Laura K. McClure (Madison, WI, 2006), 95–124, and see chap. 2, above.

51. *DMeretr.* 6.293, 8.299–300, 12.311–12, 14.320, 322–23.

52. McClure, *Courtesans at Table*, 79–105.

53. See further R. Hawley, "'Pretty, Witty, and Wise': Courtesans in Athenaeus' *Deipnosophistai* Book 13," *International Journal of Moral and Social Studies* 8 (1993): 73–91, esp. 76.

54. Euripides, *Medea*, 228–37, 241–47, trans. Helene P. Foley, in E. Fantham, H. P. Foley, N. Kampen, S. B. Pomeroy, and H. A. Shapiro, *Women in the Classical World: Image and Text* (New York, 1994), 68–69.

55. See Christiane Sourvinou-Inwood, "Medea at a Shifting Distance: Images and Euripidean Tragedy," in *Medea: Essays on Medea in Myth, Literature, Philosophy, and Art*, ed. James J. Clauss and Sarah Iles Johnston (Princeton, 1997), 253–96, esp. 279.

56. See John M. Dillon, "Medea among the Philosophers," in ibid., 211–18.

57. Thesleff, *Intro.*, 22–23.

58. See Leonardo Tarán, *Parmenides* (Princeton, 1965), 186–87, and Samuel Scolnicov, "What Is Pythagoras Doing in Plato's *Parmenides?*" in *Pythagorean Philosophy*, ed. K. I Boudaris (Athens, 1992), 195–204.

59. H. N. Fowler, *Plato, with an English Translation*, vol. 6 (London, 1926), 198–99.

60. See Leonardo Tarán, *Academica: Plato, Philip of Opus, and the Pseudo-Platonic Epinomis*, Memoirs of the American Philosophical Society, 107 (Philadelphia, 1975), 6n19. I am grateful to David Murphey for this information, in a personal communication of Nov. 23, 2010.

61. Thesleff *Texts*, 243.18. M. West, *Ancient Greek Music* (New York, 1994), 239, raises the possibility that she may have known the polymath Eratosthenes, who also was born in Cyrene.

62. For detailed commentary see Flora R. Levin, *Greek Reflections on the Nature of Music* (Cambridge, 2009), chaps. 6 and 7. See also Barker, *Greek Musical Writings*, 2: 230, 239–43, and Thomas J. Mathiesen, *Apollo's Lyre: Greek Music and Music Theory in Antiquity and the Middle Ages* (Lincoln, NE, 1999), 514–17.

63. See Sophie Gibson, *Aristoxenus of Tarentum and the Birth of Musicology*, Studies in Classics, vol. 9 (Oxford, 2005), 141.

64. Porph. *Comm.*, 22.22–23.22 (I. Düring, *Porphyrios Kommentar zur Harmonielehre des Ptolemaios*. Götesborg Högskolas Årsskrift. Vol. 38, no. 2 [Göteborg, 1932, repr. New York, 1980], hereafter referred to as Düring).

65. *Comm.*, 23.24–24.6 (Düring), trans. Barker, *Greek Musical Writings*, 2: 240–41.

66. Ibid., 241–42.

67. This quotation from here to the end is almost an exact repetition of the previous extract, but with the additional comment that followers of Aristoxenus considered both reason and sensory evidence to be inseparable.

Chapter 6 · The Letters and Treatises of Neopythagorean Women in the West

1. Thesleff, *Intro.*, 115, and Thesleff, *Texts*, 48–49.
2. John Dillon and Jackson Hershbell, *Iamblichus: On the Pythagorean Way of Life*, Society of Biblical Literature Texts and Translations, vol. 29. Graeco-Roman Religion, ser. 11 (Atlanta, 1991), 255n4.
3. Thesleff, *Intro.*, 115.
4. Waithe, *Women Philosophers*, 19.
5. Prudence Allen, *The Concept of Woman* (Montreal, 1985), 151.
6. Ian M. Plant, *Women Writers of Ancient Greece and Rome* (Norman, OK, 2004), 81.
7. See further Waithe, *Women Philosophers*, 19, 21–24.
8. Thesleff, *Intro.*, 49.
9. For full commentary, see Waithe, *Women Philosophers*, 21–26. My remarks here are largely influenced by the interpretations of Mary Ellen Waithe and Vicki Harper.
10. Ibid., 25, takes note of the implicit feminism in this passage.
11. Thesleff, *Intro.*, 115.
12. See further Sarah B. Pomeroy, *Xenophon Oeconomicus: A Social and Historical Commentary* (Oxford, 1994), 275–80.
13. See Theano I, chap. 1, above. Andrew Dalby, "Levels of Concealment: The Dress of *hetairai* and *pornai* in Greek Texts," in *Women's Dress in the Ancient Greek World*, ed. Lloyd Llewellyn-Jones (London, 2002), 11–24, esp. 119, 121, argues that the dress of respectable Greek women did not differ from the dress of *hetairai* in that both might wear saffron-dyed, sheer, flowery, and seductive clothing, but much of the evidence he cites is from comedy. In any case, the fees for a prostitute who was said to have some respectability were higher. Thus the woman who raised Neaera claimed that her young prostitutes were actually her daughters, and Neaera herself prostituted her daughter Phrynion, claiming she was the daughter of a citizen ([Demos.] 59.19, 41, 50).
14. Thesleff, *Texts*, 151, Iambl. *VP* 267.
15. Poralla, *Prosopography*[2], pp. 70–71, no. 405, lists "Kallikratidas" but does not mention Phintys.
16. Phintys is not cited in *LGPN* IIIA. On Callicratidas, see J. L. Moles, "Xenophon and Callicratidas," *JHS* 114 (1994): 70–84.
17. See A. Landi, *Dialetti e interazione sociale in Magna Grecia: Lineamenti di una storia linguistica attraverso la Documentazione epigrafica* (Naples, 1979), 135, 138, 194.
18. Thesleff, *Intro.*, 115, classifies her as third century BC.
19. Sarah B. Pomeroy, *Spartan Women* (New York, 2002), 87–89, see also on Cratesicleia, chap. 1, above.
20. See further Pomeroy, *Spartan Women*, 19–24, 82–83, 114, 121, 123–24.

21. See recently Mary T. Boatwright, "Women and Gender in the Forum Romanum," *TAPA* 141 (2011): 105–41, esp. 120–21.

22. See further Pomeroy, *Spartan Women*, 92.

23. See ibid., passim.

24. See ibid., 37–42, 45, 46, 66, 69, 79, 123, 136–37, 160.

25. Sarah B. Pomeroy, *Families in Classical and Hellenistic Greece: Representations and Realities* (Oxford, 1997), 23, 97, 110, 188.

26. Poem 8 GP = *AP* 6.353. Thus Plant, *Women Writers of Ancient Greece and Rome*, 84.

27. Xen. *Sp. Const.* 5.8, Plut. *Lyc.* 1.4.4., Athen. 686–87.

28. E.g., Xen. *Oec.* 10.2, and see Pomeroy, *Xenophon Oeconomicus*, 304–5.

29. See further Plant, *Women Writers of Ancient Greece and Rome*, 135–44.

30. Xen. *Oec.* 10.2, see further Pomeroy, *Xenophon Oeconomicus*, 19, 80, 304–5.

31. See T. Leslie Shear, "Psimython," *Classical Studies Presented to E. Capps* (Princeton, 1937), 314–16.

32. Ettore M. De Juliis, *Taranto* (Bari, 2000), 13.

33. On Cybele in the Hellenistic period, see Panayotis Pachis, "Gallaion Kubeles ololugma (*Anthol. Palat.* VI, 173): L' element orgiastique dans le culte de Cybèle," in *Cybele, Attis, and Related Cults: Essays in Memory of M. J. Vermaseren*, Religions in the Greco-Roman World, 131, ed. Eugene N. Lane (Leiden, 1996), 193–222, esp. 207–8, 213, 218–22.

34. Thesleff, *Intro.*, 17, and "On the Problem of the Doric Pseudo-Pythagorica: An Alternative Theory of Date and Purpose," 67.

35. Thesleff, *Texts*, 44, para. 4. Carl A. Huffman, *Archytas of Tarentum: Pythagorean, Philosopher, and Mathematician King* (Cambridge, 2005), 198, argues that these fragments should not be attributed to Perictione, because Perictione wrote in Ionic: apparently Huffman ignores the possibility of the existence of Perictione II.

36. Harper, 56, in Waithe, *Women Philosophers*.

37. Iambl. *VP* 267, Porph. *Plot.* 4 (from Timaeus, first quarter of 3rd c. BC), Anon. *Phot.* 438b31.

38. LSJ, s.v.

39. Poralla, *Prosopography*[2], p. 95, nr. 540. *LGPN* IIIA, s.v. cites one Myia from arch. (?) Sparta as dubious.

40. Thesleff, *Intro.*, 16.

41. Ibid., 115.

42. Pomeroy, *Xenophon Oeconomicus*, 143.

43. See further Mark Golden, *Children and Childhood in Classical Athens* (Baltimore, 1990), 123.

44. Roger S. Bagnall and Raffaella Cribiore, *Women's Letters from Ancient Egypt, 300 BC–AD 800* (Ann Arbor, MI, 2006), 76–77. Papyrus contracts with wet nurses, however, concern abandoned infants: Keith R. Bradley, "Sexual Regulations in Wet-Nursing Contracts from Roman Egypt," *Klio* 62 (1980): 321–25.

45. *Plutarch's Moralia*, xv, ed. and trans. F. H. Sandbach (Cambridge, MA., 1969),

18, n. b, p. 19, no. 114. *On the Education of Children, Moralia* 1A–14C, is a spurious work attributed to Plutarch.

46. Plut. *Consolation to His Wife*, 608.2, 609.5. See further Pomeroy, *Plutarch's "Advice to the Bride and Groom" and "A Consolation to His Wife,"* 59, 60, 79–80.

47. *Sor. Gyn.* 2.12–15, in *Soranus' Gynecology*, trans. Owsei Temkin (Baltimore, 1956), 90–103; the citations herein follow those in Temkin's version by page number.

48. See further Susan Treggiari, "Jobs for Women," *AJAH* 1 (1976): 76–104, esp. 88–89.

49. *Sor. Gyn.* 2.12.19, Temkin, 93.

50. See further Bradley, "Sexual Regulations in Wet-Nursing Contracts from Roman Egypt," 321–25.

51. *Sor. Gyn.* 2.12.19, adapted from Temkin, 91.

52. *Sor. Gyn.* 2.12.19, Temkin, 93.

53. *Sor. Gyn.* 2.26.19, Temkin, 100.

54. *Sor. Gyn.* 2.16, Temkin, 103–4.

55. In addition to the authors and texts discussed here in chaps. 5 and 6, Waithe, *Women Philosophers*, 12, includes an excerpt "On Number," which Waithe attributes to Arignote. (For testimonia: Thesleff, *Texts*, 50–51, cf. Thesleff, *Texts*, 164, 24–30). Arignote wrote about philosophy and religion, including *Bachika* ("On the Mysteries of Demeter"), *Teletai Dionysou* ("On the Rites of Dionysus"; Thesleff, *Intro.*, 11). Thesleff (*Intro.*, 11 and 27) notes that Arignote wrote in Ionic or Attic, but he does not include the following text. "Among the Pythagorean *Sacred Discourses* is a statement: . . . the eternal essence of number is the most providential cause of the whole heaven, earth, and the region in between. Likewise it is the root of the continued existence of the gods and daimones, as well as that of divine men." Furthermore, Allen (*The Concept of Woman*, 156) includes another letter from Theano II to Eurydice, one that is not found in Thesleff, *Texts*.

Chapter 7 · The Neopythagorean Women as Philosophers

1. In addition to all the considerations highlighted by Pomeroy throughout this book, I hope my detailed analysis of some of these texts will further support the plausibility of their being written by women who are seriously trying to apply a Pythagorean principle of *harmonia* to the actual conditions of women's lives.

2. See the translation and Pomeroy's commentary on Aesara, in chap. 6.

3. Though one might draw some parallels to other Platonic dialogues, including *Ti* 90 A, I shall not pursue Aesara's assertion (Thesleff, *Texts*, 49.9–11) that "the god thus contrived these things according to principle in both the outline and completion of the human dwelling place [or "body": *skanos*] because he intended man alone to be the recipient of law and justice, and none other of mortal animals."

4. See Pomeroy's discussion of the dating of these texts in chap. 3.

5. For a recent overview, see Carl Huffman's entry on Pythagoras in the online version of *The Stanford Encyclopedia of Philosophy* (Winter 2009), ed. Edward N.

Zalta. Huffman cites only four points as being well supported by early evidence: Pythagoras's fame as a believer in the immortality of the soul and a doctrine of reincarnation, as someone with expertise on religious ritual, as a wonder-worker, and as the founder of a strict way of life: http://plato.stanford.archives/win2009/entries/Pythagoras/.

6. See Huffman's online entry "Pythagoreanism," in *The Stanford Encyclopedia of Philosophy* (Summer 2010): http://plato.stanford.edu/archives/sum2010/entries/pythagoreanism/, as well as his online entries on Philolaus in the summer of 2012 (http://plato.stanford.edu/archives/sum2012/entries/philolaus) and on Archytas (http://plato.stanford.edu/archives/fall2011/entries/archytas/) in the Fall 2011 edition.

7. Iambl. *VP* 82 (DK 58 C4). Iamblichus reports that some say the latter follow Hippasus.

8. See, e.g., Aristotle's discussion of *mathematikoi* in *Metaph.*985 b and his reports of *akousmata* in fr. 197, preserved by Porph. *Pyth.* <?> 42.7. In his article, "The Pythagorean Tradition," Huffman dates the split to "sometime in the fifth century": Carl Huffman, "The Pythagorean Tradition," in *The Cambridge Companion to Early Greek Philosophy*, ed. A. A. Long (Cambridge, 1999), 78. Leonid Zhmud disagrees, arguing that there is no reliable evidence for such a division before the first century AD. Leonid Zhmud, "Mathematici and Acusmatici in the Pythagorean School," in *Pythagorean Philosophy*, ed. K. Boudouris (Athens: International Association for Greek Philosophy, 1992), 240–49.

9. Iambl. *VP* 82 (DK 58 C4).

10. *Suda* (DK 58 C6).

11. Diog. Laert. 8 18. "This is what they meant. Don't stir the fire with a knife: don't stir the passions or the swelling pride of the great. Don't step over the beam of the balance: don't overstep the bounds of equity and justice" (trans. R. D. Hicks).

12. Iambl. *VP* 81 (DK 18.2).

13. For a discussion of this method of representing numbers in Pythagorean philosophy before Plato and of its relation to the *tetractys* (the triangular figure representing the sacred number 10), see Charles H. Kahn, *Pythagoras and the Pythagoreans* (Indianapolis, IN, 2001), 30–32.

14. Burkert, *Lore and Science*, trans. E. Minar (Cambridge, MA, 1972).

15. See, e.g., Kahn, *Pythagoras and the Pythagoreans*, 23–38.

16. Carl Huffman's view in his 2009 entry "Pythagoras," in *The Stanford Encyclopedia of Philosophy*: http://plato.stanford.edu/archives/win2009/entries/pythagoras/.

Iamblichus reports the *akousmata* about harmonia, the *tetractys*, and number: *VP* 82 (DK 58 C4).

17. Sext. Emp. *Math.* 7 84–85.

18. Iambl. *VP* 82 (DK 58 C4). In *Rep.* 10 617 B-C, Plato identifies the Siren's song with the music of the celestial spheres in the cosmos. In his 2009 entry on Pythagoras, Huffman allows that the above *akousma* identifying the *tetractys* with the harmony sung by the sirens suggests that Pythagoras may have believed that the celestial bodies made music by their motions, though these motions were not likely

to be associated with spheres: http://plato.stanford.edu/archives/win2009/entries/pythagoras/.

19. Carl Huffman, *Philolaus of Croton: Pythagorean and Presocratic* (Cambridge, 1993).

20. Philolaus fr.1, Diog. Laert. 8 85.

21. Huffman, *Philolaus of Croton*, 48ff.

22. See the translation and Pomeroy's discussion in chap. 5.

23. See, e.g., Diog. Laert. 8 4–5 (DK 14.8) and the testimony of Porph. *VPyth*. in DK 14.8a.

24. I am grateful to an anonymous reviewer for pointing out the parallel to Aristox. fr. 35 (Wehrli). Aristoxenus on Pythagorean moral philosophy is discussed by Carl A. Huffman (2008), "The Pythagorean Principles of Aristoxenus: Crucial Evidence for Pythagorean Moral Philosophy," *Classical Quarterly*, n.s. 58 (2008): 104–19 (online publication date: Apr. 18, 2008).

25. See chap. 2, above.

26. Though, as Pomeroy rightfully reminds us in chaps. 2, 3, and 4, Pythagoras's reform was rather hard on the concubines.

27. In contrast to his early published (*exoteric*) works such as the *Protrepticus*, Aristotle's treatises as we know them today ultimately stem from unpublished (*esoteric*) work, possibly even lecture notes, readily available only to those inside the Lyceum. After Aristotle's death these papers were probably available to his successors in the Lyceum and possibly to others, including Epicurus and Alexandrian intellectuals. See Jonathan Barnes's discussion of the history of the treatises, esp. in *The Cambridge Companion to Aristotle* (Cambridge, 1995), 10, and Martha Nussbaum's entry on Aristotle in the *Oxford Classical Dictionary*, 3rd ed. (Oxford, 1996), 166. Our current text of the *Nicomachean Ethics* is based on an edition edited by Andronicus in the first century BC.

28. In Mary Ellen Waithe, ed., *A History of Women Philosophers*, vol. 1, 600 BC–500 AD (Dordrecht, 1987), 69–70.

29. Here I shall elaborate upon my line of argument in chapter 2 of *An Unconventional History of Western Philosophy: Conversations between Men and Women Philosophers*, ed. Karen Warren (Lanham, MD, 2009), 78–90.

30. In addition to his biological views, e.g., his views on procreation in *Gen. an.* 729 a, there are a number of passages, such as *Pol.* 1254 b 12–13, in which Aristotle asserts that "the male is by nature superior, and the female inferior."

31. Aristotle's rather mysterious comments about the immortality of the active intellect (*nous poetikos*) in the third book of *De an.* (430 a 10–25) do not point to any sense of personal immortality.

32. As Pomeroy stresses in chapter 3, these Neopythagorean texts are "the earliest prose literature to examine these subjects from a female perspective and to assert strongly that the double standard in conjugal relations is painful for married women."

33. This conviction will later be stressed by Stoic philosophers as well, e.g., by Epictetus in chapter 52 of the *Enchiridion*: "The first and most important field in

philosophy is the application of principles such as 'Do not lie.'" (*Epictetus: Discourses and Selected Writings*, trans. Robert Dobbin [London, 2008], 244).

34. Also stoutly defended by Socrates in Plato's *Meno* 77 C–78 A.

35. Thus in my commentary, *An Unconventional History of Western Philosophy*, chap. 2, 87.

36. Whether or not the husband's character could have developed differently, given a proper upbringing or greater effort on his own part in the past, is a separate question. Like a stone that has already been cast (cf. Arist. *Eth. Nic.* 1114 a), it is not in his character to rise to the occasion now.

37. See chap. 3, above, and Pomeroy's comments on the essay by Phintys in chap. 6, above.

38. See the text and Pomeroy's commentary in chapter 6, above.

39. See Pomeroy's comments on the second fragment of Perictione's "On the Harmonious Woman" in chap. 5, above.

40. The idea that it is permissible for a woman to "exhort or instruct" her parents if they are in error is noteworthy because, in fragment 1 of the same work, Perictione I allows far less latitude to a woman in relation to her husband: ". . . holding views on their common mode of life that are compatible, while acting in concert with those relatives and friends whom her husband extols. And if her husband thinks something is sweet, she will think so too; or if he thinks something is bitter, she will agree with him"; see chap. 5.

41. Phintys, "On the Moderation of Women," fr. 2. See chap. 6, above.

42. Perictione I, "On the Harmonious Woman," fr. 1, trans. VLH

43. The overall approach is that of virtue ethics, also called *aretaic* ethics because of its focus on moral excellence (*arête*).

44. Arist. *Eth. Nic.* 1104 b.

45. Theano to Euboule, trans. VLH, chap. 5, above.

46. Arist. *Eth. Nic.* 1105 a, trans. Roger Crisp (Cambridge, 2001), 27.

47. Arist. *Eth. Nic.* 1095 b. Aristotle, like Theano, mentions Sardanapolus as an exemplar of slavishness.

48. Thus my analysis in *An Unconventional History of Western Philosophy*, 82–83, and in Waithe, *A History of Women Philosophers*, 1: 49–52.

49. Porph. *VPyth*. 19 (DK 14.8a).

50. Concern for other animals is attested in Xenophanes' story about Pythagoras and the puppy (DK11 B7), but Aristotle's fr. 195 (DK 58 C3) does not attribute vegetarianism to Pythagoras himself, mentioning only a few prohibitions, such as not eating white cocks or sacred fish.

51. Thus my analysis in Waithe, *A History of Women Philosophers*, 1: 49–52.

52. See, e.g., *Eth. Nic.* 1.3, 1.6, 2.2.

53. Arist. *An. post.* 1.2.

54. Arist. *An. post.* 2.19.

55. Arist. *An. post.* 1.2, 1.13; *Ph.* 1.1, 1.2.

56. See chap. 5, above. See also Andrew Barker, ed., *Greek Musical Writings*, vol.

2, *Harmonic and Acoustic Theory* (Cambridge, 1989), 230, and Flora R. Levin, *Greek Reflections on the Nature of Music* (Cambridge, 2009), 237–39, 241–42.

57. Porphyry's *Commentary on Claudius Ptolemy's Harmonics*, in three separate quotations. Porph. *Comm.* 22.22–23.22 (extract 9.10 in Barker's *Greek Musical Writings*, 2: 239–40); Porph. *Comm.* 23, 24–24.6 (extract 9.11 in ibid., 240–41); and Porph. *Comm.* 25.3–26.5 (extract 9.12 in ibid., 241–42).

58. Porph. *Comm.* 25.3 (9.12, third extract in *Greek Musical Writings*, vol. 2); chap. 5, above.

59. Chap. 5, above, 95–98.

60. See the useful entry on Aristoxenus of Tarentum in the *Oxford Classical Dictionary*, 3rd ed. (1996), 169–70, and Carl Huffman's discussion of Aristoxenus in his entry on Pythagoreanism in the *Stanford Encyclopedia of Philosophy* (Summer, 2010): http://plato.stanford.archives/sum2010/entries/pthagoreanism/.

61. Aët. 2.7.7 (DK 44 A16) and Arist. *Metaph.* 986a, 2–12 (DK 58B4).

62. In note 141 of *Greek Musical Writings*, 2: 240, Barker recommends Ptol. *Harm.* bk. 1.6 as a useful ancient source of information on such conflicts.

63. Explored, e.g., by Levin, *Greek Reflections on the Nature of Music*, chap. 7.

INDEX

Page numbers in *italics* refer to figures and maps.

adultery: of men, 58, 60–65; Perictione I on, 57, 60, 64; Theano II on, 90–91; of women, 63–64
Aesara: date of, xiv; "On Human Nature," 99–102, 118–19; origin of, 41, 45, 49
Aeschines, 35
akousmatikoi, 119, 120
Alcman, 27, 107
Alexandria, 48, 54, 63
Alexis, xiii, 45
Allen, Prudence, 99
Anaximander and Anaximenes of Miletus, 8
Antigonus Gonatas, 44, 51
appearance. *See* clothing and dress; cosmetics; jewelry
Archytas of Tarentum, 87, 117, 119
Aretaic ethics, 129, 164n43
Arignota: date of, xiv; as daughter of Pythagoras, 5, 28; origin of, 41, 49; texts of, 161n55
Aristaeus, 6
Aristocleia, 10
Aristotle: on exercise, 13; on friendship, 126; *Metaphysics*, 121–22; Neopythagorean women compared to, 123–25; *Nicomachean Ethics*, 123, 125, 128, 130, 135; as Peripatetic, 42; on pleasure, 129–30; on sexual division of labor, 112; on slaves, 85; table of opposites, 10, 120, 121; view of women by, 10, 67–68, 124; will of, 50
Aristoxenus of Tarentum: *Elements of Harmony*, 95–96; on female contemporaries of Pythagoras, xx; as philosopher, 136; Ptolemaïs on, 98, 137; on Pythagoreans from Phlius, 7; as source, 9, 11
Arsinoë II, 44

Artemis Brauronia, 35
Aspasia, xiii
Athens, women of, xvi–xvii, 45
Attic *koine*: letters in Egypt in, xv; of Melissa, 102; of Theano II, 77, 81, 84, 88, 94
authenticity of texts, xxi, 49–53

Babelyca, 7
Bagnall, Roger S., 54, 55
bathing, 74, 116
beauty of women, 22, 102–3, 108–9
Bentley, Richard, xxi, xxii
Berenice III, 44
Bilistiche, xiii, 63
Bitale, xiii, 7, 8, 9, 39
Boeo, 7
Brontinus, xvii, xx, 5
Burkert, Walter, xxi, 42, 68, 120

Callicrates, 104
Callisto, Theano II letter to, 83–88, 130–31, 132–35
Carter, Joseph Coleman, xvii
character, role and development of, 129–30
Cheilonis, xiii, 5, 10
Cheilon the Lacedaemonian, 5
children: bathing, 74; legitimacy of, 108; Pythagoras speech to, 26–28; raising of, 78–80, 111–16, 129–30; regulations regarding, 22–26. *See also* parents and children
Chrysippus, 93
Cleachma, 7, 10, 26
Cleareta, Melissa letter to, 58, 102–3, 128

Cleobuline, 67
Cleomenes, 5
clothing and dress: of *hetairai*, 88, 159n13; Melissa on, 102–3; Neopythagorean women on, 58–59; Perictione I on, 72; Phintys on, 106; Plutarch on, 57–58; purple, 75; of Pythagoreans, 13, 33–34, 107–8; of women of Croton, 34–35. *See also* jewelry
concubines (*pallakai*), 20, 62, 89, 90
conjugal relations, 21–22, 23, 24, 56–58
contextual approach to ethics, 130–32
cosmetics, 57–58, 88, 102, 108–9
cosmic order, Pythagorean view of, 120, 121, 131, 137
courtesans, 62, 89–90. *See also* hetairai
Cratesicleia, 5, 10, 78
Crates the Cynic, 26, 50, 51
Cratinus, 45
Cribiore, Raffaella, 54, 55
Croton: as Achaean colony, xvi; address to women of, 20–21; beauty of women of, 22; Museo Archeologico Statale at, 33; Pythagoras in, xix; relations with native villages, 1; violence against young men of, 16, 18; worship of Hera at, 29–32, *30, 31, 32*
cults of female divinities, 109. *See also* Cybele, cult of; Hera
Cybele, cult of, 48, 106, 109–10

Damo: date of, xiii; as daughter of Pythagoras, 5, 28; economic status of, 47; as first among girls, 27; memoranda of Pythagoras and, 7
dating of Neopythagorean texts, 42–44, 49
daughters, 26–29
daughters of Pythagoras. *See* Arignota; Damo; Myia (daughter of Pythagoras)
dedications to goddesses, 33–39
Deino, xx, 5, 64
Demaratus, 15
Demeter, dedications to, 37–38
Demetrius of Phalerum, 59
Democritus, 68
Demosthenes, 35
dialect. *See* Doric dialect; Ionic dialect
Dicaearchus, xxi–xxii
Didymus, 6, 97
diet of Pythagoreans, 12–13
Diogenes Laertius of Cilicia: on *akousmata*, 119; on *Parmenides*, 94; as source, xx; on Theano, xxi, 5, 6, 67

Diophila, 51
divorce in Greek society, 53
Dorian women, xvi–xvii, 1
Doric dialect: of Aesara, 99; of Melissa, 99; of Myia, 111; of Perictione I, 69; of Perictione II, 110; use of, xv, 48
double standard of sexual behavior: in Greek society, 60–61, 125; Perictione I on, 75, 127–28; Pythagoras on, 19, 20; Theano II on, 125–26

Eccelo, 1, 5, 26
Echecrateia, 7
education of women. *See* literacy of women
Egypt, letters in, xv, 54–56
Erinna, xxii; "The Distaff," 52
eros, effects of, 69
ethics, contextual approach to, 130–32
Euboule, Theano II letter to, 77–80, 87, 129–30
Euclides, 41
Euripides, 75, 92
Eurydice, Theano II letter to, 60, 82–83
exercise, physical, 13, 107
exhortation, letters of, 59

fertility and cult of Hera, 36
forgery, treatises as, xxi, 49–53
Fraser, P. M., 42–43
friendship: among women, 59; disillusionment in context of, 126; in private sphere, 25–26
Fulvius Flaccus, Q., 32

gender roles, 86–87, 104–5, 112
girls reading, terra-cotta figurines depicting, 46, *47*
goddesses: as anthropomorphic, 38–39; dedications to, 33–38. *See also* Cybele, cult of; Hera
gold: crown of, 33, *34*; wearing of, 13
granddaughter of Pythagoras. *See* Bitale
grave goods, xviii
Greece: double standard of sexual behavior in, 60–61; housewife role in, 45; map of, 2–3; map of colonization by, *4*; patriarchal structure of society in, 11–12, 53. *See also* Greek society
Greeks, dialects and groups of, 139n1. *See also* Dorian women; Doric dialect; Ionic dialect

Habroteleia, 7, 10
Hannibal, 32
harmonia: numbers and, 120–21; Perictione I

on, 70–71; Perictione II on, 111; Ptolemäis on, 135–36; Theano II on, 131; in women's lives, 119, 122–23
Harper, Vicki Lynn, 66, 99, 100
Harris, William V., 8
health concerns, 81, 93
Helen, disguised as swan, 22
Hellenistic period, women in: autonomy of, 57, 63–64; as courtesans, 89–90; double standard for, 125; education of, 44, 45–47; literacy of, 46, 47, 51–52, 56; as philosophers, 50; social position of, 48; wealth of, 58–59
Hense, O., 66
Hera: cult of, xvi, 36–37; scarab with head of, 37; temple of, at Croton, 29–32, 30, 31, 32
Heraclitus, 8
Hercher, R., 66
Herodes Atticus, 25, 35
Herodotus, xx, 6, 76
Hesiod, 53
hetairai: appearance of, 88, 159n13; expense of, 89, 90, 159n13; profession of, 20, 62–63. *See also* courtesans
Hipparchia, 26, 50, 51
housekeeping, 13–14, 48, 84–88, 87
Hrdy, Sarah, 65
Huffman, Carl, 43, 121

Iamblichus of Chalcis: dates of, xiv; on exercise, 13; on female contemporaries of Pythagoras, xv, xx; on heir of Pythagoras, 6; on memoranda of Pythagoras, 8; Pythagoreans named by, 1, 41; as source, xx, 11; on speeches to children, 26; on types of Pythagoreans, 119–20
indigenous women as Pythagoreans, xv, 1
Ionic dialect, xv, 48, 69, 110

jewelry, 13, 15, 57–58, 88
Justin, 15–16

Kahn, Charles, 43
Kingsley, Peter, xxi
knowledge, experiential, 135

language of texts, xv, 48–49. *See also* Doric dialect; Ionic dialect
Lastheneia, 6–7
lebes gamikos, red figure Apulian, 9

letters: on adultery, 60–65; nonliterary, of women in Egypt, 54–56; recipients of, 55; topics of, 59–60. *See also specific authors*
Levin, Flora, *Greek Reflections on the Nature of Music*, 42, 44
linen, 13, 34
literacy of philosophers and Pythagoreans, 8
literacy of women: in classical period, 11, 70; in Hellenistic period, 44, 45–47, 46, 47, 51–52, 56; Plato on, 74; Pythagorean doctrine and, xxii, 8, 26–27
Livy, xviii, 30–31, 32
Locri, 28, 38
Lucian, *Dialogues of the Courtesans*, 89–90
Lycurgus of Sparta, 16
lyres, archaeological evidence for, 9, 12, 46–47, 83
Lysias, 61

Magna Graecia: cult of Hera in, xvi, 36–37; environmental forces at, 17–18; Pythagoras in, xix, 8; temples in, 37–38
Magnilla, 51
marriage: conjugal relations in, 21–22, 23, 24, 56–58; divorce in Greek society, 53; friendship and, 25–26; within group, 39; monogamy in, 12, 19–21; within philosophical schools, 6, 50; Pythagorean program for men and, 11–12; rules for, 23; treatment of women within, 25. *See also* adultery
mathematics in Pythagorean philosophy: education of women and, 51–52, 56; importance of, 67, 137; Ptolemäis and, 95; relation between things and, 121–22
mathematikoi, 119, 120
Medea analogy, 91, 92–93, 126
Melissa: circulation of letters of, xv, 55; on cosmetics, 109; date of, xiv; letter to Cleareta, 58, 102–3, 128; origin of, 41, 49
Ménage, Gilles, 56
Metaponto: as Achaean colony, xvi; burials at, 24, 28–29; excavations at, xvii, xviii; museum at, xvii; Pythagoras in, xix; relations with native villages, 1; temples to Hera in, 37
Middle Comedies lampooning Pythagoreans, 45, 47
mistresses. *See* concubines (*pallakai*); *hetairai*
Mnesarchus, 5
monogamy in marriage, 12, 19–21
moral psychology, 125–26

mothers, women as, 22–26, 111–16
mousike and women, 46–47
mousikoi, 136–37
music, analogies using, 82, 83, 86, 93, 131, 134, 135
lyres, 9, 12, 46–47, 83
musical theory: Neopythagoreans and, 82; Ptolemäis treatise on, 42, 47, 51, 95–98, 135–38
Myia (author): on bathing, 74; date of, xiv; letter to Phyllis, 58, 86, 111–16; origin and identity of, 41, 49
Myia (daughter of Pythagoras), xiii, 5, 6, 28

Neoplatonists, 50
Neopythagorean women: Aristotle compared to, 123–25; description of group of, xv; domestic duties of, 48; economic status of, 47–48; as innovative, 138; language of, 48–49; location and lives of, xviii–xix; origins of, 41; as philosophers, 117–18; prose texts of, xv
Nico, grave stele of, 46, 83
Nicostrate, Theano II letter to, 60, 61, 63, 64, 88–93, 103, 125–26, 130
Nigidius Figulus, 48
Nossis, 31, 34, 38, 108

Occelo, Occelus, and Occilus, 1, 5, 26
Odysseus, Pythagoras speech on, 20–21
Oeconomicus (Xenophon): on housekeeping, 84–85, 87; on literacy of women, 70; on marriage, 24; on sexual division of labor, 112
opposites, table of, 10, 120, 121
oral tradition, 9–10

pallakai (concubines), 20, 62, 89, 90
papyrus, letters written on, 54–55
parents and children: laws of Solon regarding, 155n24; Perictione I on, 128; Pythagoreanism on, 22–26, 27; relationships between, 65, 76
patriarchal structure of Greek society, 11–12, 53
Peisirrhode, 7, 10
perception, role of in Pythagorean theory, 135–38
Perictione I: on adultery, 57, 60, 64; children of, 76–77; on cosmetics, 109; date of, xiii; human psychology and, 129; life of, 69–70; as mother of Plato, 43, 44, 48, 51, 56, 70; "On the Harmonious Woman" fragment 1, 63, 65, 69, 70–76, 127–28; "On the Harmonious Woman" fragment 2, 76–77, 128; origin of, 41, 49

Perictione II, xiv, 41, 49 69, 110–11
Peripatetics, 42
Persephone, dedications to, 37, 38, 39
Pherecydes, 8
Phila of Macedonia, 44, 51
Philochorus, xx
Philolaus, xxi, 7, 119, 121, 137
philosophers, female, xix, xxii, 50–51, 56–59, 70
Philtys, 5, 26
Phintys of Sparta: on adultery of women, 64; on cleanliness, 74; date of, xiv, 103–4; human psychology and, 129; "On the Moderation of Women" fragment 1, 103–5; "On the Moderation of Women" fragment 2, 105–10; origin of, 41, 49; on women in government, 71; on women philosophizing, 44; on women riding horses, 69, 106–7
Phlius, philosphers from, 7
Photius, 5
Plant, Ian, 99
Plato: on female traits and virtues, 73–74; mother of, 43, 44, 48, 51, 56, 70; *Parmenides*, 44, 94; *Republic*, 118, 123, 130; on sexual division of labor, 112
Platonism, 43, 56, 117
Pliny, 32
Plutarch: *Advice to the Bride and Groom*, 56–58, 84, 103; dates of, xiv; on infidelity of husband, 61; *Letter of Consolation to His Wife*, 55; *Life of Lycurgus*, 107; on linen, 34; on married women, 25, 75; on mothers nursing babies, 112; on women and mathematics, 52
poetry, as preceeding prose writing, 54
politics, role of women in, 107
Polybius, 32
Pomeroy, S. B., xxii, 136
Porphyry of Tyre: on disciples of Pythagoras, 6; on literacy of Pythagoras, 8; Ptolemäis and, 42, 51, 95, 96, 136; as source, xx
practice, application of principle to, 122–23, 124, 125–29
prostitution, 45, 75. *See also* courtesans; *hetairai*
pseudonymous, works attributed to female authors as, xxi, xxii
Pseudo-Plutarch, 112, 115
Ptolemäis of Cyrene: date of, xiv, 44; identity of, 42; origin of, 41; texts of, 49; treatise on musical theory by, 42, 47, 51, 95–98, 135–38

Ptolemy (astronomer), 42, 95
purple dye, 75
Pythagoras: appearance of, 21; biography of, xix–xxii, 10, 15; children of, 5, 28; community of goods and, 17; cosmology and, 120; dates of, xiii; disciples of, xv, 6; doctrine of, 12–14; heir of, 6; on luxury, 15–16; memoranda of, 7, 8, 9; mother of, xiii, 6, 7–8, 9; rebirth of, 7–8, 9; on sexual behavior, 19–22, 57; speeches of, xxi–xxii, 14, 20–21, 26–28, 29–32; women and, xxi–xxii. *See also* Theano I
Pythagorean philosophy, 119–21. *See also harmonia*; mathematics in Pythagorean philosophy; *sophrosyne*
Pythagorean women: contemporaries of Pythagoras, xv, xix–xx; as daughters, 26–29; description of groups of, xv; as mothers, 22–26, 27; origins of, 10–11; Pythagoras speech to, 29–32; as sisters, 26; in society, xxi–xxii; as wives, 19–21. *See also* literacy of women; Neopythagorean women
Pythaïs, xiii, 6, 7–8, 9

reason, role of in Pythagorean theory, 135–38
reincarnation, 10, 122, 131–33
Rhodope, 41, 44, 46, 64, 93–94
Rome: courtesans in, 63; housewife role in, 45; Pythagoreanism in, 48

Samos, 8, 11, 15
Sappho, 69
Sara, 5
scribes, 55–56
Semonides of Amorgos, 25, 53, 71
sexual behavior: of Pythagoreans, 12, 19–22, 23, 24; of Spartans, 107. *See also* adultery; conjugal relations; double standard of sexual behavior; prostitution
slaves: Aristotle on, 85; as capital investment, 87, 109; extramarital intercourse with, 62; gender and duties of, 86–87; of Pythagoreans, xviii; as scribes, 55–56; as serving children, 80; as subjects and objects, 132–35; textile manufacture and, 35; Theano II advice on, 85–86; as wet nurses, 114, 115
Solon: brothels of, 62–63; laws of, 16–17, 19, 76, 155n24; works published by, 8
sophrosyne: Aesara on, 118; husbands as exemplars of, 19–20; Perictione I on, 71; Phintys on, 104; Pythagoras on, 28; in texts, 55
Soranus of Ephesus, 112–13, 114–15, 116
soul: justice in, 119; reincarnation of, 10, 122, 131–33; tripartite, 100, 118; as without gender, 69, 74
Sparta: *agoge* in, 79–80; educational system of, 27, 58, 78; gender practices in, 28–29; sexual behavior in, 107; women of, xvi, 10–11, 67
Sphaerus, 5
sphragis, 76, 88
Städele, Alfons, 43, 66
Stobaeus: citations of, 66; on Perictione, 70; on Phintys, 104; as source, 46, 71, 99
Strabo, xviii
sumptuary measures, 16–17
suppliants, wives treated as, 19, 24, 25
Sybaris, 1, 18

Taranto, Spartan colony of, xvi
Taras, cult of, 109
Telauges, 5, 9, 28, 39
temple of Hera Lacinia: Building B, 31; column of, 32; dedications to goddesses, 33–39; description and history of, 29–32; gold diadem from, 33, 34; Via Sacra, 30
terracottas depicting education of women, 46, 46–47, 47
tetractys, 120, 137, 162n13
textiles, 34–35
texts: authenticity of, xxi, 49–53; circulation of, 55; dating of, 42–44, 49; language of, xv, 48–49; letters, nonliterary, of women in Egypt, 54–56; letters of exhortation, 59; as philosophy, 117–18, 123–25; place of origin of, 44–49; topics of, 52–53, 55, 59–60; treatises, 59
Theadusa, 7, 10
Theano I: apothegms from, 67, 68–69; on conjugal relations, 21; date of, xiii, xiv; Dicaearchus on, xxii; Diogenes Laertius on, xxi; identity of, xvii, xx, 5–6; letters of found in Egypt, xv; marriage of, 50; as model, 58; "On Piety," 51–52, 67–68, 121–22; origin of, 41, 49
Theano II: circulation of letters of, 55; date of, xiii; epistle to Timareta, 94; on *hetairai*, 62; identity of, 66–67; letter to Callisto, 83–88, 130–31, 132–35; letter to Euboule, 77–80, 87, 129–30; letter to Euclides, 81–82; letter to Eurydice, 60, 82–83; letter to Nicostrate, 60, 61, 63, 64, 88–93, 103,

Theano II (cont.)
  125–26, 130; letter to Rhodope, 44, 46, 64, 93–94; letter to Tim(ai)onides, 94–95; as object of scandal, 94–95; origin of, 41, 49
Theocritus, *Idyll*, 48–49
Thesleff, Holger: on Aesara, 99; dating of texts by, 42, 43, 44, 49; designation of places of origin by, 41; origin of texts and, 44–45, 49, 55; Ptolemäis and, 42; *The Pythagorean Texts of the Hellenistic Period*, xvi; as source, 66
Timaeus, on Myia, 6
Tim(ai)onides, Theano II letter to, 94–95
Timareta, Theano II epistle to, 94
Timycha, xiii, 1, 5, 10
Tyrsenis, 7

Valerius Maximus, 25, 32
van der Waerden, B. L., xxi
Veblen, T., 17
Vogel, C. J. de, xxi

Wachsmuth, C., 66
Waithe, Mary Ellen, 43, 66, 99, 100
wealth: of Hellenistic households, 58–59; horses as, 107; of Neopythagorean women, 47–48; of Pythagoreans, 13, 14, 35; slaves as, 87, 109; of temple of Hera Lacinia, 33; textiles as, 35; women as means of displaying, 17
West, Martin, xvii
wet nurses, 112, 114–15
women: adultery of, 63–64; friendships between, 59; life course and life expectancy of, 23–24; as means of displaying wealth, 17; naming of, 42, 50; as philosophers, xix, xxii, 50–51, 56–59, 70; in philosophical groups, 41, 44; piety of, 67, 109; subordination of, 122–23, 124; as wives, 11–12, 19, 24, 25. *See also* concubines (*pallakai*); *hetairai*; literacy of women; Neopythagorean women; Pythagorean women; *specific women*
women's history, xvi–xviii, xxi, 11

Xenophanes of Colophon, 8
Xenophon: cosmetics and, 108; on exercise, 13; on female traits and virtues, 73–74; *The Spartan Constitution*, 107; on textiles, 35. *See also Oeconomicus* (Xenophon)

Zaleucus of Locri, 16
Zeller, Eduard, 42
Zeuxis, 22